Teaching Music Globally

Teaching Music Globally

∞

EXPERIENCING MUSIC, EXPRESSING CULTURE

∞

PATRICIA SHEHAN CAMPBELL

New York   Oxford
Oxford University Press
2004

Oxford University Press

Oxford   New York
Auckland   Bangkok   Buenos Aires   Cape Town   Chennai
Dar es Salaam   Delhi   Hong Kong   Istanbul   Karachi   Kolkata
Kuala Lumpur   Madrid   Melbourne   Mexico City   Mumbai   Nairobi
São Paulo   Shanghai   Taipei   Tokyo   Toronto

Published by Oxford University Press, Inc.
198 Madison Avenue, New York, New York 10016
www.oup.com

Oxford is a registered trademark of Oxford University Press

Library of Congress Cataloging-in-Publication Data
Campbell, Patricia Shehan.
   Teaching music globally : experiencing music, expressing culture / by Patricia
Shehan Campbell.
      p. cm.—(Global music series)
   Includes bibliographical references (p.) and index.
   ISBN 0-19-517143-8 (p : alk. paper)
      1. Music—Instruction and study. 2. World music—Instruction and study.
I. Title II. Series.

MT1.C229 2003
780'.71—dc21   2003054900

Printing number: 9 8 7 6 5 4 3 2 1

Printed in the United States of America
on acid-free paper

GLOBAL MUSIC SERIES

General Editors: Bonnie C. Wade and Patricia Shehan Campbell

Music in East Africa, Gregory Barz
Music in Central Java, Benjamin Brinner
Teaching Music Globally, Patricia Shehan Campbell
Carnival Music in Trinidad, Shannon Dudley
Music in Bali, Lisa Gold
Music in Ireland, Dorothea E. Hast and Stanley Scott
Music in the Middle East, Scott Marcus
Music in Brazil, John Patrick Murphy
Music in America, Adelaide Reyes
Music in Bulgaria, Timothy Rice
Music in North India, George E. Ruckert
Mariachi Music in America, Daniel Sheehy
Music in West Africa, Ruth M. Stone
Music in South India, T. Viswanathan and Matthew Harp Allen
Music in Japan, Bonnie C. Wade
Thinking Musically, Bonnie C. Wade
Music in China, J. Lawrence Witzleben

In memory of my parents, who led me to my earliest musical encounters of depth and substance. Lacking formal training, they nonetheless understood that the musical experience was in itself abiding love, the feeling that remains long after the sound has faded.

The hard task is to love, and music is a skill that prepares man for this most difficult task.

—John Blacking, 1973

Contents

∞

Foreword

∞

In the past three decades interest in music around the world has surged, as evidenced in the proliferation of courses at the college level, the burgeoning "world music" market in the recording business, and the extent to which musical performance is evoked as a lure in the international tourist industry. This heightened interest has encouraged an explosion in ethnomusicological research and publication, including the production of reference works and textbooks. The original model for the "world music" course—if this is Tuesday, this must be Japan—has grown old, as has the format of textbooks for it, either a series of articles in single multiauthored volumes that subscribe to the idea of "a survey" and have created a canon of cultures for study, or single-authored studies purporting to cover world musics or ethnomusicology. The time has come for a change.

This Global Music Series offers a new paradigm. Teachers can now design their own courses; choosing from a set of case study volumes, they can decide which and how many musics they will cover. The series also does something else; rather than uniformly taking a large region and giving superficial examples from several different countries within it, in some case studies authors have focused on a specific culture or a few countries within a larger region. Its length and approach permits each volume greater depth than the usual survey. Themes significant in each volume guide the choice of music that is discussed. The contemporary musical situation is the point of departure in all the volumes, with historical information and traditions covered as they elucidate the present. In addition, a set of unifying topics such as gender, globalization, and authenticity occur throughout the series. These are addressed in the framing volume, *Thinking Musically*, which sets the stage for the case studies by introducing ways to think about how people make music meaningful and useful in their lives and presenting basic musical concepts as they are practiced in musical systems around the world. A second framing volume, *Teaching Music Globally*, guides teachers in the use of *Thinking Musically* and the case studies.

The series subtitle, "Experiencing Music, Expressing Culture," also puts in the forefront the people who make music or in some other way experience it and also through it express shared culture. This resonance with global history studies, with their focus on processes and themes that permit cross-study, occasions the title of this Global Music Series.

Bonnie C. Wade
Patricia Shehan Campbell
General Editors

Preface

∞

"People make music meaningful and useful in their lives." This statement is a guiding theme for teachers who wish to shape educational experiences that result in musical and cultural understanding for their students. It is furthermore a framing perspective for thinking about music—the roles it plays for individuals and groups, the multiple behaviors of people who sing it, dance it, play it, invent it, adapt it, and listen to it, and the manner in which it is learned and taught. For teachers at all levels of instruction, the world's musical cultures can come alive in the lives of their students through their active involvement as music listeners and makers of music. Students in elementary and secondary schools (but of collegiate courses as well) can come to a discovery of music as a human phenomenon, as a means of self- and collective expression, and as an avenue of both light diversion and intensive aesthetic experience. They can come to grips with music the world over as a process and an event which invites people to participate in its making and to respond to its presence in their lives. Music is meaningful and useful to people across the globe in myriad ways, and this guiding theme can help educators to design and direct experiences that will enhance their students' development of a multimusical understanding of this overriding principle. For those who teach music to children and youth in K–12 classroom settings, and for those on their way to a teacher's life, (and even for those teaching world music courses in higher education), this book is for you.

Teaching Globally. When it comes to the study of musical expressions of the world's cultures, students of all ages may be considered *novice learners*—from children in primary and intermediate grades to high school students and students enrolled in university music courses. Novice learners are more likely than not to have been enculturated in the mediated popular music of the West, be it rock, rap, salsa, or coun-

xv

try, or any of its multiple offshoots. Many have received training in the performance of western-styled "school-music" within children's choirs and the SATB mixed choirs of secondary schools, or concert and marching bands, or string orchestras, or assorted jazz and vocal jazz ensembles. Some know through private study of piano and orchestral (and "other") instruments a repertoire of western, primarily European, art music. (The same is typically true of their instructors whose training was taken at tertiary-level institutions where Western European art music, or "WEAM," has reigned supreme since the inception of music programs there.)

Yet few students know music with a capital "M," Music, for its global and cross-cultural manifestations. Such knowledge can only come by discarding "the west is best" perspective (which all too frequently becomes "the west is the only" position). This is accomplished by taking the grand leap into attentive and engaged listening, participatory-performance experiences, and creative composition and improvisation projects that provide firsthand encounters with a broader representation of the world's musical expressions. It is a brave quest, too, on a sometimes lonely journey, to challenge a curricular model that is rooted in nineteenth century values and infrastructures. School music programs in North America, Europe, Australia and New Zealand, and in parts of Asia, Africa, and Latin America have been successful in developing western-oriented musical skills and understandings, and are celebrated for the effectiveness of pedagogical approaches that produce musically literate singers and players. Yet this is but one model, and a colonial one at that, which fixes European music (and its staff notation) and its pedagogical processes highest in a hierarchy atop the musical expressions and instructional approaches of so many other rich traditions. Should such a model be continued in the twenty-first century, in a time of postcolonial and democratic reconsiderations of cultures and their perspectives?

I suggest a continuation of successful curricular models in K–12 settings, but with strong and substantive efforts to bring students thorough-going experiences in the music of the world's cultures where the West is just "one of them." This volume guides teachers to teach globally, so that a commitment can be made to shaping students' understanding of music in its multiple human dimensions, thus reflecting the pluralistic perspective of our era. It is meant for teachers of students in secondary school instrumental and choral programs as much as for teachers of music to children in elementary schools, for its aim is to transform while also preserving aspects of curricular content and method that have "worked" for generations. Further, if a global approach to teaching music is to be successful with elementary and secondary school students, it will need to infiltrate courses in higher education as well, from appreciation courses to methods classes for teachers, so that a broader perspective becomes the norm rather than the exception across the board.

Teaching Musically. Novice learners, both children and adults, benefit from personal encounters with music. Rather than teach only *about* the music (which is nonetheless a useful technique for expanding music's contextual meaning), teaching musically calls for interactive experiences with the music itself. Listening is key, including *(a)* the development of a sound awareness of music in its multiple uses and meanings in people's lives, *(b)* teacher-directed "attentive listening" that offers a first-entry exploration of sound components of particular musical genres and traditions, *(c)* "engaged listening" that calls for active participation in the music by way of singing, playing, or moving to the recorded musical selections, and *(d)* "enactive listening" that occurs as the singer or instrumentalist is performing music "live," listening intently and pointedly to recorded models as a reference for approaching the authentic performance of music. The essence of teaching musically is to center the instructional experience on the music itself, and to facilitate the involvement of students aurally, kinesthetically and viscerally, in the music. In this important way, *Teaching Music Globally* shares an affinity with Keith Swanwick's *Teaching Music Musically* (1999). Regardless of age, learning proceeds through keen and focused listening to the musical events as they unfold in time, and in the making of music alone and together with others. Musical understanding is furthered by knowing about the music: who performs it, why, where, when, and how, and in what ways a musical culture thinks about and values the song or selection. When the music studied spreads across time and distance, and various historical periods and cultures are represented in the selections for listening, participation, and performance, a multimusical understanding can evolve. The musical sound and its power to involve its listeners is core, however, and is the impetus for this volume, while the ideas that surround or spin out from the music serve to add meaning and thus to deepen one's musical understanding.

Chapter Content. The chapters of this volume are intended to offer teachers across levels and venues, especially those in K-12 settings, the means for bringing inexperienced learners into listening to and interacting with the world's musical cultures. In Chapter 1, I discuss the learning styles of musicians in world cultures and students in American classrooms, and note how the oral/aural techniques of musical learning in many traditions can be applied to students in school and university classrooms. There are suggestions for the curricular infusion of music of the world's cultures into particular instructional contexts—ranging from children's classes and secondary school vocal/choral and instrumental performance programs to academic courses that combine aspects of music's theory with practice, and history with culture, at the secondary and tertiary levels. Sample schedules are outlined for the inclusion of music cultures in curricular units of varying lengths, and a pathway ahead is suggested for the development of global perspectives on repertoire and method.

The volume is replete with instructional activities that can fill lessons and courses sessions that last an hour, a week, a term, or an entire academic year. Chapter 2 begins with the premise that all students are musically capable of listening with comprehension, once they are aware of the musical fabric that envelops them in their homes and families, their neighborhood communities, the places of their worship, their social gatherings—where they meet, eat, shop, and "hang." There are experiences for the development of students' sound awareness of music (or awareness of musical sounds) in their lives, and in local, mediated, and world cultures. In Chapter 3, I consider approaches for guiding students to listen with careful attention to music's details and its overarching essences. Listening "maps" point the way of instrumental entries, textures, and sonic events, and brief notations function as illustrations of melodic themes here and structural pitch sets there. As well, "listenpoints" direct the listener to timbres, tunings, pitches, durations, and formal designs—all attempts to develop attentive listening. The contents of Chapter 4 draw students through engaged listening experiences into singing, playing along, and getting the musical groove into their bodily movement. The strategies described (some with complete notated excerpts) are intended to lead students directly into the musical expression, by attending to discrete components and the integral whole of the music and by becoming musically expressive themselves even as the recording leads them and buoys them in their efforts.

From these participatory experiences, the emphasis in Chapter 5 is on performance possibilities through enactive listening (some with the assistance of notation), so that solo and unison vocal lines, partial choral works, and pieces on pitched and nonpitched percussion, and inexpensive or accessible, instruments can be realized. In fact, this is enactive listening, whereby students listen to a specific selection or a sample from the same genre in order to know the stylistic nuances of performing parts or full selections of the music "live." I provide initiatives and sequences for mentoring student-created improvisations and compositions of works in the style of featured selections in Chapter 6. There is a shift in direction in the last chapter, from music-as-music to matters that surround an understanding of music's place in culture and curricular studies. In Chapter 7, I provide guidance for teachers who wish to consider music-as-culture, and suggest a model that offers avenues for music's beginnings, continuities, and meanings so as to inform students more fully of the musical traditions they study. There, suggestions are found for building bridges through curricular integration between music and the study of language, social studies, science and math. Considerations are also given to ways in which ethnomusicological issues such as globalization, acculturation, gender, nationalism and musical identity might be probed by students. The final pages offer references and resources within the series, *Global Music: Experiencing Music, Expressing Culture*, as well as beyond it.

The Series. This book is one of two framing volumes for the Global Music Series. The other framing volume, *Thinking Musically*, offers an exploration of basic ideas and materials of music across cultures, and is a launching point for students of all ages to think in musically analytical ways as they listen to selections from the world's peoples. It fully describes musical concepts and processes within specific cultures and in a comparative manner across cultures that are only briefly noted here in this volume, and provides a glossary that is relevant to concepts in both framing volumes. *Teaching Music Globally* is a compendium of ideas for the musical education of K–12 and collegiate students (and their teachers), aimed at suggesting experiences and stimulating thought concerning pedagogical possibilities for teaching the world's musical cultures. The individual culture-case volumes, within the series, probe more deeply the musical expressions and forms from Africa, the Americas, Asia, and Europe. Teachers and students—in preparation for teaching—will find it useful to lay *Thinking Musically* and *Teaching Music Globally* side by side in order to note how the first explores music-culture concepts while the second provides extended ideas for how to enhance the exploration of these concepts by students. These two volumes share the same CD, so that teachers can be fully informed—and multiple steps ahead of their students—in conducting lessons and class sessions with multicultural and global aims in mind. This shared CD contains a wide spectrum of brief music-culture samples from the world, including Western art, jazz, and popular music, each of them selected as illustrations of musical features discussed in *Thinking Musically* but which subsequently have found their way into the instructional experiences suggested in this volume as well. The individual culture-case volumes of the Global Music series can be consumed, too, their pages read with care and the CD selections played again and again, and choices can be made from among the musical cultures featured in Africa, the Americas, Asia, and Europe. Teachers can then turn to the instructional manuals on the website that accompany each case, as well as to *Teaching Music Globally*, for suggestions on how to bring these musics to life in the classroom. These instructional manuals, designed by curriculum specialists with expertise in world music education offer everything from stand-alone performance and listening lessons to printable worksheets and assessments of students' learning. Alone and together with the series components, I hope that this volume will provide answers to questions of who-should-teach-what-to-whom.

ACKNOWLEDGMENTS

This Global Music Series can be traced to conversations with Bonnie C. Wade, coeditor, and Maribeth Anderson Payne, former Oxford University Press music editor. We met in Seattle, in Berkeley, and over a fine set of summer days at a Rhode Island beach house to consider the possibilities of this collaboration. It has been a pleasure and a privilege to know them both and to benefit from their insights. I thank Bonnie's vision on so many facets of this project, and for her *Thinking Musically*, which is central to the series and a companion to this volume here. There has been a team effort all the way through the realization of this project, and I wish to acknowledge the assistance of the Global Music Series authors: Matthew Allen and T. Viswanathan (South India), Greg Barz (East Africa), Benjamin Brinner (Java), Shannon Dudley (Trinidad), Lisa Gold (Bali), Scott Marcus (Middle East), Adelaide Reyes (United States), Timothy Rice (Bulgaria), George Ruckert (North India), Stanley Scott and Dorothea Hast (Ireland), Daniel Sheehy (Mexico/Mexican-American), Ruth Stone (West Africa), Lawrence Witzleben (China), and John Murphy (Brazil). Special thanks go to my colleagues in music education with their specialized study and attention to the pedagogy of the world's musical cultures for curricular inclusion, and for their skillful work as educational consultants to the series and designers of the web manuals: Bryan Burton, Victor Fung, Rita Klinger, Marie McCarthy, and Ellen McCullough-Brabson. I appreciate the professional expertise of Oxford's editorial team, and I thank especially Jan Beatty, editor, Lisa Grzan, project editor, and Talia Krohn, editorial assistant, all of whom have dedicated long hours to moving the series forward. I am grateful for the keen ear and careful notation of Eric Wiltshire, who was there even during the thick of marching band season to assist me in the transcriptions and "finale-ization" of CD selections.

This book is dedicated to the many teachers who have helped guide me to an understanding of music of the world's cultures, and who have inspired me to teach music musically and globally. I count among my influences those in music education and ethnomusicology who have long straddled the two fields to bring them closer together: William M. Anderson, Charlie Keil, Barbara Lundquist, William P. Malm, Terry Miller, Bruno Nettl, and Tony Seeger. As well, artist-musicians and culture-bearers have guided me into their music through my studies with them and/or through our collaborative projects, especially Euclides Aparicio, Munir Beken, Jarernchai Chonpairot, Kimi Coaldrake, Han Kuo-huang, Kovit Kantasiri, Nusrat Fateh Ali Khan, Phong Thuyet Nguyen, Pornprapit Phaosavadi, Ramnad Raghavan, and Sam-Ang Sam. My many encounters with students, from elementary school children and secondary school youth to university students-becoming-teachers, have been enriching, and I have been enlightened by them on matters of music and teaching in far more ways than they could know. As ever, Charlie, and now Andrew as well, are the sources of my solace, support, and inspiration.

CD Track List for the Accompanying Volume, Thinking Musically, by Bonnie C. Wade

∞

1 First *sura* of the Koran, *al-Fatiha* (Islamic recitation). Ceremony of the Qadiriya Sufi brotherhood, Mevlevi Sufi, Turkey. *Archives internationales de musique populaire (Musée d'ethnographie, Geneva, 1988)*.

2 *"Gunslingers"* (Trinidadian steelband). *The Steel Drums of Kim Loy Wong*. From *University Settlement Steel Band*, ed. Pete Seeger (Folkways, 1961).

3 "Partridges Flying" (Chinese ensemble). China Records (Zhongguo Changpian, n.d.).

4 "Mi bajo y yo" (*salsa*). Oscar d'Leon, bandleader. From *Exitos y Algo mas* Company, n.d.

5 *Atsiagbeko* (Ghanaian narrative dance). West Africa drum ensemble. Recording and notes by Richard Hill, n.d. Courtesy of Lyrichord Discs.

6 "All for Freedom"; "Calypso Freedom" (American protest song). Sweet Honey in the Rock. From *On to Mississippi* (Music for Little People, c. 1989).

7 "The Ballad of César Chávez" (*corrido*). Pablo and Juanita Saludado. From *Las Voces de los Campesinos*, n.d. Courtesy of the Center for the Study of Comparative Folklore and Mythology, UCLA.

8 "Ketawang Puspawarna" (Javanese *slendro*, pentatonic). Istana Mangkunegaran and the Surakarta court gamelan. From *Javanese Court Gamelan*, vol. 2, c. 1977. Courtesy of Nonesuch Records.

9 Navajo corn-grinding song. Joe Lee, lead singer. Recorded in Lukachukai, Arizona, 17 August 1940, by Laura Boulton. From *Navajo Songs* (Smithsonian Folkways, 1992).

10 "Vikrit recitation." From *The Four Vedas: The Oral Tradition of Hymns, Chants, Sacrificial and Magical Formulas* (Folkways 01426, c. 1968). Courtesy of Smithsonian Folkways Recordings. Used by permission.

11 "Raga Purvi-Kalyan" (North Indian *sitar*). Pandit Ravi Shankar. Ocora Records, 1995.

12 "First Wine Offering: A-ak" (Chinese Confucian music in Korea). Confucian ritual ensemble. Orchestra of the National Music Institute, Seoul, Korea, Kim Ki-su, director. Recorded by John Levy. Lyrichord Discs, 1969.

13 Didjeridu (aboriginal aerophone). A selection from northwestern Australia/Arnhem Land, performed by an unidentified blower (or "puller," as they are called). From *Tribal Music of Australia* (New York: Ethnic Folkways Album P 439, c. 1953).

14 "Conch call" (Tibetan Buddhist ritual). Conch. From *Musique rituelle tibetaine* (Ocora Records OCR 49, [1970]).

15 "Hifumi no Shirabe Hachigaeshi" (Zen Buddhist music). Goro Yamaguchi, *shakuhachi*. Japan Victor, n.d.

16 "Festival Music" (offstage (*geza*) ensemble). From *Music from the Kabuki*. Nonesuch H-72012, [1970].

17 Korean *Komungo Sanjo: Chinyango, Chungmori, Onmori*. Han Kapdeuk, *komungo*; Hwang Deuk-ju, *chang-gu*. Recording offered by the National Center for Korean Traditional Performing Arts, Seoul.

18 "Travelling in Soochow" (Chinese folk instrumental music). Chinese *di-tze* (flute). China Records, n.d.

19 "Kiembara xylophone orchestra," Famankaha, Sous-Prefecture of Korhogo, Ivory Coast, West Africa. From *The Music of the Senufo*. Bärenreiter, UNESCO Collection. *Anthology of African Music*, vol. 8, n.d.

20 Cantonese opera (Chinese vocal, Cantonese style). Fung Hang Record Ltd. (Hong Kong, n.d.).

21 Georges Bizet, "L'amour est un oiseau rebelle" (Habanera) from *Carmen*. Robert Shaw Chorale and Children's Chorus from l'Elysée Francaise. Robert Shaw, Conductor. Fritz Reiner conducting the RCA Victor Orchestra. Carmen: Rise Stevens; Don José: Jan Peerce; Micaëla: Licia Albanese; Zuniga: Osie Hawkins; Moralès: Hugh Thompson. English translation of the libretto by Alice Berezowsky. RCA Victor Records, c. 1951.

22 Andean panpipes: three cortes (sizes). An example of the Peruvian "Toril" genre, in *conima* style. Performed by Patricia Hinostroza, Jesus Jaramillo (*chili* melody); Vanessa Luyo, Jose Carlos Pomari (*sanja* melody); Illich Ivan Montes, Hubert Yauri (*malta* melody). Followed by a traditional *sikuris* ensemble, including panpipes recorded in the Andean highlands, city of Puno, during the festival La Candelaria, in 1991. Courtesy of Raul Romero Cavallo, Centro de Etnomusicologia, Pontificia Universidad Catolica del Peru, Lima.

23 "Ma Ram" "Dancing Horse" (Thai *pî phât* ensemble). From *Traditional Music of Thailand*, 1968. Institute of Ethnomusicology, UCLA Stereo ier-7502. Courtesy of the UCLA Ethnomusicology Archives (David Morton Collection)

24 Paul Desmond "Take Five" (jazz). The Dave Brubeck Quartet (Dave Brubeck, Paul Desmond, Joe Morello, Gene Wright). Copyright © 1960, renewed 1988, Desmond Music Company (USA) Derry Music Company (world except USA); used with permission; all rights reserved.

25 "Maqam Rast" (naming intervals: mode and mood). Egyptian instrumental ensemble with vocal, c. 1958. Umm Kulthum, singer. "*Aruh li min*," composer: Riyad al-Sinbati; poet: `Abd al-Mun 'im al Saba 'i Sono Cairo.

26 "Hyōjō Netori" (Japanese *gagaku* ensemble). Gagaku Music Society of Tenri University, n.d. Courtesy of Koji Sato, Director, Gagaku Music Society of Tenri University.

27 "Te Kuki Airani nui Maruarua" (Polynesian homogenous choral song/chant from the Cook Islands, in the joyous old style called *ute*). Singers from the Cook Islands National Arts Theatre. From *Festival of Traditional Music: World of the South Pacific* (New York: Musical Heritage Society, c. 1974).

28 Witold Lutosławski, "Mini Overture" (1982). Meridian Arts Ensemble: Jon Nelson, Richard Kelley (trumpet), Daniel Grabois (horn), Benjamin Herrington (trombone), Raymond Stewart (tuba). Courtesy of Music Sales Corporation and Channel Classics CCS 2191, c. 1991.

29 "El Gustito." From *Mariachi Music of Mexico* Cook 5014, c. 1954. Courtesy of Smithsonian Folkways Recordings. Used by permission.

30 Sargam (North Indian vocal solfège). From Bonnie C. Wade, *Khyāl: Creativity within North India's Classical Musical Tradition* (Cambridge:

Cambridge University Press, 1984). Cassette tape master in the collection of the author.

31 Balinese *gamelan*. Recorded by Lisa Gold.

32 "West End Blues" (New Orleans jazz). Louis Armstrong, trumpet, et al. Courtesy of MCA Universal.

33 "Marieke." Words and Music by Eric Blau, Jacques Brel, Gerard Jouannest. Recording and text translation courtesy of Suzanne Lake. Recorded by Suzanne Lake, *The Soul of Chanson*, CD. © Copyright 1968 Universal-MCA Music Publishing, a Division of Universal Studios, Inc. (ASCAP) International Copyright Secured. All rights reserved.

34 Frédéric Chopin, *Waltz in C-sharp Minor*. Performance by Jean Gray Hargrove. Recording courtesy of Jean Gray Hargrove.

35 Bruce Springsteen, "Born in the USA." Columbia CK 38653.

36 Dave Brubeck, "Three to Get Ready and Four to Go" (jazz). The Dave Brubeck Quartet (Dave Brubeck, Paul Desmond, Joe Morello, Gene Wright). Copyright © 1960, renewed 1988, Derry Music Company; used with permission; all rights reserved.

37 "Tar Road to Sligo" and "Paddy Clancy's Mug of Brown Ale" (Irish jigs). Becky Tracy, fiddle; Stan Scott, mandolin; Dora Hast, whistle. From *Jig Medley* cassette. Courtesy of Becky Tracy, Stan Scott, and Dora Hast.

38 "Makedonsko horo" (Bulgarian *tambura*). Recorded by Tsvetanka Varimezova, 29 December 2001. Courtesy of Tsvetanka Varimezo and Timothy Rice.

39 "Unnai Nambinen" (South Indian *Ādi tāla*). *Rāga Kirawāni* (21st *mela*). T. Vishwanathan, singer; David Nelson, *mṛdaṅgam*; Anantha Krishnan, *tāmbūra*. Music by T. M. Swami Pillay, Text by Muttutanuvar. Courtesy of Matthew Allen, T. Vishwanathan, David Nelson, Anantha Krishnan.

40 Richard Strauss, *Also Sprach Zarathustra*, excerpt. Columbia MK 35888, 1980.

41 "Seki no To" (Japanese *shamisen* and vocal). Example of *Tokiwazu*, a section from the *Kabuki* play *Tsumoru koi yuki no Seki no to*, music by Tobaya Richoo I, text by Takarada Jurai. 1784. From *1,000 Years of Japanese Classical Music*, vol. 7, *Tokiwazu, Tomimoto, Kiyomoto, Shinnai*. Nihon koten ongaku taikei. (Tokyo: Kodansha, 1980–82).

42 Balinese *gender wayang* (paired tuning). Recorded by Lisa Gold.

43 Western orchestra tuning process. University of California, Berkeley, Orchestra.

44 "Frère Jacques" (*"Are you sleeping?"*). Recorded by Viet Nguyen and Jane Chiu.

45 Western major scale. Recorded by Viet Nguyen and Jane Chiu.

46 "Oriental" scale. From *Cante Flamenco Agujetas en Paris* (Ocora, 1991).

47 Western vertical intervals.

48 Progression of pitches (roots of chords).

49 "Sumer is icumen in" (medieval European *rota*). Courtesy of the Chamber Chorus of the University of California, Berkeley, Paul Flight, director, 2001.

50 *Kotekan "norot"* (Balinese *gender wayang*). Recorded by Lisa Gold.

51 *"Yaegoromo"* (Japanese *sankyoku* ensemble). Jiuta Yonin no Kai Ensemble (Tokyo: Ocora, n.d.).

52 Scottish bagpipe drone. Recording by John Pedersen. Courtesy of Lucia Comnes.

53 "Rāga Miyāṅ ki Ṭoḍi" (North Indian vocal). Dagar Brothers, CD 4137.

54 Ludwig van Beethoven, *Symphony No. 5*, excerpt. London Symphony Orchestra, Wyn Morris, conductor. MCA Classics, n.d.

55 Episode from *woi-meni-pele* (Kpelle epic performance). Liberian *Womi* epic pourer. Courtesy of Ruth Stone.

56 "The Great Ambush." Tsun-yuen Lui, Chinese *pipa*. Courtesy of Tsun-yuen Lui and the UCLA Archives of Ethnomusicology.

57 "Iron Duke in the Land" (Trinidadian *calypso*). Julian Whiterose, 1914.

58 "Kumbaya." Kenyan. Courtesy of Greg Barz.

59 *"Riachao"* (Brazilian *capoeira*). São Bento Pequeno de Angola e São Bento Grande de Compasso. From *Capoeira: A Saga do Urucungo* (Luzes: Silvio Acaraje, n.d.).

CHAPTER 1

Cultures, Courses, and Classrooms

∞

Because music is made meaningful and useful by people in every nook and cranny of the world, music—all music—has been learned and transmitted, directly or not, by a knowledgeable maker of the music. On the docket for this chapter is a discussion of the presence of music and music teachers in our lives, and the subject of learning styles among practiced and proficient musicians, as well as aspirant musicians and music participants. Techniques by which musical learning transpires are described, and possibilities are suggested for instructional techniques that honor both the ways of many of the world's musicians as well as our students in school and university classrooms. The chapter makes headway into a discussion of the infusion of world musics into particular instructional contexts ranging from children's classes and secondary school music programs, to theory, history, and culture courses, with several sample schedules for the inclusion of global musics into curricular units serving as illustration of curricular change and transformation. This volume is intended as a guide for teachers of children and adolescents in band, choir, orchestra, general music—and any other gatherings of students—who strive for the comprehensive musical understanding and skill-building of students living in a global era. Thus, the schedules suggest up front, and in advance of the actual experiences, a myriad of ways of educating the student within the current frameworks of courses and programs.

SURROUND-SOUND

Through the open door of my university office, I can hear strains of a jazz ensemble at work, overlapped by a soprano's bright and shining vocalise, and punctuated by the pulsive rhythms of an Ashanti drummer and his students. Earlier in the day, I was touring classrooms, studios, and rehearsal halls in the elementary and secondary schools of a nearby district, and my ears were filled with the sounds of young singing voices, the instruments of adolescents at play in a homophonic wall of sound, and even the timbres of children's voices in conversation and at play. There was music on the car radio as I drove from school to school and over to campus, in the waiting room of the dentist at an appointment I had wedged in between these school visitations, and in the deli where I grabbed a quick lunch. Tonight, there will no doubt be musical segues between bits of the TV news that I tune into, and probably a little "unwind music" by me at our piano, musical etudes by our teenage son on his saxophone, and one or another selection from his favorite CDs wafting out from under his bedroom door. As I reflect upon these varied musical encounters, I am reminded of the findings of Susan D. Crafts, Daniel Cavicchi, and Charles Keil, in *My Music* (1993), Tia DeNora's *Music in Everyday Life* (2000), and my own *Songs in Their Heads* project (1998), that music permeates our very identities. All the day long and well into the night, in varied venues, the music flows and envelops those of us who choose to listen or not. Our surroundings are as musical as they are visual, and the unavoidable sonic textures blanket us in our every circumstance.

People are passive recipients of music that filters into their ears, but they are also potential participants in the music-making in our surroundings. Noted ethnomusicologist John Blacking argued long and hard—and most famously in his classic work, *How Musical is Man?* (1973)—against an exclusionary view of musicality, and pressed tirelessly for acceptance of the precept that musical ability is inherent within all normal humans. All are wired to hear music and to respond to it, as they are also capable of singing, playing instruments, and moving to music. Children exhuberantly manifest their musical leanings in their chants, songs, dances, and rhythmic movement, and it is only because of the natural development of inhibitions in late childhood and adolescence that the music goes "under cover" (usually in Western cultures). All too often, musicality lies dormant in adulthood, and many are complacent and may even find it humorous to quip "I've got a tin ear" and "I can't sing my way out of a paper bag" rather than to reckon with the music that has settled so deeply inside of them. Still, it is there, a penchant for people to listen to music with rapt attention, and to make music. The music is wrapped around and through them, and when circumstances are right for it, passive recipients are once again active in the process of making music, and in making sense of music.

In the rushed lives people lead, music is a constant, and yet it may not always be consciously heard nor experienced. One of the charges of an effective teacher, and the mission of a solid course or class on the subject of music, is to develop in students a conscious attention to sonic surroundings and musical matters that are "out there," alive and evident in local communities as well as preserved in recordings from around the world. Beyond the initial stage of mere awareness of music's presence lie opportunities for thorough-going experiences in the music they hear, ushered in and guided by teachers with the knowledge of and experience in making it. In his riveting theory of *Musicking* (1998), sociologist Christopher Small described music as part of our social and self-definitions, and logically argued that our musical involvement is an important means of exploring and celebrating our relationships with others. Deep-listening to musical expressions, and the participatory experiences that allow musicking to occur between and among people, requires inventive teachers with the ideas and enthusiasm for facilitating the connection between music and the individuals who comprise their classes.

THOSE WHO CAN, TEACH

From Madras to Manhattan and from Seoul to Soweto, those who are truly driven to make music—to sing it, dance it, and play it—are often compelled to share it, to facilitate experiences for others to know it, to pass it on. These highly motivated music-makers find themselves engaged in the act of teaching; they are the music teachers. Their teaching of music is accomplished in schools, universities, and conservatories, in community ensembles, in studios and storefronts, in homes, in jam sessions and among friends and family members. Most teachers are working within systemic settings (that is to say, institutions), and thus they brave on a daily basis the societal, artistic, and educational complexities of transmission. As Estelle Jorgensen has posited in her philosophical frameworks for both *In Search of Music Education* (1997) and *Transforming Music Education* (2002), they work in directive and liberative ways, didactically and as facilitators of heuristic-styled learning, and move from subject-centered to student-centered approaches according to the circumstances of their instruction. These wise and knowing teachers kindle and rekindle the sparks within individuals to want to make music, as they nurture the musicality of their students and encourage their creative musical expression. When music teachers—musicians all—care enough to commit themselves to imparting musical techniques, repertoire, and meaning, music learning results.

Those who can, teach. More than just another career option, the teaching of music is a rare and honorable calling. Teachers in elementary and secondary schools, or in universities are privileged to be living their lives within the balance of music and people. In Thailand, a *wai kru* ceremony is prepared by students to honor their teachers, and the traditional apprenticeship in Japan may require students to run errands for their teachers—or even clean their floors—in exchange for the valuable knowledge they will receive in lessons and just by being in the presence of their teachers. Among the Lummi Indians of the Pacific Northwest, a traditional song-bearer is held in high regard at the upper end of the community's hierarchy of roles and positions, and student members of a gharana in Calcutta or Varnasi (Benares), India, study hard and pay respectful homage to the teachers who lead this family-like training arrangement. Some are born teachers, gifted with the natural talent to deliver and entice learning from their students, while others learn to teach through experience and training. Yet it is the intersection of musical abilities with the teaching craft that brings about the professional pursuit of music teaching in settings ranging from preschool to post-graduate programs. The act of music teaching at any level and in any venue is a privilege that brings the coupling of music and people and the marriage of keen artistic expression with positive social interactions. The phrase, "those who can't (perform), teach," is no longer in vogue (nor may it ever have been of relevance), nor is it rational, for one of the principal attributes of effective music teachers is their ability to perform and to engage others in performance and participation in the music itself. Brought to its highest form of development, teaching music is about teaching musically.

Good teachers know their music, and they understand the musical needs of their students. They are personable and sensitive in their interactions with naive or less expert learners, and they communicate both their enthusiasm and the tools vital to making and understanding music. They possess characteristics which students prize: qualities of caring and enthusiasm, a sense of fairness, and a flexibility that allows them to adapt to student interests. They know when to sing or to play their instrument, when to listen, and when to provide evaluative remarks. They can shape the musical knowledge and skills of their students step-by-small-step, fashioning a sequence that fits individual and collective learning paces and styles. They have developed a sense of instructional timing and flow, and they understand the balance of their words and actions with that of their students.

As to the practice of good teachers, their mentoring, modeling, and mastery of performance of a particular technique or segment of the repertoire inspire and engage students. Far beyond words of explanation that can fall short of even the best teaching intentions, the manner in which teachers can demonstrate a musical phrase or technique cuts through the words to respond to the core questions of student musicians, "How should the music sound?" and "How do I make that musical sound?" Good teachers of many musical traditions have developed a musicianship that includes keen aural skills for picking up musical nuances or even complete musical works (and the patterns and processes that comprise them), a high level of dexterity that enables them to move their fingers and to shift the positions of their hands, arms, and even feet to sound pitches on time and in sometimes quickly moving rhythms, and in some traditions, a sharp eye for reading notes at sight and observing the correspondent gestures of a strong musical performance. Good teachers, for example, in southern India, eastern Africa, northern Europe, and the western Pacific perform well, understand through experience and/or training music's structural and expressive content, and listen carefully to the performances of their students for what feedback they can provide. They understand and value the aesthetics of a musical culture, and strive to bring their students within the realm of a quality of sound deemed acceptable by the cultural tradition. As they were also once student musicians, good teachers recall the challenges of making music in musical ways in a process that gradually unfolds with practice.

There are considerable challenges in teaching musically, and they are shared by teachers from Bali to Bulgaria. It is one thing to teach scales, exercises, modal segments, micromelodies, and rhythmic passages, and quite another to lead students in rendering them as musically expressive "moments" that flow with all of the nuances of rhythmic accentuation and dynamic change. Practice pieces, and solo and ensemble works, can be dull drudgery, expressionless routines, and note-after-note sequences of sounds with little outlay of thought or emotion. Lessons and rehearsal sessions are made into vital musical events as students mirror the musical vibrancy of their teachers. As main (perhaps only) models in the attainment by their students of a musical performance, diligent musician-teachers apply watchful ears and eyes as they shape raw sonic material into musically meaningful ideas.

The making of music strongly reflects how it has been learned, and is informed by the particulars of its transmission—the what, who, why, when, where, and how of music's teaching. Teachers of music in cultures across the globe are wrapped up into the musical content itself and are connected to the lineage of musicians and teachers from whom they come, the meaning and value of the musical expressions, and the time, place, and function of the musical events within their culture. Such particulars vary from one setting to the next, so that music's transmission as well as the sound of it will reflect the cultural ways in which the teacher-musicians and their students live.

LEARNING STYLES OF THE WORLD'S MUSICIANS

As musicians learn their craft, they employ techniques that appear widespread across traditions and cultures. From teacher to student, from master to apprentice, from parent to child, and through formal and informal experiences, people become more musical through their enculturation, training, and schooling. Learning is a multisensory experience, and the aural, visual, and kinesthetic capacities are called into play in acquiring techniques and repertoire. Students listen, observe, and imitate the teacher or master musician in lessons and sessions for Japanese syamisen, Bulgarian gaida, Shona (Zimbabwean) mbira, Peruvian charango, Indian sitar, Trinidadian steel pan, Persian santour, Senegalese kora, and Chinese qin. As they listen to the performance of the masters (who are also their teachers), they watch and finally become active themselves in the kinesthetic process of performance. Musicians throughout the world carefully exercise their aural capacities as they develop their technical skills to their maximum potential.

Imitation is a critical device in learning music in formal and informal settings. The Maori of New Zealand sing, sway, leap, and lunge as a result of long years of participation as children in their musical communities, and then through intensive training in their select *kapa haka* groups. Children of Balinese gamelan players come to rehearsals, watch their elders perform, and then imitate the melodies, instrumental techniques, and dance gestures while at play during the period prior to their own formal training. Students of Irish fiddle in specialized schools and informal sessions listen, learn, and retain certain characteristics of the jigs and reels for safekeeping in the aural and kinetic memory. Chopi xylophone players of Mozambique watch, listen, and learn from experienced players the patterns and passages of complexly layered music. In most traditions, verbal explanation does not play a large part in the training of musicians, and notational systems, if existing at all, is an option that teachers incorporate or leave out of their lessons. Notation may be used more to trigger the memory following a lesson than to supercede the musician-teachers as the reliable source of critical musical information. Importantly, notation is simply not helpful in some tra-

ditions, where the direct teacher-to-student passage of music-making
is key.

Mnemonic devices are utilized by musicians, so that aural (and oral,
spoken) cues may serve the memory well in storing and later recalling
certain passages. Many of these syllable systems may be employed—
solmization systems such as European-based solfege and Tonic Sol-Fa—
and many local vocalization techniques are utilized to train the ear and
fortify the memory. There is an elaborate mnemonic system for desig-
nating durations and drum strokes among tablā drummers of North
India. Drumming throughout much of the sub-Saharan continent of
African employs mnemonics that cue the duration, timbre, accents, and
strokes of instruments. Japanese instruments—including syakuhachi,
syamisen, biwa, noh kan flute, and various drums—each have their own
sets of syllables that designate pitches, playing positions, and rhythms.
South Indian students of vīṇa will typically sing phrases and whole
melodies that they will eventually play. Student musicians of many traditions and styles may well be chanting and singing the phrases they
will later transfer to instruments, utilizing syllable systems as they go.

LEARNING STYLES OF STUDENTS
IN CLASSROOMS

Many are drawn to music for its listening pleasures, or to dance it, while
some take great joy in singing and playing musical instruments. These
categories are not mutually exclusive either, as students may well be
inclined to multiple types of musical involvement: they sing, they dance,
they play—or are certainly capable of it. Students are variously motivated to pursue musical interests in and out of school, depending upon
their individual personal traits as well as exogenous factors. Parental
beliefs and practices enter into the picture, as well as the values which
siblings, grandparents, even aunts, uncles, and cousins place upon musical participation. Students who grow up with live music within their
environment are thus socially enculturated into it, so that for one who
lives with a father who plays the guitar, a mother who sings in a church
choir, and a brother who plays trumpet in the school band, it will be
"natural" to become musically involved in one or more ways. The sociocultural context accounts for the willingness of students to begin and
to continue musical study, which extends to the involvement of peers
and neighbors in music as well as the nature and circumstances of musical opportunities. The music teacher's own musical knowledge and

skills, as well as the teacher's personality characteristics that include enthusiasm, warmth, patience, tact, trust, adaptability, and positive encouragement are likely reasons for students to want to learn to make music and to learn musical matters.

Theories of child development suggest that musical learning is a graduated process that begins with young children's fully sensorimotor experience in the acquisition of knowledge, so that they learn through what they are able to touch, taste, smell, see, and hear, and how they are able to interact with it through physical movement. Particularly, as they play with sounds and sound-makers, young children from infancy through their preschool years grow in understanding of how music works. From this period of enactive engagement, they develop a sense of concrete concepts of what it means for music to sound high or low, loud or soft, fast or slow, and how to articulate these descriptive terms and understand symbols that represent them. Perception of pitch and rhythm grows rapidly in childhood, with foundational concepts becoming stable by middle childhood (by approximately eight or nine years of age). By adolescence, most young people have the intellectual and physical maturation, not only to understand music's structures but also to know how to create original expressive pieces, perform them vocally or instrumentally, and to analyze and verbally discuss musical expressions across styles and traditions. At least, the capacity for musical expression is there (and is aided by earlier training), awaiting the stimulation and guidance of a perceptive teacher.

The long-standing age-level theories, for example, Piaget's Hierarchy of Children's Intellectual Development, that adhere to a universal schedule of musical development are tenuous or fading as a movement emerges for the greater acceptance of environmental influences that propel one twelve-year-old (or twenty-year-old) to have acquired a sophisticated level of performance, analytical, and expressive skills while another may be at a decidedly earlier stage of musical fluency. The ability to understand and to make music is directly linked to the musical and music-educational influences of family, friends, and teachers. As one would expect, students with musical training and ensemble experience will display much higher levels of musical perception and discrimination skills than students who lack such experience. Students from "singing cultures" are likely to sing as they talk, easily, with range and volume, and without embarrassment. Students from families of professional musicians may well have had opportunities for early instrumental study and consistent nurturing. Young adults who have enjoyed music in the home, the community in which they grew up, and through opportunities at school, achieve a high level of musical accomplishment that is the undergirding of their musical engagement all their lifetime long. Likewise, cultures which pay homage to a "star system" in which the talented few "speak" (sing, play, and dance) for the untalented masses will raise people who are uncomfortable with their voices as musical instruments and with their bodies as an expressive means of responding to music. Many who grow up in societies worldwide where the "star system" predominates will find an invitation to participatory experiences in music intriguing but perhaps off-putting (and occasionally even threatening to their secure roles as passive music-consumers). Classrooms at all levels contain students at various points of a spectrum of music-making experience, and teachers are challenged to intrigue and entice them to know music in thoughtful listening and active participatory ways.

Students in elementary, middle and high school classrooms (and one might argue, at the tertiary level as well) learn well by listening. Lowell Mason, a nineteenth-century American pioneer music educator, advised teachers to "teach sound before symbol," as it can be logically reasoned and consistently observed that students learn music best by observing musical practice, listening to it, and then attempting to imitate it. Mason and his contemporaries cautioned against theoretical discussions and lectures about music when step-by-step musical performance and participation experiences for students were more directly the point of their musical learning. (Intriguingly, this nineteenth-century American perspective, rooted in the work of European educationists such as Heinrich Pestalozzi, is also integral to music learning in India, then as now.) The doing of music, informed by listening, is what brings musical learning and what brings home the conceptual understanding and skill-building that students require. Regardless of the age of the student, music-as-music—the aural art, and one certain avenue of self-expression—is best understood by knowing its structures and meanings through live and recorded sources. Listening that is attentive and focused develops into thoughtful music-making experiences all the way to aurally-informed performances that can be rendered with sensitivity to style and nuance.

ORAL/AURAL TECHNIQUES

There are several instructional techniques concerned with the teacher's oral transmission, the teacher's facilitation of sound sources, and the student's aural reception, that have been found effective in teaching music in many cultural locations and classroom contexts. Whether the music to be taught and learned is preserved in notation or not, oral and aural means remain central to the discovery of essential features of a song or an instrumental piece. Notation is a significant invention that can enhance listening experiences, and it may serve as a graphic map to melodic and rhythmic components of the music. Still, attention to the musical sound itself is the surest way to knowing music analytically and for its performance possibilities.

From Chicago to Shanghai, and from London to Lima, teacher-to-student practices aimed at achieving a satisfactory level of performance follow a modeling-and-imitation strategy whereby the expert or master musician-teacher sings or plays a musical section with the intent of demonstrating to the student not only rhythm and/or melody but every intricate expressive element that cannot be fully captured in notation. It is the task of the teacher to demonstrate musical phrases and segments well within the style, to select appropriate musical lengths that can be perceived and immediately recalled by the student, and to cue, listen intently, and provide feedback to the student who will follow in imitation of the teacher. This instructional strategy is evident within the context of Chinese pipa (lute) study as well as within a session of Peruvian charango (lute) players. It is the way of much studio instruction for aspiring pianists and orchestral musicians, and it is also applicable to the musical education of students in classrooms of every level. For maximal effectiveness, this oral/aural technique requires a teacher who is either born and bred or (if nonnative) intensively trained in the musical tradition, and who is committed to transmitting it live-and-in-person to the students.

The teacher utilizing the modeling-and-imitation strategy becomes an artist-in-residence within the classroom, performing for students what they will know and may well work up to performance level. There are no intervening factors in the use of this strategy, but instead the music flows in a direct line from the teacher to the student. In the case of vocal and choral settings, and in band, orchestral, and other instrumental sessions, students hear their teacher's demonstrations and follow suit. Repeated demonstration and imitation of musical segments may be necessary, as well as the breaking down of what may seem to the teacher as brief and easily comprehendible phrases, if students are confused or unable to imitate them accurately. Sometimes the tempo of a segment will need to be downshifted to a slower pace, too. But partial phrases grow to whole pieces, so that some of the liveliest, most sincere, sensitive, and spirited performances are a result of having learned them from the teacher "by ear."

There are variations of the modeling-and-imitation strategy that bear noting. As teachers of K–12 and tertiary music courses diversify their repertoire, they alone and individually can rarely present the music of multiple cultures in ways that are true to the traditions. It is unreasonable to expect a teacher trained in one or even several musical genres to know the vocal and instrumental techniques of a vast assortment of cultures, and a lifetime of study is not conceivably long enough to develop the expertise to model a grandly varied repertoire. In aiming for musical diversity within the content of a course or program but still with the intent of developing an acceptable level of performance quality by students, a teacher wisely taps into other musical sources and resources. Culture-bearers, musicians living and working in the community, are contracted as teachers of songs, instruments, and choral and instrumental pieces for short- or long-term periods of instruction. Recordings provide models of musical sounds, and can either be stopped and started at the push of a button, or may even come already made with phrases sung, chanted, and played one-by-one, along with the silent time it takes to repeat the phrases in imitation before moving on to the next phrase. Video-recordings may make even better models of some traditions where the visuals may underscore and complement the aural information, or when movement is integral to the song or instrumental piece; the stop-and-start use of segments of a performance may again provide the means for concentrated study, discussion, or, of course, immediate imitation of the musical moment.

When performance is not the goal, but rather an understanding of the music through listening analysis, oral/aural techniques are nonetheless in play. Singing and rhythmically chanting musical phrases and patterns draw students immediately into the musical center of a work or style. Getting the groove of a musical work by patting the musical pulse, its subdivisions, or a rhythmic pattern, or by tapping, conducting, or "dancing" it can effectively bring the listener into sharp focus on musical components. A teacher will thus utilize oral/aural strategies with considerable frequency to engage students in participatory experiences, knowing that the greater the participation of the students, the more deeply their musical understanding may be.

Regardless of whether the goal is performance or musical understanding through attentive and engaged listening, successful units of musical study include occasions for students to hear the whole composition without interferences, interjections, breakdowns, or conversational pauses. From a 20-second "blip" to a 10-minute form, music deserves to be known in its entirety. When it can be seen as well, live or via VCR and DVD formats, so much the better. The deep and enriching experiences happen then, when the observer can give full attention to the qualities and processes in motion within the piece. Listening to live and recorded models with attention to specific aural events is an entry point to learning, and repeated listening can make the point of music's structures and meanings. The oral/aural way is thus put into place, as it logically should be, in knowing the musical art.

CURRICULAR INFUSIONS OF THE WORLD'S MUSICS

Because of the cultural diversity of populations across the globe and within our very own local communities, there is musical diversity. Further, because schools operate within societies that prize cultural democracy, their curricular subjects for study, including music, are intended to be taught and learned from the perspective of more than a single "dominant culture." James Banks, American multiculturalist, sought to develop through research, policy, and curricular designs, effective ways in which an equity pedagogy could be achieved so that all children and youth regardless of culture (particularly their ethnicity) might benefit from instruction that fits their learning needs and styles; his visionary ideas figure prominently in the *Handbook of Research in Multicultural Education* (Banks and Banks, 1995/2001). In music education practice, the growth of multicultural awareness among teachers resulted in attempts to diversify the repertoire for students of all levels and venues. The collaborative efforts of educators and ethnomusicologists in *Multicultural Perspectives in Music Education* (Willliam M. Anderson and Patricia Shehan Campbell, editors, 1989/1996) made available instructional materials from various world music cultures, and the transcriptions and contextual descriptions of ethnomusicologist Jonathan Stock's *World Sound Matters* (1996) were likewise a means for broadening the musical repertoire of classroom practice. Instructional issues and curricular designs on world music education were surfacing in symposia (*Teaching Musics of the World*, Margot Leith-Phillip and Andreas Gurtzwiler, editors, 1993), collected essays (*World Musics in Education*, Malcolm Floyd, editor, 1995); *World Musics and Music Education: Facing the Music*, Bennett Reimer, editor, 2002), interviews with ethnomusicologists (*Music in Cultural Context*, Patricia Shehan Campbell, editor, 1996), bibliographic compilations (*Musics of the World's Cultures*, Barbara Lundquist and K. Szego, editors, 1998), and historical chronicles of the multicultural and world music movements in schools (Terese M. Volk's *Music, Education, and Multiculturalism* 1998). Cultural diversity is on the radar screen of music teachers and musical diversity is valued in principle, but the curricular infusion of musical expressions of the world is yet in its infancy.

The teaching and learning of the world's musics can happen in courses and curricular programs from preschool through post-graduate studies, in academic-styled courses or performance ensembles. Even the youngest learners can sing, play, move, create, and listen in focused ways. They can engage in the music-making that children in selected cultures may know and perform, from singing games to percussion ensembles, in what American music teachers refer to as "general music" classes. For older children from middle childhood through adolescence, the possibilities increase for their participation in a host of vocal/choral and instrumental performance, and in analytical listening and creative composition and improvisation experiences. By middle school, in grades 6, 7, 8, and 9, and through their high school careers, students are capable of sophisticated performance and expressive skills, and given sequential instruction, can advance rapidly in the development of techniques necessary for performing a broad array of music for band, choir, orchestra, and jazz ensembles. Likewise, secondary school students in North American schools have proven themselves articulate performers in what have been referred to as "nontraditional ensembles" (meaning ensembles not traditionally found in most schools) such as West African drumming, Shona-style marimbas, Trinidadian steel drums (or "pans"), Mexican mariachis, and world vocal/choral ensembles that feature Bulgarian, South African, and other multipart traditions. High school students are able to engage in a highly technical level of musical analysis, perceiving melodic themes and their development, layers of syncopated rhythms that sound simultaneously, and musical sections that repeat and are varied. The results of such analysis are also to be found in their improvisations and composition projects, when the awareness by students of how musical structures fit together across cultures are reflected in what they create. For university students, whether they are music majors or students enrolled in music as an elective course, the potential is there to engage in performance and participatory experiences, in analytical listening and creative projects, and in the discourse on issues such as globalization, identity, and authenticity that surround the music. At all levels and in every setting, the study of music as a global phenomenon is possible—and may already be successfully in play.

The design and delivery of innovative instructional units and revised curricular and course emphases that reflect the world's musical cultures rests in the work of thoughtful teachers to follow into practice the principles of teaching in a cultural democracy, and who persevere in teaching with cultural sensitivity and in a socially conscious manner. In pursuit of curricular pathways that bring about for students the broadest possible understanding of musical expressions, teachers need to keep in mind these action-items: (1) Recognize each musical culture for what it offers in the way of understanding music as music, as human experience, as culture, and in context, (2) study unfamiliar music cultures by listening, reading, viewing, tapping into the expertise of local musicians, culture-bearers, and scholars as resources, (3) teach in culture-specific units, for example the music of East Africa or Samoan choral music, so that students can become immersed in the music and its cultural meanings and functions, (4) teach in a comparative manner, selecting "lutes," "triple meter," "drones," "court ensembles," or "protest songs," finding multiple examples of a concept across cultures, (5) honor the pedagogical system in which the music is embedded, for example, teaching via oral/aural techniques if they are traditional to the musical culture. Programmatic changes that strive to globalize musical studies for students of any age are likely to succeed and to be met with enthusiasm and interest by students when caring and conscientious teachers take these matters into their hands.

SAMPLE COURSE SCHEDULES

When embarking into the realm of a musical education that is globally oriented, it is useful to consider designs that have proven successful for teachers in a variety of circumstances and situations. Below are found sample schedules of "global musics" over longer and shorter durations, in use in elementary and secondary schools, and in university settings. They entail attention to music's structural and expressive components, and to aspects of music's cultural meaning to the people who make it and value it. Included are shorter instructional units, semester-length courses, and whole-year plans of study. There are suggested designs for cross-cultural comparative music courses, and culture-specific study units. While some of these plans may work with students of any age, it may be useful to envision them at specified grade levels. They are not set-in-stone prescriptive models to be preserved intact, however, but hypothetical possibilities to be played with and reshaped according to the interests and needs of teachers and students. Further, they will be made more relevant and real as the chapters ahead unfold their suggestions for explicit music-cultural experiences.

These sample schedules are mere "shells" that outline courses and units that can be found in K–12 settings, along with a small assortment of university-level music appreciation and methods courses for teachers. The content to fill the sessions is found throughout the chapters of this volume, from exploratory listening (Chapter 2 and 3) to participation (Chapter 4), performance (Chapter 5), and creative-expressive experiences (Chapter 6), and thoughtful teachers will find that the outlines can be fleshed out from the vast array of suggested activities on the pages that follow. These courses can be enhanced through the use of other components of the Global Music series, too, through excerpts from the companion volume, *Thinking Musically*, and from specific culture-case studies and their websited instructional manuals. Of course, video footage can make for compelling instruction, and suggestions in the appendix can complement the audio components noted in the outlines. Students themselves can be tapped for musical cultures they know, too, for they are not blank slates but experienced listeners—and quite possibly performers, too. Finally, the expertise of guest artists and culture-bearers is certain to give spark to a teaching unit, as they may be willing to perform, lead students in participatory experiences, tell traditional tales, contextualize the music, and offer an understanding of music as personally meaningful. Thus will sample schedules move beyond the sparse outlines that follow.

20-Session School Unit on Music as a Global Phenomenon. For children in intermediate grades 3 through 5 (or 6) within elementary schools but also for middle school students in grades 6, 7, 8 (and 9), a broad survey of music and ways of entering into the musical experience can be useful. Teachers may spread the twenty sessions over twenty weeks, or ten, or just a month, depending upon the scheduling of the music class. The teacher can lead a discovery of music as a global phenomenon by using a selection of developmentally appropriate activities in later chapters of this volume, all of which maximize active student involvement. An in-school performance of several songs and instrumental pieces can be one of the goals to be realized, and an ongoing project by individual students to interview and develop oral histories of the preferred music and musical experiences of family members can enliven and build a recognition by children and youth of the use and meaning of music in people's lives.

20-SESSION SCHOOL UNIT ON MUSIC AS A GLOBAL PHENOMENON

Session 1	What is Music? (Sampling of listening selections)
Sessions 2–3	Exploring Musical Sound (See assorted activities in Chapter 2)
Sessions 4–7	Listening with Attention and Engagement (See assorted activities in Chapters 3 and 4)
Sessions 8–14	Performing (See assorted activities in Chapter 5)
Sessions 15–18	Composing Original Works (See assorted activities in Chapter 6)
Sessions 19–20	Preparing for the Public (Rehearsals of music to be performed)
Culmination	Public Performance of Varied Musical Expressions; (also known as an "Informance," an informal sharing of learned music)

30-Session All-Level Survey of "Big Cultures." A longer duration of study can entail thirty class sessions (more or less) in which "big cultures" of the world's major regions are probed for the musical expressions that are made by professional and amateur musicians, in work and worship, for dance and listening pleasure, and as a means of expressing personal and cultural identity. Beginning with two sessions of awareness in the musical cultures that live locally, which can be developed via live appearances of musicians (including parents and grandparents, and other family members who have songs to sing and instruments to share), the survey then can proceed to an exploration of a sampling of musical selections from North American, European, African, Latin American, East Asian, Southeast Asian, Australian, Pacific, South Asian and Southwest Asian (Middle Eastern) cultures. As the recorded selections of each cultural region are intended for use in listening, participatory, performance, and creative experiences in the classroom, the teacher of music courses in upper elementary and secondary school may pick-and-choose those activities that may best fit the timing of the course and the students' needs. A final segment of the course can shift the focus of study from music-by-region to cross-cultural comparisons of concepts, which can be approached as a class or through small-group projects.

30-SESSION ALL-LEVEL SURVEY OF "BIG CULTURES"

Sessions 1–2	Music Where We Are: Listening to Surround-Sounds (Neighborhood and community music)
Sessions 3–4	Music of North America (CD tracks 6, 7, 9, 24, 29, 32, 35, 36)
Sessions 5–7	Music of Europe (CD tracks 21, 28, 33, 34, 37, 38, 40, 49, 52, 54)
Sessions 8–11	Music of Africa (CD tracks 5, 19, 55, 58)
Sessions 12–15	Music of Latin America (CD tracks 2, 4, 22, 57, 59; Also U.S./Latin 7, 29)
Sessions 16–18	Music of East Asia: China, Japan, Korea (CD tracks 3, 12, 14, 15, 16, 17, 18, 20, 26, 41, 51, 56)
Sessions 19–21	Music of Southeast Asia, Australia, and the Pacific (CD tracks 8, 13, 23, 27, 31, 50)
Sessions 22–24	Music of South and Southwest Asia (CD tracks 1, 10, 11, 25, 27, 30, 39, 46, 53)
Sessions 25–30	Comparisons (Flutes, lutes, theatre music, dance music, singing games, seasonal and holiday music, love songs, pop styles, ceremonial music examples)

Exploratory Middle School Music-Culture Modules. Schools operating on block schedules, particularly middle schools, may have need for short exploratory courses or modules. Even in the case of longer courses, a module of study may nonetheless be of interest to teachers and their students who look for a series of intensive, focused musical experiences (for example, six weeks of guitar study, followed by study of the music of Africa, then recorder study, East Asia, keyboard, American popular music, and compositional techniques). The two modules below offer examples of how exploratory music-culture modules might unfold in a middle school setting, beginning with a listening sampler that is followed by participatory experiences in assorted musical traditions, and ending with a review and assessment of the music of the given region. These suggestions can be enhanced and extended through activities noted in later chapters of this volume.

6-WEEK MIDDLE SCHOOL MODULE: AFRICA (EAST AND WEST)

Week One	Introduction to the Music of Africa. Explore by listening to CD tracks 5, 19, 55, 56. Determine transcontinental pan-African music: Percussive and pulsive timbral/quality, call-response technique, brief melodic motifs, open-ended forms, layered textures. (Identify components in African music recordings.)
Week Two	Drumming. CD track 5: Listen and learn to play. Extend open-ended piece.
Week Three	Mallet Music. CD track 19: Listen and learn to play. Extend open-ended piece.
Week Four	The Story-Song. CD track 55: Listen to solo and choral response. Learn "Chawe Chidyo Chem'chero."
Week Five	The Choral Song. CD track 58: Listen and learn to sing. Sample other choral songs.
Week Six	Review African styles by listening, engaging in participation in and performance of all previously learned pieces. Reassess the function, content, and value of pan-African music.

6-WEEK MIDDLE SCHOOL MODULE: MUSIC OF ASIA

Week One	Introduction to the Music of Asia. Explore and categorize Asian regions by listening to CD tracks 3, 12, 14, 15, 16, 17, 18, 20,

	26, 41, 51, 56 (East Asia); 8, 23, 31, 40 (Southeast Asia); 1, 10, 11, 25, 27, 30, 39, 46, 53 (South and Southwest Asia). Identify instruments and vocal timbres, melodic and rhythmic qualities, textures, forms.
Week Two	East Asian Percussion. Listen to CD track 16 as style example. Learn to play Japanese Percussion Ensemble (Matsuri Bayashi) piece.
Week Three	East Asian Melodic Ensembles. Listen and follow graphs to CD tracks 12, 14, 15, 17, 18, 20.
Week Four	Southeast Asian Xylophones. Listen to CD track 50, and play separate and interlocking patterns.
Week Five	Southwest Asian Melodic Ensemble: Egypt. Listen to CD track 25, and play dombek (drum) and riqq (tambourine) parts.
Week Six	Review Asian styles by listening/engaging in participation in and performance of all previously learned pieces. Reassess the function, content, and value of Asian music.

Secondary School Ensemble Sessions. Performance ensembles at the middle and high school level are typically involved in the reading and preparation of scores for public performances, including concerts, school assemblies, festivals, parades and social events of the school and community. A distinctive repertoire for secondary school bands, choirs, and orchestras has evolved over time to fit the particular nature of the instruments of these ensembles and the developing choral voices in varied stages of maturation, and many young people have become accomplished musicians through the study of musical repertoire that fits these standard school ensembles. Indeed, school ensembles comprise their own unique musical cultures whose continuity are a source of pride to their communities. Yet even in cases of the most successful of traditions, change can be a refreshing renewal to standard routine and repertoire, and may make for invigorating experiences in rehearsals and even new sounds to filter into public performances. Some of the best teachers of band, choir, and orchestra have the flexibility to allow in some of the world's musical cultures to their classes, thus bending the ears and stimulating the minds of their young musicians.

"Break-out" sessions in performance classes are one means of diversifying the music-educational experience of students in secondary schools without losing sight of the standard repertoire. While greater lengths of instructional time are likely to be more effective, even five- or ten-minute "spots" can be worked into band, choir, and orchestra periods for students to listen to, discuss, and participate in a global view of the musical world into which they are heading. These "break-out" experiences are wedged within the more traditional curriculum, or they may occasionally replace it (for the day, the week, or the every-other-Thursday session). The key is a systematic instructional approach, one which is preplanned and carefully structured to link one step, activity, and session to the next. If the goal is something deeper than mere exposure to a musical culture, then multiple "spots," longer sessions, linked sessions, and a clear sense of techniques and strategies will be vital to achieving it.

Directors of bands, choirs, and orchestras can select some of the Attentive Listening and Enactive Listening Experiences (see Chapters 3 and 4), depending upon the strengths and needs of their students. They may guide their students to identify musical characteristics of a selection, to compare unfamiliar music to music they know well and have even performed, to follow graphic depictions, including notation, as they listen to selections. They can be led in the partial performance of musical selections, via participatory experiences, by playing or singing a melody in unison, chanting a rhythm, performing a polyrhythm using instruments or body percussion in interactive sections, or selecting out one part of a multipart piece to listen to and then to perform (with or without notation).

Closely related to the realm of "break-out" sessions is the matter of developing musicianship, as one so typically does in an opening period of warm-ups and exercises, through new musical experiences for the ear that embrace multiple offerings from the world's musical cultures. For example, along with playing selected major and minor scales, band and orchestra students could be challenged to listen to musical selections and to determine the scales and modes upon which the melodies are based. (Several of these scales and modes are found notated in Chapters 3 and 4.) Choral students can vocalize on single phrases that can be repeated at different pitch levels, for example the first phrases of the "Navajo Corn-Grinding Song" (CD track 9, page 136), "Habanera" from Carmen (CD track 21, pages 140–42), or "Iron Duke in the Land" (CD track 57, page 121). Instrumentalists can likewise play snippets of melody, such as a phrase or more of "Gunslingers" (CD track 2, page 95), Kiembara xylophone orchestra (CD track 19, page 138), and "Tar Road to Sligo/Paddy Clancy's" (CD track 37, page 149). Percussionists can be challenged to listen and learn, or to read the nonpitched notation for "Mi Bajo y Yo" (CD track 4, page 99), "Atsiagbeko" (CD track 5, page 129), or Episode from *wei-meni-pele* (CD 55, page 120), or to accompany their melody-making colleagues with stylistically appropriate rhythms.

Occasionally, just following a major performance, in between concerts, or at other times when the pressure is off to learn another program of music repertoire at a rapid pace, more thorough-going explorations of a musical culture may be designed and offered to students of secondary school ensembles. Should students show a curiosity or penchant for a specific musical culture, several sessions may be devoted to the study of it. Modules can be designed to probe the music of Bulgaria, or North India, or West Africa, or Bali, or Brazil, by gathering recorded selections and experiences from this volume and from *Thinking Musically*. Comparisons and contrasts of musical cultures, and of specific musical components and concepts, can easily fill a series of sessions, and can be delivered by the ensemble director or by special guest artists and culture-bearers.

Nonstandard Secondary School "Academic" Music Courses. Beyond the time-honored instrumental and choral ensembles of school programs, and the public perception of the characteristic repertoire they perform and typical functions they fulfill, there are increasing occasions in middle and high schools for the development of other courses and ensemble classes. Young people who enjoy music as a listening, performance, or creative outlet may be drawn to a course or ensemble class that is globally oriented or culture-specific in nature. A "global musics" course that serves as a cross-cultural survey of music (see the "30-Session All-Level" Survey of Big Cultures cited previously), and which makes use of a wide selection of the types of experiences offered within this volume, may proceed region by region, concept by musical and cultural concept, or activity by activity. Such a course may run a single term or for an entire scholastic year, and it may remain close to its musical-sound center or turn the corner into an integrated music with arts, humanities, or social studies course. Taught by an individual teacher or by a team, as an elective or advanced placement offering, with large-group lectures or small-group and individual projects, a global musics course may appeal to a significant number of secondary school students seeking multicultural and international perspectives on music—or through music to culture (see Chapter 7). When contemporary events bring attention to the need for further study of a nation or region, such as in the case of tensions in the Middle East, drought on the African continent, or a rapidly changing economic scene in the Asian trade market, a partnership effort by teachers across several subjects may recognize and value the design and delivery of a specialized course that utilizes music as a centerpoint or a launch into understanding these events.

Nonstandard Secondary School Music Ensembles. Academic courses aside, secondary schools are turning toward the establishment of nonstandard school music ensembles. Occasionally a population of students may request the development of a gospel choir or a mariachi band, framing their proposal on the basis of their ethnic identity, but more frequently ensembles emerge due to the appeal of the music itself to the teacher and students. The driving sound of a Brazilian samba band, the resonant blend of voices in a "world music choir" performance of South African and Polynesian songs, the toe-tapping jigs, reels, horas, hambos, branles, and tsamikos of various European string traditions, the deep groove of a Ghanian drumming ensemble or an Afro-Cuban salsa band—these are the musical traditions which, once heard and learned, may be the means by which a music program can grow to serve secondary school students who are drawn to musical study other than the standard school fare. Teachers can develop skills through their own outside school performance in various ensembles, and through workshops and weekly lessons, and year-by-year can add yet another ensemble to the schedule of music-making possibilities for their prospective students. The budget for contracting specialist teachers might well be given over to a visiting artist, too, whose residency can build the musical skills of students and teachers. The benefits of such a residency to both musical growth and the development of cultural sensitivity are not to be underestimated, for they are considerable.

University World Music-Culture Courses. Shifting from K–12 school programs to the university, as there may be readers charged with teaching university world music-culture courses now or later in their professional teaching career, the study of the world's musics is typically required of music majors or it may serve as one of several elective courses under the "music literature" or "music history/culture" rubric. For students of other majors, a course in music cultures of the world may function as one of several to select within distribution requirements in the arts or humanities. Whether for majors or not, a world music-culture course typically functions as an introduction to music across the globe. It may run for a 10-week quarter or 15-week semester, or may take the shape of a sequence of courses, such as "Music of Asia" and "Music of the Western Continents" (Africa, the Americas, and Europe) or separate big cultures courses (of Africa, Asia and the Pacific, Latin America, North America). More than a single course in world music-cultures is rare, however, so that the typical one-term university course resorts to either a surface-level survey of the musical world or an in-depth study of three or four selected cultures anchored by general precepts of music and culture. In the latter model, the selected cultures are spinouts from a musical and cultural framework that illustrate such principles as the organization of time or the role of gender relevant to music-making.

A semester-length university course consisting of three hours weekly conceivably would begin with general constructs of music exemplified in a wide variety of cultures, graduate to the concentrated study of specific cultures, and then close with a review and comparison of the constructs under study across the selected cultures. As is vital to learning music (and learning about music) at every level, active involvement through participatory experiences is again the recommended way to a thorough-going and long-lasting study of music. An ongoing fieldwork project can draw students out of their study carrels and into the community, help in sorting out the concepts as they relate to a living local culture, and lead to making connections with real musicians and musical audience members. The final weeks can serve as opportunities for review and comparison, visiting artists and culture-bearers, and presentations by student of their fieldwork projects. (Of course, the imaginative teacher will also observe that this schedule is applicable as well to students in a secondary school course.)

UNIVERSITY WORLD MUSIC-CULTURE COURSE

Week One   Thinking about Music: People, Music,
                  Meaning, Use, Transmission, Musical
                  Instruments
                  (See *Thinking Musically*, Chapters 1–2)

Week Two	Time: Rhythm, unit organization, speed Pitch: Horizontal, vertical (See *Thinking Musically*, Chapters 3–4)
Week Three	Structures: Improvisation, composition, themes and sections Issues: Culture contact, authenticity, media (See *Thinking Musically*, Chapters 5–6), Test 1
Week Four	Music Culture Choice #1 (For example, South India)
Week Five	Music Culture Choice #1 Continued
Week Six	Music Culture Choice #1 Continued, Test 2
Week Seven	Music Culture Choice #2 (For example, Japan)
Week Eight	Music Culture Choice #2 Continued
Week Nine	Music Culture Choice #2 Continued, Test 3
Week Ten	Music Culture Choice #3 (For example, Ireland)
Week Eleven	Music Culture Choice #3 Continued
Week Twelve	Music Culture Choice #3 Continued, Test 4
Week Thirteen	Review and Cultural Comparisons
Week Fourteen	Artist-Teachers and Culture-Bearers
Week Fifteen	Student Fieldwork Project Presentations, Test 5

Teacher Education Methods Courses. The materials contained within this volume are useful for study and practical application, when possible, in undergraduate and graduate methods courses within university-level teacher education programs. (Here again, readers may be students in these courses, or their course instructors, and more than a few may fill professorial roles for these courses in the years ahead— thus the description here.) A generic music education methods course may do well with insertions of suggested activities within this volume for making musical, multicultural, and pedagogical points. Courses in elementary music education methods, secondary general music methods, choral methods, and instrumental methods typically have jam-packed agendas, but when one of the principal aims is a broadened view of music repertoire and instructional style, the content of this volume becomes more relevant. Whereas a straightforward review of the various issues, the skills, and the materials for teaching choral, general, and instrumental music is vital for prospective teachers (and also helpful to those teachers already in practice), a globally conscious understanding of what to teach and how to go about it may entail at least supplemental use of recordings, readings, and experiences that will develop this way of thought and action. A choral methods student could be geared to developing conducting skills and rehearsal strategies as they pertain to a broad sampling of the world's vocal traditions, while an instrumental methods student might recognize that alonsgside the maintenance of school band and orchestra programs, there are the overarching musical goals of developing in students comprehensive skills and understandings in music listening, varied performance practices, and creative-expressive possibilities. Meanwhile, a teacher of music to children, who utilizes Orff or Kodaly techniques, or who strives for integrating music into language arts and social studies classes, may recognize the value of gathering repertoire and strategies for teaching from a global perspective.

Specialized courses for undergraduate students, graduate students, and inservice teachers, under such titles as "Multicultural Music Education," "World Musics in the Classroom," or "Ethnomusicology in the Schools," may benefit from the use of a combination of *Teaching Music Globally* with *Thinking Musically*, the shared CD, and with a selection of one or several music-culture case studies. Such courses may cover the discussion of sociopolitical issues that have rocked the foundation of society and its schools. They frequently give appropriate attention to the cultural diversity of student populations, their learning styles and instructional needs. (Suggestions for readings on these issues may be found in the appendix.) Still, these courses require the substance of music at their core, coming from students' own experiences within their local communities as well as from across the globe, to sing, play, move to, create, and reflect upon. Diversity, both musical and cultural, are best addressed by music teachers through music, which comprises the bulk of these volumes.

It is accepted practice that whatever the experiences that are designed for K–12 classrooms, whether choral, general, or instrumental, they can be applied to students in teacher education courses. The suggested experiences in the chapters to follow can be taught by methods course instructors to students. They can also be selected by students to trial-teach to young people in schools for a 10-minute lesson segment here or a full-fledged 50-minute lesson there. Further, these experiences can (and should) be evaluated for the instructional sequence and effectiveness with children and adolescents in various venues, as student responses will most certainly be affected by the instructional circumstances and settings. The array of activities are meant as much for teachers-in-preparation, students in pursuit of music education certification, as for full-time teachers, in the hope that the actual doing of them will result in the development of a familiarity and confidence so that they can be applied to students in schools.

WORLD MUSIC PEDAGOGY

Sitting somewhere between the scholarly discipline of ethnomusicology and the practice of musically educating students in the world's musical cultures is a newly emergent phenomenon known as world music pedagogy. Ethnomusicologists study music in culture and music *as* culture, including the art, traditional, tribal, and popular musical cultures of nearby neighborhoods as well as those of remote and far-flung locales across the globe. Those serving on university faculties are responsible, through their lectures and seminars, for teaching music from perspectives steeped in anthropological theory, musical and cultural analyses, and area studies. Music educators, whether in the K–12 schools or on universities faculties of music or education, typically come from backgrounds in the performance of music that is overwhelmingly European (or Euro-American) in style. Changing demographics, societal forces, and multicultural mandates, however, have begun to turn educators toward viewing their educational missions in more inclusive terms, and to searching for a wider variety of musical sources for their teaching repertoire. The two streams of music professionals have accomplished much in their specialized work, and prospects for the crossing of their areas of expertise are rich with possibilities for the phenomenon of world music pedagogy.

Beyond the theoretical understandings of music in and as culture, and the aim for global expansion of repertoire in vocal and instrumental music, the pedagogy of world music strives to reach beyond queries of "what" and "why" to the question of "how." World music pedagogy concerns itself with how music is taught/transmitted and received/learned within cultures, and how best the processes that are included in significant ways within these cultures can be preserved or at least partially retained in classrooms and rehearsal halls. Those working to evolve this pedagogy have studied music with culture-bearers, and have come to know that music can be best understood through experience with the manner in which it is taught and learned. These "world music" educators, working as ethnomusicologists and educators, have ventured to the borders of their fields to blend the expertise and insights of the two into a pedagogical system that is sensitive to transmission systems within the culture. While they hardly "reenact" music learning in the South African bush, or the Indian gharana, or the Brazilian samba school, they are conscious of and pay tribute in their teaching to other notational systems (or their inapplicability), oral/aural techniques, improvisatory methods that may be integral to a style, and even what customary behaviors precede and immediately follow lessons and sessions within particular traditions. World music educators understand that less is more—at least at the entry stages to a musical culture, and that an understanding of even a single musical piece through deep and continued listening, participatory, performance, and creative experiences, and study of its cultural context and meaning, are likely to make an important impact in the musical education of students at every age and level of development. The world music pedagogy they profess is sensitive to both music and culture, with culture interpreted as both "old" (original culture of the music) and "new" (instructional culture). The "how" of world music pedagogy requires bridging the two cultures.

Ethnomusicology will continue its scholarly course through interdisciplinary themes and theoretical analyses to understand music as human expression. Likewise, music education's directive, to guide children and adolescents in knowing music firsthand for its composite aesthetic, expressive, and historical-cultural aims, will hold its place as a compelling component of many curricular programs. What remains to be seen is how the blending of expert and committed scholars, musicians, and teachers forge their collective interests into a scholarship of teaching that is reflective of the available knowledge on music, culture, and instructional/ learning processes. The phenomenon of world music pedagogy will be the obvious beneficiary of these blended efforts, as will the students of teachers who are musically and globally attuned.

A PATHWAY AHEAD

A pathway lies ahead for developing the musical understanding of K–12 students, so that they might come to grips with it as a global and cross-cultural phenomenon. This pathway is best traveled by teachers who possess an open reception to the breadth of music's multiple manifestations, a sensitivity to the cultural uses and meanings of music by its singers and players, an earnest interest in students' experiences and needs regarding knowledge of their own and other musical cultures, and a willingness to balance new global approaches to school music instruction with long-standing traditions that have been successfully in place for generations—and even centuries. Along with *Thinking Musically*, *Teaching Music Globally* (and the companion CD) offers the means for traveling this pathway, a tour guide for teachers working with elementary and secondary students (with relevant information as well for some who teach university courses). A portion of the pathway will appear as familiar territory to teachers, including some of the excerpted jazz classics and symphonic themes, the very use of notation to convey the melodic and rhythmic features of a musical phrase, and quite possibly the format of graphic listening guides. More unusual and innovative components for teachers' use will be the musical selections that are derived from places far distant from the Western origins of standard school repertoire, the exploratory nature of developing in students of various experience levels a sound awareness of the many realms of the world's musical cultures and contexts, and the three phases of musical involvement that require a keen ear for taking full advantage of attentive, engaged, and enactive listening.

The process of teaching music in its cross-cultural array is mapped out in the chapters that follow for teachers who will work with children in bands, choirs, orchestras, general music classes, and assorted other academic and applied music venues. The map is not definitive, however, for explicit directions are not likely to be pertinent to so many varied circumstances and settings of music instruction. Instead, practical suggestions are offered for the use of exploratory music-culture experiences, straight-ahead listening, participation, performance, and creative-expressive events across diverse venues and levels. Thoughtful teachers will take note of those musical selections and suggested experiences that seem to fit the philosophical aims of their real (and perhaps even ideal and imagined) instructional practices. The pathway ahead is not straight and narrow in a fully prescriptive way, but with prospects for turn-offs, cloverleafs, crossroads and cul-de-sacs. Speed will be a factor in following the pathway to teaching music globally, and teachers will want to exercise caution in considering (and even trial-teaching) which musical selections and strategies may work best with what students, and why. A pathway lies just ahead that is well worth pursuing, as it is certain to lead teachers, who can thus lead their students, in knowing music with a capital "M," Music, as it sounds and functions across the globe.

PROBLEMS TO PROBE

1. What is your musical "surround-sound," the sonic and musical environment in which you live and work? Spend a day listening with care, jotting down the flavor and tone of your aural surroundings, their sources, magnitude, and duration. Compare notes with colleagues.

2. Challenge yourself to learn a song or short instrumental segment totally by ear. Describe the strategies undertaken in doing so. Discuss whether there are occasions for learning music through notation or aural/oral means, and what benefits and deficits there are to either way.

3. Select one of the sample course schedules. Scan the CD for sounds and flip through the chapters for experiences, and sketch out how you might undertake teaching the course from a globally-conscious position. Return to the sketch to make adjustments following your further experience in the study of world musics in education through the chapters ahead.

CHAPTER 2

A Sound Awareness of Music

∞

Music is a many-splendored thing. Now as in the historical past, people are making music meaningful and useful in their lives, as singers, players, dancers, creators, and listeners. In many traditions, they may be musically interactive in all of these roles at once, where no demarcations are found to cubbyhole them into one realm only to keep them out of another. Across the earth, the palette of musical possibilities is as varied as technology can provide and as deeply involving as the time that people will allow it into their lives. Music calls individuals to embrace it intimately, and to share in it as social experience and as members of a community of musicians and listening audiences. For people of the world's cultures, music is vital to their very being, whether they know it as "makers or takers," active participants or passive consumers. Music teachers traditionally aim for the active participation of their students in musical experiences and, as such, they match well the manner in which so many of the world's people are musically involved, both in their own neighborhoods as well as in far-flung places across the globe.

Practically speaking, there are three central features to consider in developing a sound awareness of music: instruments (and voices), elements, and contexts. We grow in awareness of the music by knowing about the instruments (and voices) that produce the sound—their timbral quality, how they are constructed, what ideas people have of their instruments and their associations with spirituality, gender, and cultural status, and whether the instrument is viewed as a "thing" of beauty or an item of technology (or both). We come to terms with music's structures through analysis of its elements of time (rhythm, its organization, and speed), pitch (both horizontal, as in melody, and vertical, as in the textures of pitches sounding together). We recognize that our own conceptions of music are personally and culturally evolved, and that we must commit ourselves to the study of music's functions and settings within the culture from which it is derived if we are to truly understand it. When we make an effort to know the singers, players, dancers, composers (improvisers and arrangers, too), and avid listeners, to talk with them, to observe them in "live" musical action, we can get to the heart of context and what the music truly means to the people within the culture and why it is a valued human expression. Our understanding of music depends upon the information we can gather about these features.

The process of musically educating children and youth requires a continuous commitment to multiple courses of action, from basic musical awareness experiences to the thoughtful creation and re-creation of music. For the sakes of our students, whether they are the very young elementary school children rooted to their homes and families or the more musically sophisticated secondary school adolescents, we are compelled to consider, on the way to providing them with applied performance and creative skills, their *sound awareness of music*. Who are our students, musically speaking? What music do they find familiar, less familiar, or even "exotic"? What musical experiences do they bring from outside the context of instruction into the classroom? How aware are they of music's features and processes? How can their awareness, both of locally grown music and music from distant cultures, be extended and intensified? By raising these questions and seeking responses, the musical education of our students can be made more relevant.

Teachers do well when they awaken in K–12 students the deeper meanings of the music of their own familial experiences. They do well, too, when they develop their students' awareness of musical genres and expressions that have been outside their experience but which can be brought within their reach through effective curricular considerations. Through a kind of discovery zone of suggested "sound awareness activities" described next, teachers can guide students in ways for knowing musical sound through the music-makers, and the instruments and voices, that are able to be accessed. Independently conceived although similar in spirit to the development of ideas prescribed a generation ago by Canadian composer R. Murray Schaefer in *The Thinking Ear: Complete Writings on Music Education* (1986), these activities stretch from local to global conceptions of musical sources, elements, and contexts. Some of the three dozen suggestions are student-independent, while others require the teacher's guidance and facilitation in class to set up and show students the way. The activities are wide-ranging, too, some of which will prove to be quite elementary and intended for young beginners while others will challenge even an experienced first-chair flutist or a ten-year veteran of piano lessons. As for where to begin, which activities to use (and even which to discard), the decision is dependent upon teachers, students, and programs. Perceptive teachers will fit the activities to the needs of their students, although levels of difficulty (initial, intermediate, and advanced) are designated in an advisory way. As might be expected, the activities can be used intact as described or adapted by teachers and their students.

DISCOVERING THE SPLENDORS OF SOUND

As babes-in-the-womb, we had our first experiences through what our mothers sang to us, and we could hear through her the music our parents preferred listening to, and that they may have sung and played together. The sense of hearing develops first, and is fine-tuned through infancy and toddlerhood. Creeping and crawling, we listened to the sounds of family members in the home, and then as young children in the yard, we heard our neighbors talking, singing, playing their recordings, and maybe even a playing a musical instrument or two. We discovered our world partly through our sound-sense, and our musicality developed through the music that appeared within our range of hearing. Yet as the world crowded in on us by middle childhood and into our adolescence, it is not surprising that our sound awareness may have dimmed and diminished some, and that the scope of our musical experience became fixed on just that music that was most commonly "in the air" around us and thus easily available to us.

The world is rich with musical sounds which distinguish one culture from the next, and even the most local and familiar sound environments, heard in a moment's time, are reflective of a culture. It is captivating to listen with fresh ears to the sounds that emanate from local "home" cultures. Open the door into a family home, and there are people talking, walking, humming, whistling, laughing, dogs barking, and appliances whirring or buzzing—from washers and dryers to electric drills and saws, or TVs and radios and recordings playing. From the other direction, open the door to the outside, and an active neighborhood may be heard—from songbirds and the wind in the trees, to the motors of near and distant vehicles, to the dull thumping music that pours out of restaurants, stores, cafes, and passing cars. The doors that open into and out of these cultures lend themselves to widely varied sound-palettes, so that even the languages or inflections of a family's speech, or the melodies of particular songbirds perched nearby, or the music from a specific TV station or restaurant, will differ and thus distinguish a given place as having its own very local sonic culture. In knowing the wider world of music, then, we go forward with our ears perked to explore with our students the musical possibilities of our immediate environs and of a sampling of sound that is captured on a single CD.

SOUND AWARENESS ACTIVITY 2.1   Discovering Environmental Sounds. *(Initial) Alone or in groups, take stock of the sounds in an immediate environment. In the classroom, elsewhere in the building, or outdoors, maintain silence for five minutes in order to listen and jot down all ambient sounds. Discover which sounds appear to have definitive musical qualities of pitch (high, low, changing), duration (long, short, fast, slow, steady or not), timbre (from dull to brilliant), and intensity (soft, loud, changing). Note how sounds seem to collide and combine in polyphonic textures, and how others seem to "stand out." Which sounds are predictable and familiar? Which sounds might be telling symbols of who people are, of ideas and objects that people value, that is, signifiers of cultural value?*

SOUND AWARENESS ACTIVITY 2.2   Constructing an Environmental Sound Composition. *(Initial) Using a variety of sound sources, including voices, body percussion, musical instruments, and other available objects like paper, cups, pens, chairs, keys, and desk tops, try to reproduce with others a 30-second piece comprised of the ambient sounds observed in 2.1. Experiment with not only the timbral qualities but also duration and intensity, and textural variety (one sound source versus many). Note the challenges in re-creating natural and mechanical or motorized sounds, if that is your intent, and in developing the textures that come from the combination of sounds occurring simultaneously. Create a miniature composition based upon this environmental sound-palette. Evaluate its impact as a musical composition or as a mere exercise in sound exploration.*

SOUND AWARENESS ACTIVITY 2.3 Instrumental Sound-Spectrum. *(Initial) Find at least five musical instruments, or objects with music-making potential, in your home and community. Play them, or ask others to play them, and explore the mechanisms by which sound is produced. Make a list of these instruments and categorize them by their sound-making capacities (by plucking or bowing a string, blowing into a tube or cone, striking the instrument's surface, shaking the instrument).* See Thinking Musically, *Chapter 2, as you consider various other ways to categorize these instruments, including the material from which they are made.*

SOUND AWARENESS ACTIVITY 2.4 The Personal Voice. *(Initial) The most personal instrument of all is the voice. Listen to your singing voice as you sing. The shower is a place of good resonance where the sound feeds back to you from the shower wall, or a tape recording is an obvious source of feedback to you as to your sound. Describe your vocal quality: High, medium, low in pitch? Bright, light or darker, heavier? With vibrato or "straight" in tone? With or without rasp, or buzz, or breathiness, or twang? Large or small range? Once you have decided what it will do, try various singing qualities or styles: Western art/operatic, Country (western), Pop-styled, other. What music are you most comfortable singing? Which ones will you learn?*

SOUND AWARENESS ACTIVITY 2.5 Other Voices. *(Intermediate) Listen to the voices of others on the CD selections. Without reading their official descriptions from the CD list, make notes of the vocal quality and estimate which culture the voices belong to. What led you to these descriptions and speculations? (Suggested ten selections: CD tracks 1, 7, 9, 10, 20, 21, 27, 33, 39, and 46.)*

SOUND AWARENESS ACTIVITY 2.6 Instrument ID-by-Ear. *(Intermediate) Listen to ten selections from the CD, and identify them according to the following process:* (a) *description of materials from which the instrument is constructed (for example, wood or brass or gourd),* (b) *description of how it's played,* (c) *country or region of the world where the instrument is played,* (d) *"educated guess" as to the English-language name of the instrument. Check your answers with the CD list description, and discuss which ones were most challenging, and why. (Suggested ten selections: CD tracks 2, 3, 5, 8, 13, 14, 22, 25, 32, 52).*

SOUND AWARENESS ACTIVITY 2.7 Making Your Own Instrument. *(Intermediate) Based upon the sound-making properties of which you are aware through your examination of instruments, look into the possibilities for making your own instrument. Nonpitched percussion instruments, such as drums, wood blocks, and shakers, may immediately come to mind, and numerous materials found at home or at school could be adapted to make musical sounds. Consider what instruments could be made, including strings and winds, from the following materials: hollowed-out bamboo stalks, PVC or other plastic pipes, "Easter eggs" and rice, pots and pans, rubberbands, 2 × 4 boards, sticks, cans, strings (including metal guitar strings), drinking straws, or cheesecloth.*

SOUND AWARENESS ACTIVITY 2.8 Sleuthing for Styles. *(Intermediate) Scan radio, TV, and Internet sources to sleuth out as many musical styles as is possible. If descriptive words are applied to them (or occur to you), jot them down. Visit the local record shops for style descriptors, too, as you take note of the dividers and bins in which the recordings are kept. In small groups, list all of the different styles of music you have gathered.*

Check off those styles that you know and write the name of a composer, artist, or song/composition that is identified with this style. Compare your findings with those of your peers.

GETTING THE FOCUS ON MUSIC AND CULTURE

People often take music for granted. Sounds from every source, every song and instrumental piece, may converge into an aural collage and become too much "a part of the scenery." Occasionally, music will stand out and be transformative in the experience we have with it, but for most music to be greatly valued and viewed for its remarkable contribution to human life, it is often necessary to study it. The mission of a musical education in schools and institutions of higher learning is to develop in students a deeper understanding of the structures and meanings of music; thus it is vital for teachers to teach musically and culturally. Developing in students a sound awareness of music necessitates that they focus on music and its cultural significance, a noble goal that can be achieved through their involvement of activities presented here. The volume *Thinking Musically* is a useful guide to further explanation of the concepts behind these "focus" activities, and both its glossary and the CD are vital components in the study of music as a cultural expression.

A musical culture may be as tightly conceived of as what is heard within one family home or as expansive as a neighborhood, a community formed by ethnicity or religious practices, or region defined by geographic, ecological, or political boundaries. One family's sound surroundings may differ from the next, and so do neighborhoods vary in the music people listen to, make, and value. What music may sound in the center of a city may not be the same as what may be heard on the east side, or the south side. As communities develop around main streets, churches, schools, parks, business districts, and shopping centers, the music of the people who live there is part of what distinguishes them. First-generation Eritreans bring with them the musical heritage of their home country, and it uniquely defines them, as does the heritage-music of first-generation Russians, Koreans, and Venezuelans. Those whose families have lived away from these home countries for two, three, or more generations may yet be musically linked to their old-world heritage, and music, like the food, traditional clothing, and religious practices, may emerge at weddings, funerals, family reunions, and holiday celebrations. Americans whose roots may be traced to Ireland, Mexico, Japan, Italy, and the Philippines may live as mainstream Americans on most days but enjoy the festive occasions that recall their ancestry and underscore their ethnic identity.

SOUND AWARENESS ACTIVITY 2.9 Defining Music. *(Initial) Survey friends and family members, asking them to define what is (and is not) music. How close do they come to the definition of music as "humanly organized sound"? Or to referring to music as "a process" that requires the efforts of performers and listeners? Do any of the collected definitions take in dance as well (as in the case of the Indian word for music, sangita)? Do any of the definitions separate vocal and instrumental music by the use of separate words, as in the case of the Macedonian "pesne" for song and "musika" for instrumental music?*

SOUND AWARENESS ACTIVITY 2.10 Exploring Musical Heritage. *(Initial) Gather information on the music of your family's cultural heritage. What musics do your parents prefer? Your grandparents? Siblings, aunts, and uncles? Ask them about favorite songs, artists, and styles. On what occasions do they hear his music? Do they sing or play an instrument (or did they)? To what kind of music do they dance? Review their collections of recordings (CDs, tapes, LPs) and videotapes/DVDs of a musical nature. Compile a list of significant musics that define their heritage. Discuss any surprises (to you) concerning your family's musical heritage.*

SOUND AWARENESS ACTIVITY 2.11 Determining Musical Identity. *(Initial) Who are you, musically speaking? Beyond the ties to your family's musical heritage, the music you listen to, and perform, uniquely defines you. Maintain an accurate record of your daily musical involvement over a week's time. Be specific about the nature of your listening (To what? By whom? For how long?), performing (What instrument? What piece?), dancing (Type of dance? To what music?). Tally the amount of your musical involvement per day, with subtallies on activity types and musical styles (or artists), and determine the average amount over the week. Compare to the musical preferences of other family members, and classmates.*

SOUND AWARENESS ACTIVITY 2.12 Knowing Musical Beauty. *(Intermediate) Play a sampling of musical selections from the CD, and discuss what might be considered beautiful about the music. For example, CD track 3 features embellishment and variation in Chinese music, a beautiful approach to "adding flowers" to the otherwise plain melody, and CD track 5 presents a community of musicians (from West Africa) who come together in a socially responsive manner to interlock their short segments of rhythm and pitch to create a satisfying musical sound. To know musical beauty one must not only be familiar with the music, but also come to an understanding of what the music means. Music's power is inherent in its ability to stir deep emotions in the listener. Further, this power may be personally and culturally constructed. Discuss what music has been particularly beautiful, and powerful, and why. If the selections do not sound beautiful to you on initial or even multiple hearings, pinpoint and probe for reasons why not.*

SOUND AWARENESS ACTIVITY 2.13 Discovering Music's Functions. *(Intermediate) Music's meaning is often associated with its function within culture, and many songs and genres are referred to and are categorized by what function they fulfill. Play and discuss examples of music's functions as sacred expression and worship (CD tracks 1, 10, 14), social protest (CD tracks 6, 7), tribute and honor to nobility (CD tracks 8, 26), work (CD track 9), storytelling (CD tracks 55, 56), dance, movement, and martial art (CD tracks 2, 4, 37, 38, 59), religious ritual (CD tracks 12, 26), vocal art (CD tracks 20, 21), instrumental art (CD tracks 11, 17, 51, 54), festive celebration (CD tracks 16, 27), expression of national identity (CD tracks 2, 23, 29, 34, 35). Discuss the use of music in daily life.*

SOUND AWARENESS ACTIVITY 2.14 Musician-Speak. *(Intermediate) Interview a musician who represents a musical culture you know little of but would like to know better. Go to a performance by the musician, if possible, or a rehearsal, or some way hear him or her perform live. Interview that musician about the use, meaning, and value of music to him or her personally, and its role and place within the cultural community. Ask questions about the musician's musical experience and training: When he/she learned? Where? From whom? How? Ask about favorite pieces in the repertoire, and why they are preferred. Record the interview (and performance, if possible), listen to it and study it, write up a description of the performance and interview, and conclude with your personal reflections and reactions to the experience of knowing a musician of an unfamiliar culture.*

SOUND AWARENESS ACTIVITY 2.15 Going Global on Styles. *(Advanced) If there is diversity in the music that is near to us, that diversity multiplies by magnitudes as we consider the global possibilities. There are no limitations anymore to the music that we can know, given the technological possibilities of tapping into music cultures on radio and TV, over the Internet, and through the brisk recording market that seems to be prolifer-*

ating in every conceivable corner of the world. In many cultures, there are indigenous and "roots" styles, folk and traditional expressions, high art or classical forms, jazz, and popular music. There are fusion styles, too, where one musical culture may interface with and influence another and a new form emerges, as in the case of European and African-American components merging into jazz, or Afro-pop arising from the combination of traditional West African and Western popular elements. The splendors of music are nearly endless, and access to knowing it is well within reach. On the basis of these assumptions, proceed in one of these three directions: (a) choose a culture and research it for which musical styles are performed by people from within that culture (and collect audio-examples to share); (b) consider the people living in your local community, and research which music of their ancestral homeland they know best and actively preserve in your/their local community (and find out how that preservation is taking place); (c) listen to fusion music, and dissect by listening and through interviews with musicians or astute listeners just what components of various styles are interfacing to create the new blended sound.

OPENING THE EAR I: RHYTHM AND INSTRUMENTS

Musical awareness has its beginnings in experiences with the elemental features that comprise the musical sound itself. When we open our young students' ears to music, they cannot help but notice the elements that make it what it is: the rhythms, timbres, pitches, small structures and larger forms. As they listen, they consciously and unconsciously find items that draw their attention and aid their understanding and liking of the music. They connect to one feature and then another, listening for instruments that are familiar to them, wondering about those that are unfamiliar, gauging the qualities of singing voices and the languages they express, searching for a groove or lingering amid sounds that wash over them without a perceivable pulse. With our commitment as facilitating teachers, the musical experiences of our elementary and secondary school students gain depth through an understanding of the musical elements and their treatments by singers and players. Element by element, our students can know an expansion of musical riches as they are led to new discoveries that unfold before them with each further listening opportunity. Beyond an awareness of our sonic environments and following a focus on musical cultures close by and at some distance, the experiences that follow allow occasions for understanding the musical "insides," the features that make the music work its wonders on listeners. By opening our students' ears to the technical matters of time and timbre, they are certain to develop a fuller awareness of musical sound.

SOUND AWARENESS ACTIVITY 2.16   Beat Detection. *(Initial) Find the beat (also known as the pulse) in musical selections from the CD, and pat it, tap it, clap it, or in some other way, move to it. Note also those which do not appear to have a perceivable beat but which may unfold in free and flexible rhythm. Take this activity further by beats that are accented, performed with greater stress, and those that are performed with lesser stress. The following are a sampling of CD selections for beat detection: CD track 1 (no beat), CD track 2 (beat, accent on 1, no accent on 2-3-4), CD track 3 (free, no-beat introduction, followed by beat section with an accent on 1, no accent on 2), CD track 11 (free, no-beat), CD track 24 (beat, accent on 1, lesser accent on 4, no accent on 2-3 and 5), CD track 33 (beat, accent on 1, no accent on 2-3), CD track 49 (beat, accent on 1, no accent on 2), CD track 52 (no beat). Can you find other examples of a clearly perceivable beat?*

SOUND AWARENESS ACTIVITY 2.17   The Body as a Sound Source. *(Initial) Amid the various categorizations of musical instruments according to the manner in which the sound is produced, including those known as aerophones (vibrating columns of air), chordophones (vibratings strings), membranophones (vi-*

brating skin), and idiophones (sounds made by striking, shaking, rubbing), there is a category called corpophone that refers to "body-sounds," including hand claps, finger snaps, foot stomps, chest slaps, and the like. Listen to these CD selections that incorporate corpophone sounds: CD tracks 6, 27, 39, and 58. Explore the varied sounds that can be produced by the body, including singing. Create a piece that utilizes a repeated rhythmic pattern of corpophone sounds alongside an invented melody and/or harmonies.

SOUND AWARENESS ACTIVITY 2.18 Metric Challenges. *(Initial to Advanced) In understanding meter as a pattern of strong and weak counts, the beat selections for 2.16 are workable for this activity. Find strong and weak movements to correspond to strong and weak beats; for example, step or stamp for strong beats and clap or pat for weak beats. In small groups, try a variety of movements to express the strong-and-weak beat patterns, determine one that fits best, and share the movement patterns that the meter of strong and weak beats inspire with other small groups in the class. Notice how the movement seems dance-like in its repeated metric pattern. Some CD selections that present interesting metric challenges for more advanced students are track 22 (♫ ♫) alternating to (♪ ♪ ♪), track 36 (changing meters from triple to quadruple), and track 38 (♫ ♪ ♪).*

SOUND AWARENESS ACTIVITY 2.19 The Human Voice. *(Intermediate) Compare the vocal styles of musical traditions for their range of pitches, their open-throated, raspy, breathy, and nasalized qualities, their plain or ornamental styles—and syllabic (one pitch to a syllable) or melismatic (multiple pitches to a syllable) styles, their solo or group presentations, their special* techniques *(yodels, glottal stops, vibrato, tremolo) and their unaccompanied or instrumentally accompanied forms. Listen and describe the female voice of Cantonese opera (CD track 20) with the female voice of European bel canto (CD track 21), the male voice in a Navajo corn-grinding song (CD track 9) with the male voice of a South Indian kriti (CD track 39), and the choral sounds of an African American freedom song (CD track 6), a Cook Island ute (CD track 27), a European medieval rota (CD track 49), and an eastern African rendition of the well-known "Kumbaya" (CD track 58).*

Comparisons: The Singing Voice

	Example CD track 9 (Navajo)	Example CD track 39 (South Indian)
Pitch Range	Small (m6)	Medium (octave +)
Vocal quality	Raspy, Nasalized	Nasalized
Plain/Ornamented	Ornamented	Highly ornamented
Syllabic/Melismatic	More syllabic	Melismatic
Solo/Group	Two voices in unison	Solo
Special Techniques	Vibrato, some glottal stops	Tremolo
Accompanied/ Unaccompanied	Unaccompanied	Accompanied

SOUND AWARENESS ACTIVITY 2.20 Instrumental Comparisons. *(Intermediate) Flutes, fiddles, and xylophones: What remains the same, and yet how also are they distinguished, across cultures? Consider and chart the timbral qualities, materials from which the instrument may be constructed, tuning, playing position, culturally-influenced melodic or rhythmic conventions of the instrument in various traditions. Listen to examples of the* *flute (CD tracks 3, 12, 15, 22), xylophone (CD tracks 8, 19, 23, 31, 50), and fiddle (CD tracks 8, 20, 21, 25, 37) to make these comparisons.*

SOUND AWARENESS ACTIVITY 2.21 Keeping the Tāla. *(Advanced) Indian musicians refer to meter as tāla, and recognize its composite of subunits of even and uneven numbers of beats (or counts). One frequently-used tāla in the Karnatak music of South India is called adi tāla, whose eight beats are grouped into three sections consisting of an even number of beats in each, 4 + 2 + 2. As the discernment of the tāla is of vital importance to audience members as it is to performers, it is common to see and hear clapping and waving on the strong (and initial) beat of each subunit, and a finger-ticking movement on the weak beats. (The right hand claps into the left hand, waves out away from the body with the back of the hand leading it; on the finger ticks ("f.t."), the right hand thumb moves inward to touch the tip of the little finger (for the two-beat subunits) also the ring and middle fingers (for the four-beat subunit). Practice "keeping the tāla" of adi tāla by following the movements below, counting as you go. Once it is comfortable and "second-nature," play CD track 39 (Unnai Nambinen) and keep the tāla while listening to the claps.*

Beat/count:	1	2	3	4	5	6	7	8
Subgroup	4				2		2	
Movement	clap	f.t.	f.t.	f.t.	clap	f.t.	wave	f.t.

For further rhythmic intrigue, there are stroke patterns for the tablā and mridangam drums found in North and South India, respectively, each with their own correspondent speech syllables, that are spoken as the tāla is kept. See examples of the Hindustani spoken drum patterns (called thekā) for tablā, and the placement of the gestures for keeping their tālas in *Thinking Musically*, (page 68).

SOUND AWARENESS ACTIVITY 2.22 Modes of the Middle East. *(Advanced). In the music of much of the Middle East, the metric feeling of the music centers around a rhythmic mode. Beyond the number of beats in a unit, a rhythmic mode is also distinguished by the way it is performed on a drum or other percussion instrument such as tambourine or finger cymbals. Percussionists learn to play by chanting "dumm" for deep and/or muted sounds and "takk" for high and/or bright sounds. Experiment with a goblet drum, tambourine, and finger cymbals to find the best "dumm" and "takk" sounds. Then chant and play the maqam's rhythmic mode:*

Beat/count:	1	2	3	4	5	6	7	8
	♪	♩		♪	♩		♩	
Chant:	dumm	takk	–	takk	dumm	–	takk	–

At 1'27" on CD track 25, the Egyptian ensemble enters into the maqam's rhythmic mode. Listen for the improvisatory sound of the dombek (drum) and tambourine (riqq), and try to insert the rhythmic mode by chanting or playing it. At 2'35", the drum briefly takes on the actual rhythmic mode.

SOUND AWARENESS ACTIVITY 2.23 Free within the Cycle. *(Advanced) Choose a tāla, such as the eight-beat adi tāla (See 2.21), or the eight-beat Middle Eastern rhythmic mode (See 2.22). Create a short unison melody (for example, of 16- or 32-beats) for all melody instruments to play together. Allow the percussionists to perform the rhythm cycle through several repetitions, followed by the entrance of melodists together. Intersperse the tutti performance of the melody with individual improvisations, also of the length of 16- or 32-beats. Decide together that tonality may (or may not) a consideration of improvisatory segments, or whether the players will be completely free within the cycle to create their own melody.*

SOUND AWARENESS ACTIVITY 2.24 Leadership Roles. *(Advanced). Consider that while some of the world's ensembles have a visible leader, such as the conductor who is positioned on a podium in the center-front of the orchestra to lead the one hundred-plus instrumentalists in tempo, dynamic shadings, and interpretive decisions, other ensembles such as the jazz combo or rock band appear to be more egalitarian and collaborative in their music-making. Still other ensembles, such as a West African drumming ensemble, or a Trinidadian steel band, or a Central Javanese gamelan, look to certain individuals (the African master drummer, the arranger of the steel drum band music, or the Javanese kendang drummer) to steer the group through the subtleties of performance. For these leaders, there may be no designated head-spot location within the ensemble, no special garb, no highly visible gestures, but there is leadership nonetheless. Select a vocal or an instrumental ensemble (choir, marching band, string quartet, Latin dance band, drumming circle), and observe the interactions of musicians in rehearsal to determine what roles they play. Arrange for an interview with an apparent or not-so-apparent leader, to determine what it takes to achieve this position—and to guide musicians toward musical coherence.*

OPENING THE EAR II: PITCH AND FORM

The development of musical sensitivity requires a focus on not only elements of rhythm and timbre but also of pitch and form. Many of the instruments, and certainly the singing voices as well, are capable of creating patterns, phrases, and whole pieces that sound a vast array of pitches, in many tunings, performed one-at-a-time or with multiple pitches sounding simultaneously. The pitches and their plain or ornamental qualities vary by culture, and their colorings and shadings are what give life to the melodies and textures that are sung and played. Patterns of pitches and rhythms, and the timbral varieties that perform them, fall into germinal ideas called motifs, brief patterns that are repeated, varied, extended, and constrasted with others. Taken together, these patterns and phrases are grouped to constitute larger sections and forms that make the music coherent and cohesive. As we open our students' ears to the possibilities of pitch and form, as well as to rhythm and timbre, the fuller sense of music's elemental structures—those that give it logic and beauty—will become clear to them.

SOUND AWARENESS ACTIVITY 2.25 The High and Low of it. *(Initial) Explore the pitch possibilities belonging to one or more instruments. Produce the highest and lowest pitches on each instrument, and chart the extent of the range between the pitch extremes. Notice how some instruments span larger pitch ranges than others. Approach the pitch ranges of singing voices in the same manner. Classify instruments and voices as treble or bass, and then strive for greater definition by fitting the voices or instruments into soporano, alto, tenor, and bass categories by pitch range. Across instruments and cultures, notice how the size and materials from which the instrument is constructed affect the pitch possibilities.*

SOUND AWARENESS ACTIVITY 2.26 Openings. *(Initial) As conceived by composers and musicians in some traditions, the beginning of a piece is often a time to make a significant musical statement. Listen to the opening musical statements in Western European art music (CD track 40 and CD track 54) as examples of this. Gather other examples of this compositional practice (for example, Copland's "Fanfare for the Common Man," Stravinsky's "The Rite of Spring," and symphonies by Haydn, Mozart, and Beethoven). Note the strategy of other musical traditions to allow a gradual unfolding into important musical statements, including the opening sections of music from North India, Thailand, and Java. Can you find other examples of powerful musical openings?*

SOUND AWARENESS ACTIVITY 2.27 Calling and Responding. *(Initial) One of the most socially interactive forms music can take is the call-and-response mode, when a soloist singer or instrumentalist offers a musical phrase that calls out to others for a response. That response may be sounded by another soloist, by two or more in a unison (and preset) manner, or by a group in a fully expansive melodic, rhythmic, or harmonic way. Examples of call-and-response are prominent in the music of much of Africa, and in places where Africans have traveled with their traditions. Listen to CD track 59 for an example of the form in an Afro-Brazilian treatment. Look for further examples in popular and rock music, and in jazz.*

SOUND AWARENESS ACTIVITY 2.28 Graphic Melodies. *(Initial to Intermediate) How do individual pitches connect to form a melody? Listen to the rise and fall, or static stay-on-one-pitch, pathway of the melody to "Sumer Is Icumen In" (CD track 49). Trace in the air the melodic maneuverings, using fingers or a hand to "paint" overall melodic shape. Take a pencil to paper and sketch or graph the direction of melodic phrases. Compare the graph to the recorded sound, or even try singing the sound from the graph.*

SOUND AWARENESS ACTIVITY 2.29 A Note by Any Name. *(Intermediate) Sing a major scale, using the names designated by various systems: Arabic-inspired letter names, the number system common in China and Indonesia, European solfege (also known as Tonic Sol-Fa in England), and Hindustani syllables found in North India. Sing at a steady tempo. On cue, sing the scale twice as fast while retaining the same beat, and then four times as fast. Discuss which systems are easier or more challenging to sing, and explain reasons why. Once the systems*

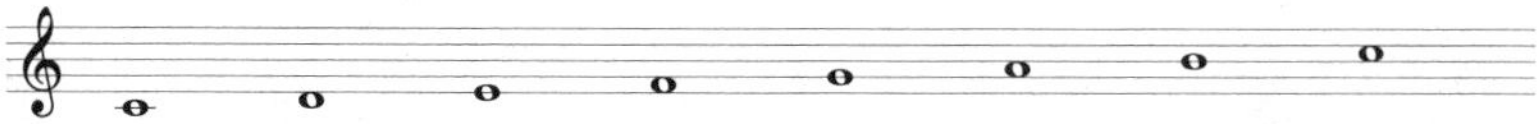

C	D	E	F	G	A	B	C
1	2	3	4	5	6	7	8 (1)
Do	Re	Mi	Fa	Sol	La	Ti	Do
Sa	Re	Ga	Ma	Pa	Dha	Ni	Sa

FIGURE 2.1   *A note by any name*

feel comfortable for scales, try applying the various systems to singing familiar melodies (Frere Jacques, Row Your Boat, Amazing Grace, Auld Lang Syne). (See Figure 2.1)

SOUND AWARENESS ACTIVITY 2.30 Harmonious Sounds. *(Intermediate) Listen to examples of pieces that feature harmony, and respond to the challenge of detecting by ear which chords are sounding. Like an aural transcription, listen, write them down as letters or Roman numerals (C, F, G or I, IV, V) in order of their progression. Sing the root tones of the chords with the recordings, and then attempt to sing them chorally or play them. Songs with clear chordal harmonies include CD tracks 6, 7, 29, 33, 35, 57, and 58.*

SOUND AWARENESS ACTIVITY 2.31 Alone and Together. *(Intermediate) (a) Find examples of solo vocal and instrumental pieces on the recording, such as CD tracks 1, 13, 14, 34, and 52. Notice the capacity of some instruments to sound only melody while others can offer a fuller harmonic envelope of sound. Experiment with other instruments that play horizontally one pitch after another and those that can also play simultaneous pitches in a vertical manner. (b) Select examples of groups of voices and instruments, as they sound in unison (CD track 49, at the* beginning), in interlocking parts (CD track 50), in a heterophonic texture (CD track 25), in homophonic style (see Sound Awareness Activity 2.30 for examples), and polyphonically (CD track 49). Listen to and list pieces of other groups across a variety of styles and traditions, and determine what musical textures they perform.

SOUND AWARENESS ACTIVITY 2.32 Closings. (Intermediate) Note the manner in which performers and composers choose to end their music. Do they fit these categories? (a) A cadence of repeated melodic and/or rhythmic phrases, (b) a cadence linked to chord progression ending on the home-tone (I) and possibly preceded by the dominant (V), (c) a fading out of familiar material (technologically possible on recorded pieces), (d) a loss of interest by the audience or artist(s) (possible in live performances). Choose a familiar song and explore some of these ways of closing the music.

SOUND AWARENESS ACTIVITY 2.33 In Tune and Out of Tune. (Advanced) While cultures seem to be in solid agreement on the division of pitches into octaves, the pitches in between the high and low end of an octave vary with the tradition. People select the precise set of pitches that give their music its identity, and it is so thoroughly in tune to them that any other set of pitches may appear out of tune. Listen to pitches and tunings in a variety of examples: CD track 40 and CD track 54 as examples of Western European art music, CD track 25 as an example of Southwest Asian (Middle Eastern) music, CD track 23 as an example of Southeast Asian music, remembering that to people within the culture, the tunings of the instruments are exactly right for giving the tradition its flavor. Musicians take time to tune instruments, too, as can be heard on CD track 42 (when two Balinese instruments in a pair are tuned intentionally to sound slightly different frequencies) and CD track 43 (when instruments of the orchestra zero in to match the "A–440" pitch of the lead oboe).

SOUND AWARENESS ACTIVITY 2.34   Drones and Microtones. *(Advanced) To fully grasp the meaning of tones and tunings, pair with a friend who sings a drone tone while you sing a gradually rising tone that makes its way to from the drone pitch to a quarter-, then half-, then wholetone higher than the drone. Do the same in the opposite direction, gradually lowering the pitch from the drone tone. Try this as well in a group of singers who are divided into "drones and microtones." Advanced instrumentalists might rise to the challenge of experimenting with a fretless stringed instrument like a violin or a bass. Play a scale to match as accurately as possible the tuning of a piano keyboard. Then, alter the scale pitches, playing each one audibly flatter and then sharper than those of the piano. Sing along with these microtonal changes to the familiar Western tempered tuning, if you can—a tremendous challenge to the ear and the voice.*

SOUND AWARENESS ACTIVITY 2.35   Home- and Away-from-Home Tones. *(Advanced) Experiment with the home-tone or tonal center and its critical role in offering a sense of musical solidity, by identifying and then singing familiar songs that end on tonic ("do," or "1") and then comparing the sound-sense of ending on the supertonic ("re" or "2," as in the Japanese children's song, "Zui Zui Zukkorbashi," the mediant ("mi" or "3," as in "De Colores") or dominant ("sol" or "5," as in the "The Riddle Song" (I Gave My Love a Cherry) instead.*

Listen and sing the home-tone for the following selections: CD track 52, which is also the drone-tone of the Scottish bagpipe, and CD track 53, which can be heard among the drone pitches of the North Indian singer.

SOUND AWARENESS ACTIVITY 2.36   Melodic Moods. *(Advanced) Consider the Indian and Middle Eastern selection of particular melodic modes for seasons, days, times of days, and the traditional association of these modes to moods. (The books on North India and South India in this series offer descriptions and illustrations of rāga as associated with moods.) Find examples of modes which, while not likely to specify times of performance, nonetheless do create particular moods. Sing or listen to familiar songs in major and harmonic minor scales, and in modes such as Dorian (as in "Wayfaring Stranger," "Scarborough Fair," and at least one version of "Greensleeves") and Mixolydian (as in the Canadian song, "The Banks of the Nile," and a Northumberland version of "Cuckoo"), and discuss what moods their pitches seem to communicate.*

LOCAL AND GLOBAL IDENTITIES

Music is rampant, widespread in our daily lives, and when the antennae are up, it is remarkable what a rich tapestry of sonic surroundings we know. Music makes up the urbanscapes of city neighborhoods, where people are tuned simultaneously to their own local musical identities and also to the expressions of cross-town communities. It is present in the increasingly rare rural settlements of music-makers who play and sing for each other on front porches, in closed circles, and on communal grounds, and is undergoing change by the same rural people who are now becoming wired to the outside world of sound possibilities. Music is sounding, whether we are aware of it or not: snippets of tunes and segments of rhythm, sporadic music scatterings or solid walls of sound. The route to musical understanding begins with a discovery of our own personal and familial music, and then extends to the expressions of others. Thus the exploratory excursions featured in this chapter leads to a recognition of the very local identities of our students as well as the global musical identities that are there for the listening. As well, the concept of people making music meaningful and useful in their lives becomes real to them through these explorations. For teachers striving for a broad-based musical education for their children and youth, these are vital excursions to take, parts of the bigger musical journey that stretches across their lives.

PROBLEMS TO PROBE

1. Evaluate the effectiveness of the sound awareness activities *(a)* as a student participant in them, and/or *(b)* as a teacher who has facilitated them with K–12 students. What musical aims were accomplished through them? How were they modified or extended? Make your remarks in the margins of this book for your future reference, and note which activities you would use in the future, or discard, or further adapt—and why.

2. Gather with colleagues to brainstorm ways of developing a meaningful exploration of one world of musical sound. Choose a single musical culture (for example, Navajo, Nigeria [Yoruba], or North India), and consider starting with just a single selection (such as found on the CD). List some of the principal musical elements that define the musical culture (selection). Then, choose several Sound Awareness Activities, or invent others, that can introduce and open students' ears to elemental features of the culture (selection).

3. Review your sketch of a sample course schedule, selected in Chapter 1, and insert three Sound Awareness Activities to fit the schedule. Think: Which experiences will be meaningful to developing my students' (in, for example, band, choir, general music, or a world music cultures course) knowledge of Music with a capital "M"?

CHAPTER 3

Learning through Attentive Listening

∞

Because listening is central to musical understanding, its presence is integral in musical analysis, participatory experiences, and performances in preparation and for public concert and program offerings. First-timers to musical works, forms, and genres—our students—do well to have their ears opened to "big picture" items, noting timbres, and textures, and melodic and rhythmic components of the music. Our students are further enlightened when we lead them into a discovery of the nuances of music in its cultural variety, and when they are able to come to terms with the extremes and subtleties of dynamic expression, the give-and-take of tempo and timing, the slight turns of melodic pitches that are higher and lower than standard or expected. What challenges are found in the breath rhythm of a Korean A-Ak ensemble? How are dynamics treated in the performance of Balinese gamelan or a Japanese syakahachi? What is the flavor of a drone on a Scottish bagpipe, and in a vocal khyal from North India? How is a melodic motive used in a Beethoven symphony, or by Navajo singers? For teachers who hope to develop the musicianship of our elementary and secondary school students, it is worth noting that the more involved they become in the listening process, the more enriched and complete their musical understanding can be.

"LISTEN-TO-LEARN" PHASES

There are three phases of musical involvement that bring about the development of musical knowledge and skills, and that deepen an individual's valuing of music as an important part of daily life. They are based on the premise that one learns music by listening; hence, they are referred to as the three "listen-to-learn" phases. They are linked to the instructional processes which a teacher can put into place within K–12 classrooms: (1) Attentive Listening, directed listening that is focused on musical elements and structures, and that is guided by the use of specified points of focus or diagrams (including notation and "maps" that lead a listener from one musical event to the next), (2) Engaged Listening, the active participation by a listener in some extent of music-making (singing a melody, patting a rhythm, playing a percussion part, moving eurhythmically or in an actual dance pattern) while the recorded (or live) music sounds, and (3) Enactive Listening, the performance of the work, where the intensive listening to every musical nuance of a selection for the purpose of re-creating in performance the music in as stylistically accurate a way as possible. The first listening phase, Attentive Listening, is the focus of activities in this chapter. In fact, some aspects of this directed listening phase were already evident in some of the Sound Awareness Activities of Chapter 2. Experiences in Engaged Listening that are "participatory" are found in Chapter 4, and Enactive Listening experiences, with notation and suggestions for aurally-informed performance possibilities—or invitations to perform the piece "sans notation" and totally by ear—are found in Chapter 5.

The three central features that help to develop a sound awareness of music—instruments, elements, and context—are also folded within instructional processes that lead to "attentive," "engaged," and "enactive" listening. A discovery by our choral, general, and instrumental students of the potential of musical instruments (and voices), the elemental musical qualities and their treatments, and the contexts in which people make music meaningful and useful in their lives lead to their deeper levels of musical understanding. These three features are briefly noted for selections so as to enable teachers to provide their students the fullest possible extent of the "listen-to-learn" premise and process by which it unfolds.

ATTENTIVE LISTENING EXPERIENCES

The experiences that follow are associated with numbered selections from the accompanying CD, so that the musical structures and meanings can be known through the enhanced listening that occurs when specified points of focus or graphic visual means are merged with the sound experience itself. Some items diagram contours of the melody, or several melodies at once, while others depict rhythmic components of a piece, and still others offer the identification of instruments and their entrances within a work. About half the experiences are associated with outlines of musical sections, called "listen-points," on which to focus one's listening. More than a single listening opportunity, and even five or more listenings per selection, is advisable so that students may be able to shift their focus from one musical dimension to another. Occasionally, just because it will be natural for our students to do so, suggestions to sing, hum, conduct, move, and pat pulses or rhythms will be inserted alongside the more analytical directions for students' attention. These suggestions then play into the need to diversify our instruction so as to suit the learning styles of our students.

The selections constitute a varied sampling of vocal and instrumental styles across a wide span of musical cultures. There are sacred and secular expressions, music for solo and ensemble performances, and music that can be classified as art, traditional, or popular. The musical selections differ in intent and function, too: music for ritual and worship (such as the call of a conch in a Tibetan Buddhist monastery), songs that accompany work (such as the Navajo corn-grinding song), music of the royal courts (including those of Indonesia and Thailand), concert-hall music (such as the symphonic works of Beethoven and Richard Strauss, the chamber music of a Japanese sankyokyu ensemble, and the North Indian duo of sitar and tamboura), music of celebration (such as the choral sounds from the Cook Islands), and music for performance in the great outdoors (such as the Scottish bagpipe). Instruments include those that may be familiar to student listeners—for example, the brass instruments of Lutoslawski's overture—and those, like the komungo (zither) of Korea and the pi nai (quadruple reed) of Thailand, that have been rarely heard in western classrooms or through the media. The rich variety of vocal timbres are sampled here, too, including styles from Turkey, Indonesia, the Navajo nation, North India, the Pacific, and Japan). Altogether, these selections comprise a taste of the musical diversity that exists in the world for the listening ears of our students.

The numbers at the front of each experience refer to the CD track. All Attentive Listening Experiences name relevant musical elements, called "notable elements," that pertain to the music; these elements are defined within the glossary or main text pages of *Thinking Musically*. Matters of context that clarify aspects of the music's role within the culture are briefly noted, and "teaching commentaries" that suggest a goal and which may guide the instructional activity are suggested. The diagrams and "listen-points" can be reproduced for individual student use or full classes of students, or can be used by teachers independently to clarify what concepts might be raised as focal points in the brief listening experiences which students will have. Students of all ages and experience can be enriched through these listening selections, because teachers who choose to use them will know how to gain the attention of their students through questions and colorful commentary. Some of the terms may appear too technical for the very young or inexperienced, so that instructional levels (elementary or secondary school) and venues (choral/vocal, general, instrumental, other) are suggested—although they are not prescribed. Teachers are invited to think broadly of the uses of these Attentive Listening Experiences, and to listen and determine for themselves just which musical selections might best suit their students and classes.

ATTENTIVE LISTENING EXPERIENCE 3.1   *CD track 1,* First sura of the Koran, al-Fatiha *(Islamic recitation, Turkey)* Possible Use: *Secondary, choral/vocal* Instruments: *Male voice* Notable Elements: *Chant, syllabic and melismatic melody, monophonic, unmetered* Context: *In Islamic culture, the recitation of verses from the Koran is not viewed as musiqa (music); that term is reserved for secular music with no perceived links to religious life and practice. More than elsewhere in the Arab world, reciters in Turkey recognize the similarity of Koranic chant to music, and some reciters even train in singing as well as in recitation. The text of the opening phrases to the recitation by members of the Qadiriya Sufi brotherhood translate as "In the Name of God, the Merciful, the Compassionate."* Teaching Commentary: *Follow the rise and fall of the melody as depicted in graphic form. Trace the melodic contours with a finger on the page or in an expanded graph on the wall or overhead via a projector. Use the hand to "paint" the contour across space, brushing higher lower, and sustained pitches in the air. (See Figure 3.1)*

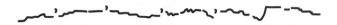

FIGURE 3.1   *Graphic form of the first* sura *of the Koran, al-Fatiha, (Islamic Recitation, Turkey) CD track 1.*

ATTENTIVE LISTENING EXPERIENCE 3.2   *CD track 8,* "Ketawang Puspawarna" *(Surakarta court gamelan, Indonesia).*
Possible Use: *Elementary or secondary, general music, instrumental*
Instruments: *Rebab (fiddle), kendang (drum), saron and slentum (xylophones), suling (flute), gongs, female voice, male voices*
Notable Elements: *Nonmetrical introduction, gamelan ensemble, gong cycle, soft-playing style*
Context: *The musical identity of Javanese people in the country of Indonesia is wrapped into the sound of the gamelan, and the ensemble's uniquely communal practice of homogenous sound (versus soloistic performance) reflects the larger principle adhered to within the culture, of collaboration and cooperative support of one another. In the Central Javanese gamelan found in the court at Surakarta, the instruments have been fashioned by a gongsmith to match one another's tuning, and all are intended to be played together rather than soloistically. Court musicians play a melody set within the slendro tuning of five pitches (or sometimes the pelog tuning of seven pitches). Singers perform the poetry of old Javanese language that is little known today, and they blend their voices into the sound of the gamelan rather than to set themselves apart as superior to the instruments.*
Teaching Commentary: *Follow the instruments and voices as they enter and join with others in the fuller texture of a Central Javanese gamelan sound. Through repeated listenings, follow one instrument even as others enter and alter the texture. (See Figure 3.2)*

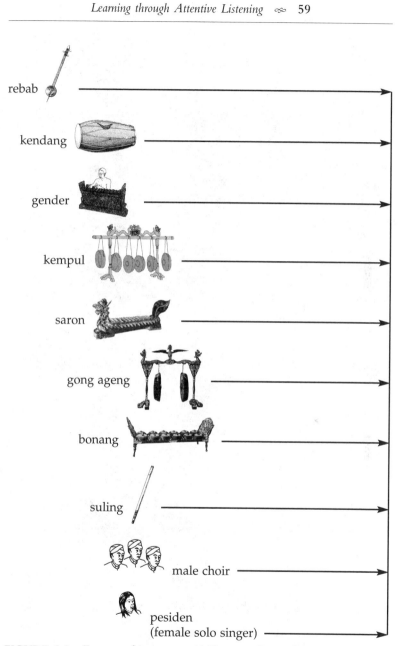

rebab

kendang

gender

kempul

saron

gong ageng

bonang

suling

male choir

pesiden
(female solo singer)

FIGURE 3.2   *Entrance of instruments in Ketawang Puspawarna (Surakarta court gamelan, Indonesia).   (Instruments from* Musical Instruments of the World *[Diagram Group, 1997]. Used with permission by The Diagram Group.)*

ATTENTIVE LISTENING EXPERIENCE 3.3 *CD track 9,*
Navajo Corn-Grinding Song *(Joe Lee, Arizona)*
Possible Use: *Elementary or secondary, choral/vocal, general*
Instruments: *Male voices (two)*
Notable Elements: *Vocal timbre, phrases, pulse*
Context: *When the Navajo of Arizona and New Mexico learned to grow corn from neighboring Pueblo Indians, they used milling stones to crush the hard kernels into meal, one heavier flat stone under the kernels and a lighter movable stone shaped like a flattened cylinder on top. For the girls' puberty ceremony, the grinding of corn endows her with strength, good nature, and good health for her adult life ahead. Beyond that, Navajo men have taken corn-grinding songs into their own use as a means of lightening various types of labor. They may sing without accompaniment, or may add a thumping sound from a moccasin or a doubled up belt on an inverted basket, always featuring repetition or partial repeats. Corn-grinding songs are now heard on the radio and during corn-grinding exhibitions at tribal fairs, Indian heritage programs, an occasional powwow, and even during the annual Miss Navajo contest.*
Teaching Commentary: *Follow each of the listen-points, one point per listening time, and then all points together in a final listening. Imagine and tune the inner-hearing sensibility to the pulse.*

Listen-points
Challenge yourself to hear

• two male voices singing in unison
• pulsive, wavering vocal quality of the longer, sustained tones
• repeated phrases
• phrases that fall into this form: a-a-b-b-c-c (+ phrase segment) a-a

Imagine the sound of a thumping moccasin, a belt tapping a basket, or a beaded gourd, sounding the pulse. Softly pat the pulse.

ATTENTIVE LISTENING EXPERIENCE 3.4 *CD track 10, "Vikrit recitation" (North India)*
Possible Use: *Elementary or secondary, choral/vocal, general*
Instruments: *Male voices (two)*
Notable Elements: *unison, repeated phrases, small melodic range*
Context: *In India, the chanting of religious texts is a long-standing tradition that dates as far back as 1500 BCE. Sacred texts called the Vedas are taught by Brahmin priests to Brahmin students in an oral-aural manner without the use of printed words or notation. A memorization technique is utilized in which text phrases are arranged in patterns and chanted repeatedly until they are thoroughly committed to memory. The text to the Vedic recitation here is as follows: "The gods gave birth to the goddess of speech, spoken by animals in all forms. This cow, lowing pleasantly, who gives strengthening libation with her milk, as speech when well spoken should come to us."*
Teaching Commentary: *Focus on the listen-points that document the sung syllables and phrases, and note the design of the memorization technique. Play with the possibilities of this design by creating a text phrase that could be maneuvered to follow this form (see following example).*

Listen-points
Follow the memorization schema for the krama and mala patterns.

krama pattern	a b / b c / c d / d e
mala pattern	a b / b a / a b / b c / c b / b c / c d / d c

Follow the word syllables for the krama and mala patterns.

krama pattern	devim vacam / vacam devim
	devim ajanayanta / ajanayanta devim
mala pattern	devim vacam / vacam devim
	devim vacam / vacam ajanayanta
	ajanayanta vacam / vacam ajanayanta
	ajanayanta devas / devas ajanayanta

> ajanayanta devas / devas tam
> ajanayanta tam devas / devas tam
> visvarupah pasavo / pasavo visvarupah
> visvarupah pasavo . . . .

Create krama and mala patterns from familiar phrases.
Example: "Let's go together."

krama pattern	Let's go / go Let's
	Let's together / together Let's
mala pattern	Let's go / go Let's
	Let's go / go together

ATTENTIVE LISTENING EXPERIENCE 3.5 *CD track 11*, Rāga Purvi-Kalyan *(North India sitār).*

Possible Use: *Elementary or secondary, general, instrumental*
Instruments: *Sitār, tānpura*
Notable Elements: *Melodic ornamentation, rāga, ālāp, non-metric*
Context: *North Indian classical music will often begin with a nonmetrical section called ālāp that is intended through improvisation to introduce the features of the rāga. The freedom to explore the pitches and their ornaments without rhythmic restrictions allows the performer an opportunity to orient the listener to the melodic material that will resurface later within the metric cycle called tāla. This intimate chamber music may be heard in house concerts, small recital halls, or (with proper amplification) full-sized concert halls. It is music of the highest artistic integrity which, even centuries from its origin, is still rooted to a devotional inspiration.*
Teaching Commentary: *Follow the graphic rise and fall of the sitār's melody over the tānpura's drone. Graph the drone's stationary pitch and melody's movement on paper or using two hands in the air. (See Figure 3.3)*

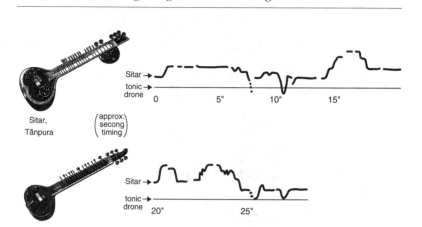

FIGURE 3.3 *Graphic form of the Rāga Purvi-Kalyan, CD track 11 (North Indian sitar). (Instruments from* Musical Instruments of the World *[Diagram Group, 1997]. Reprinted with permission by The Diagram Group.)*

ATTENTIVE LISTENING EXPERIENCE 3.6 *CD track 12,* "First Wine Offering: A-ak" *(Korea)*
Possible Use: *Elementary or secondary, general, instrumental*
Instruments: *Clappers, lithophones, high and low drums, flutes*
Notable Elements: *Breath rhythm, transparent texture, A-Ak ensemble*
Context: *Some of the earliest Chinese instruments underwent a process resulting in their marginal survival: they were taken abroad and were preserved at the borders (and beyond) of the culture even while "newer" musical expressions were taking hold at China's geographic centers. Instruments of natural materials constituted the "eight sounds" (ba yin) of China's (and then Korea's) music: metal, stone, skin, gourd, bamboo, wood, silk, and earth clay. The A-ak, or Confucian ritual music, came to Korea as a gift from the Chinese emperor in the twelfth century. Two short pieces survive and are performed at the semiannual homage to Confucius and at concerts by the National Center for Korean Traditional Performing Arts in Seoul.*

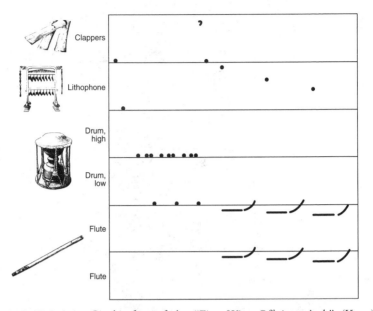

FIGURE 3.4 *Graphic form of the "First Wine Offering: A-ak" (Korea). (Instruments from* Musical Instruments of the World *[Diagram Group, 1997]. Reprinted with permission by The Diagram Group.)*

Teaching Commentary: *Follow the graphic display of instrument entries and sketches of their durational contributions to the piece. Breathe with the instruments, feeling their phrases and the breaks between them. (See Figure 3.4)*

ATTENTIVE LISTENING EXPERIENCE 3.7 *CD track 13,* Didjeridu *(Arnhem Land, Australia)*
Possible Use: *Elementary, general*
Instruments: *Didjeridu, log drum, time sticks*
Notable Elements: *Melodic and rhythmic pattern*
Context: *The indigenous Aboriginal peoples of Australia are internationally known for the sound of their didjeridu. Branches of the eucalyptus tree are hollowed out and decorated with paint,*

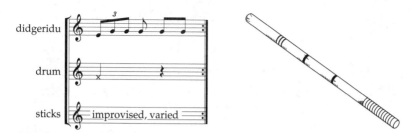

FIGURE 3.5 *Musical Motive of the Didjeridu (Arnhem Land, Australia).* *(Instrument from* Musical Instruments of the World *[Diagram Group, 1997]. Reprinted with permission by The Diagram Group.)*

and players use circular breathing (blowing through the tube while intaking air through the nose) to create a constant, gap-less sound. As many as nine different tone qualities are possible within the range of an octave and a third. Cans and plastic tubes are also used by Aboriginal peoples today to construct a didjeridu, and time sticks and log drums are frequently heard to accompany the wind instrument. The fusion of didjeridu and the melodies and rhythms that are traditional for it, is well within the artistic expression of contemporary Aboriginal Australians, and groups like Yothu Yindi retain the sensibilities of their musical traditions even including the instrument in their performances of popular music styles.
Teaching Commentary: *Find and follow the pattern of the didjeridu, drum, and sticks. Hum the melodic pattern and pat the drum's pulse. (See Figure 3.5)*

ATTENTIVE LISTENING EXPERIENCE 3.8   *CD track 14,* "Conch call" *(Tibetan Buddhist ritual)*
Possible Use: *Elementary, general*
Instruments: *Conch shells (two)*
Notable Elements: *"Buzz" quality, sustained tone*
Context: *Although it is a landlocked and mountainous country at the "top of the world," Tibet's monasteries ensure that the*

FIGURE 3.6 *Graphic form of conch shells' call (Tibet Buddhist ritual).*

conch shell will sound. *Classified as a "peaceful instrument," the conchshell is used as a signal to call monks to assemblies, and as part of the ritual orchestra. It would not be played in rituals that focus exclusively on Fierce deities; for these, metal trumpets are substituted. The conch came with Buddhism to Tibet from India, where it also plays an important musical role. In Tibet, it symbolizes the sound of Buddha's voice, which penetrates everywhere, and is not mistaken by Buddhists for any other instrument.*
Teaching Commentary: *Study the graphic depiction of two conch shells for their entrances and their functions as drone and "elaborating" sounds. Match the sustained pitch by singing. (See Figure 3.6)*

ATTENTIVE LISTENING EXPERIENCE 3.9 *CD track 15,* "Hifumi no Shirabe Hachigaeshi" *(Japan, syakuhachi)*
Possible Use: *Elementary or secondary, instrumental*
Instruments: *syakuhachi (flute)*
Notable Elements: *breath rhythm, pitch variance, dynamics*
Context: *The syakuhachi flute of Japan has continued its role in making a spiritual connection with nature and Zen Buddhist meditation, yet is enjoyed in concerts of solo and chamber music. The instrument is made of a hollowed-out bamboo stalk with a mouthpiece that is cut obliquely outward, a small piece of ivory inserted so that the playing edge is less susceptible to wear. The*

Shakuhachi

or

FIGURE 3.7 *Transcription of Hifumi no Shirabe Hachigaeshi, (Japan, Syakuhachi),* CD track 15. *(Instrument from* Musical Instruments of the World *[Diagram Group, 1997]. Reprinted with permission by The Diagram Group.)*

five holes of the standard syakuhachi produce D, F, G, A, and D tones, but it is the system of half-holing and embouchure changes that give the instrument its unique abilities to vary and decorate the tones. A correct performance of the endings of each breath phrase, including the proper performance of grace notes, marks the professional syakuhachi player.
Teaching Commentary: *Follow the transcription of the flute's melody. Notice the manner in which the player's breath draws the instrument to places above and below the pitches indicated, and provides dynamic contrast to a single pitch. (See Figure 3.7)*

ATTENTIVE LISTENING ACTIVITY 3.10 *CD track 17,* Korean Komungo Sanjo: Chinyango, Chungmore, Onmori Possible Use: *Secondary, instrumental* Instruments: *Komungo (zither), changgo (drum)* Notable Elements: *Timbral decay, triple meter, elastic rhythm, tremolo, sanjo* Context: *There are several forms of Korean folk music, the leading ones which are p'ansori, a dramative form for solo voice and drum, and sanjo, virtuoso music performed by a single instrument*

with changgo drum. The komungo, the lead instrument in court ensembles, is a six-string fretted long zither played with a pencil-shaped wooden plectrum. Three of its six nylon strings are raised by tall frets, while the other three are supported by movable bridges. One of the aesthetic highlights of komungo performance is the percussive plucking, often with characteristic vibrato, and then the quick fading of the pitches. The double-headed changgo drum is played with a stick on its right side and with the hand on the left side.

Teaching Commentary: *Over multiple listenings, concentrate on one listen-point during each listening time, and then all of them at once. Conduct or pat the meter while focusing on other points. (See Figure 3.8)*

Listen-points
Challenge yourself to hear

• triple meter
• stretched "elastic" breath rhythm that "gives and takes"
• tremolo "wiggles" on the strings of the komungo
• high tap-like drum sound of the changgo
• low thud-like drum sound of the changgo

FIGURE 3.8 *Komungo, Changgo. (Instruments from* Musical Instruments of the World *[Diagram Group, 1997]. Reprinted with permission by The Diagram Group.)*

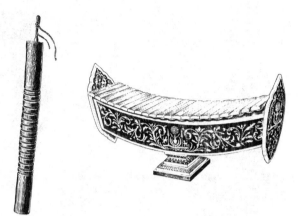

FIGURE 3.9 *Pi nai, Ranat-ek.* *(Instruments from* Musical Instruments of the World *[Diagram Group, 1997]. Reprinted with permission by The Diagram Group.)*

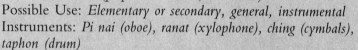

ATTENTIVE LISTENING EXPERIENCE 3.11 *CD track 23, "Ma Ram" (pi phat ensemble, Thailand)*
Possible Use: *Elementary or secondary, general, instrumental*
Instruments: *Pi nai (oboe), ranat (xylophone), ching (cymbals), taphon (drum)*
Notable Elements: *metric versus nonmetric sections, scalar passages, pi pha ensembles*
Context: *As rare as the ensemble is, pi phat music is still considered by the Thai to be central to their musical identity. Most Thai rarely hear the pi phat music on recordings, or see it on TV, but the music continues to be a presence at the royal court (and is enthusiastically supported by HRH Princess Maha Chakri Sirindhorn, in particular, who has studied many of the instruments). There are from six to twelve players in the pi phat, and they are spread across instruments that include a pair of wooden xylophones (ranat ek, ranat thum), a pair of knobbed gong circles, a quadruple reed oboe (pi nai), smaller and larger cymbals, a hanging knobbed gong, and several drums. Pi phat instruments*

are tuned to a seven-tone equidistant scale, although in reality there is a five-tone core of pitches that are ornamented in particular ways.

Teaching Commentary: *Identify the instruments and formal sections of the piece through repeated listenings. Explore the virtuosic performance of the ranat ek (or ranat thum) xylophone by experimenting with mallet techniques on a xylophone or marimba. (See Figure 3.9)*

Listen-points
Challenge yourself to hear

• pi nai, quadruple reed oboe
• ranat, wood xylophone
• ching, small bronze bell-like cup cymbals
• taphon, double-headed drum
• nonmetrical section
• metrical section
• halt midway into selection
• fast scale-like passages that ascend and descend

Notice the rapid mallet technique, in which the player alternately hammers two mallets on a wooden key in order to sustain the sound of a pitch. Take two pencils or pens and rapidly "play them," one then the other, on a flat surface. Try "playing" four "notes" in a row, accenting the first pulse of the tremolo for each new new note. Shift to a xylophone or marimba, hammering four times on each key, then playing four consecutive keys in a row—rapidly.

ATTENTIVE LISTENING EXPERIENCE 3.12 *CD track 26,* "Hyōjō Netori" *(Japanese gagaku ensemble)*
Possible Use: *Secondary, instrumental*
Instruments: *Sho (free-reed gourd), hichiriki (oboe), kakko (drum), ryuteki (flute), biwa (lute), koto (zither)*

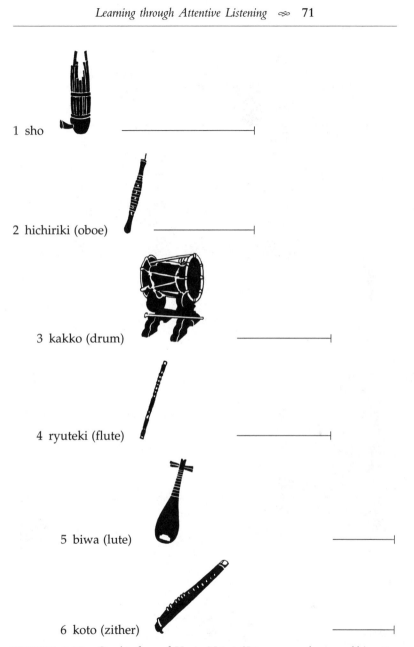

1 sho

2 hichiriki (oboe)

3 kakko (drum)

4 ryuteki (flute)

5 biwa (lute)

6 koto (zither)

FIGURE 3.10   *Graphic form of Hyojo Netori (Japanese gagaku ensemble).   (Instruments from* Musical Instruments of the World *[Diagram Group, 1997]. Reprinted with permission by The Diagram Group.)*

Notable Elements: *breath rhythm, gagaku ensemble*
Context: *Japan's court music, called gagaku, dates back to the Nara and Heian periods (the eighth through the twelfth centuries), and is preserved yet today where it remains a national treasure of the Imperial Court in Tokyo. The instruments of gagaku are broadly varied, from a central core of wind instruments to percussively plucked lutes and zither, to drums and gongs. The wind instruments lead the others in the embrace of a breath rhythm that functions elastically and flexibly. No conductor is necessary since gagaku musicians have mastered the technique of breathing deeply together, listening intently, and expelling the breath slowly. Gagaku music includes both instrumental music (for listening) and music for dance.*
Teaching Commentary: *Identify instruments as they enter, playing in pairs, and follow their breath rhythm. Breathe with the instruments as they play. (See Figure 3.10)*

ATTENTIVE LISTENING EXPERIENCE 3.13 *CD track 27, "Te Kuki Airani nui Maruarua" (Cook Islands)*
Possible Use: *Elementary or secondary, choral/vocal, general*
Instruments: *Female and male voices, claps, stamps.*
Notable Elements: *Ute, call-and-response form, melodic repetition, harmony (homophony)*
Context: *On the Cook Islands in the southern Pacific, voices of male and female singers blend in an homogenous style to produce both unison and chordal textures. Text is typically important in the music of Pacific Islanders, and the textures ensure that*

FIGURE 3.11   *Transcription of Te Kuki Airani nui Maruarua, CD track 26.*
(Cook Islands)

*the words can be understood. While guitars and other lutes ac-
company many song forms, there are still those like the ute, a
song-chant of considerable exhuberance, that relies on voices and
accompanying body-sounds to communicate feeling.*

Teaching Commentary: *Attend to the listen-points through
multiple listenings, noting especially the melodic repetition, and
the absence of instruments as voices and "corpophones" (body
sounds) fill the performance. (See Figure 3.11)*

Listen-points
Challenge yourself to hear

- women's voices
- men's voices
- vocal harmony (also called homophony)
- corpophones: claps, stamps
- vocal interjections
- call-and-response form

Follow the principal melody.

ATTENTIVE LISTENING EXPERIENCE 3.14 *CD track
28,* "Mini Overture" *(Lutoslawski, Poland).*
Possible Use: *Secondary, instrumental*
Instruments: *Trumpet, trombone, French horn*
Notable Elements: *Chromatic phrases, brass, dynamics*
Context: *Polish composer Witold Lutoslawski (1913–1994)
wrote a fanfare for brass instruments that is energetic and with a
strong forward-drive feeling to it. The piece opens with a descending chromatic passage and then shifts to the use of three-
pitch patterns. There is sense of momentum in the underlying
quick-moving pulse of the lower brass instruments even as the
trumpets sail their motivic melody above it. The composer's use
of minor seconds adds to the musical tension, and the sudden shift*

of dynamics from loud to soft and back again create excitement that keeps listeners on their toes.

Teaching Commentary: *Note the listen-points, giving focus to each one over multiple listening opportunities. Follow the sounds of a selected brass instrument through its motivic play and dynamic changes.*

Listen-points
Challenge yourself to hear

- initial entrance of the trumpet in descending chromatic passage
- entrance of trombones
- sections of solo and ensemble
- sections of loud and soft dynamics
- 3-pitch rhythms
- varied pitch ranges of the all-brass ensemble

ATTENTIVE LISTENING EXPERIENCE 3.15   *CD track 30, "Sargam" (North Indian vocal solfège)*
Possible Use: *Secondary, choral/vocal, general*
Instruments: *Male voice, tablā (drum), tānpura (drone), harmonium*
Notable Elements: *Pitch, ornamentation, sargam*

Re   Ni   Sa   Re - Ni   Pa
(opening phrase)

Sa Re Ga Ma Pa Dha Ni Sa   Sa Re Ga Ma Pa Dha Ni Sa

FIGURE 3.12   *Transcription of Sargam (North Indian vocal solfège), CD track 30.*

Context: *In North India, the seven pitches that lie within an octave are named by syllables, called sargam (or solfege). In ascending order, the syllables are Sa, Re, Ga, Ma, Pa, Dha, Ni; they compare to the French syllables Do, Re, Mi, Fa, Sol, La, Ti. The famous singer Ustad Amir Khan sings a melody using sargam, opening with a phrase that begins on the second degree (Re), lowering the pitch below the home-tone (Ni), and settling on the fifth (Pa). As he proceeds, the syllables associated with the pitches take on rich ornamentation so that no tone is "plain"-sounding. The syllables are far more than a musical drill, and may be incorporated into improvised sections of the vocal art music of India.*
Teaching Commentary: *Aurally follow the solfege syllables, called sargam, that the singer performs. Listen for the opening phrase (notated). Sing a major scale using the sargam syllables, then sing another scale using the same syllables. (See Figure 3.12)*

ATTENTIVE LISTENING EXPERIENCE 3.16   *CD track 31,* Gamelan *(Bali)*
Possible Use: *Elementary, general*
Instruments: *Gamelan: bronze or metal xylophones (gender and gangsa)*
Notable Elements: *Dynamics, gamelan ensemble*
Context: *On the far eastern Indonesian island of Bali, the gamelan sound is bright and boisterous when compared to its sedate, muted cousin ensemble on the island of Java. The lead bronze metallophones, the gender and gangsa, are paired as "female" and "male" instruments of slightly lower and slightly higher pitched tuning, respectively. When played together (as they are intended to do), their differentiated tunings "beat" against each other to cause a brilliant shimmering sound. Hard wooden mallets function to draw out an even brighter timbre, as opposed to the subtle and muted quality that comes from the padded mallets*

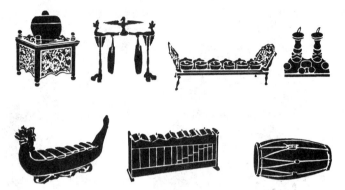

FIGURE 3.13 *Gamelan (Bali).* *(Instruments from* Musical Instruments of the World *[Diagram Group, 1997].* *Reprinted with permission by The Diagram Group.)*

in the Javanese gamelan. Along with the metallophones, the Balinese gamelan also includes two small but clashing sets of cymbals, two drummers, and a single row of knobbed gongs called trompong. Balinese gamelan music is known for its hocketed melodies, in which melodies from two xylophones interlock in order to contribute to a joint resultant melody.

Teaching Commentary: *Draw attention to the listen-points, particularly the timbral quality of Balinese gamelan. Locate selections of varied musical features. Draw comparisons with other metallophones. (See Figure 3.13)*

Listen-points
Challenge yourself to hear

- bright timbral quality of bronze xylophones
- rapid running sections versus sustained pitch-ringing sections
- loud-playing ensemble
- sudden starts and stops
- audience reactions to performance

Compare the sound of the Balinese gamelan to the Javanese gamelan (CD track 8). Write descriptive words for the distinctive sounds of the two gamelans.

CD track 40:

Also Sprach Zarathustra
(Richard Strauss)

Trumpet

Low Strings

Timpani

FIGURE 3.14 *Also Sprach Zarathustra (Richard Strauss), CD track 40.*

ATTENTIVE LISTENING EXPERIENCE 3.17 *CD track 40,* Also Sprach Zarathustra *(Richard Strauss, Austria)*
Possible Use: *Elementary or secondary, general, instrumental*
Instruments: *Trumpet, timpani, symphonic orchestra*
Notable Elements: *Fanfare, melodic motive*
Context: *Richard Strauss (1864–1949) was a widely acclaimed German composer of symphonic poems and operas. He enjoyed using dissonance that resolved to consonance, very full and some-*

FIGURE 3.15 *Trumpet. (Instruments from* Musical Instruments of the World *[Diagram Group, 1997]. Reprinted with permission by The Diagram Group.)*

times harsh orchestration, and chains of modulations that always returned to the tonic home-tone. He is credited with seven symphonic poems, from "Aus Italien" in 1887 to "Don Quixote" in 1898. "Also Sprach Zarathustra," composed in 1896, is as straightforward as a melodic motive can be, sounding almost like a signal or a fanfare in its opening, and giving little clue to the lush orchestral harmonies that lie ahead within the same piece.
Teaching Commentary: *Follow the motive that opens this symphonic poem. Sing the tonic drone pitch and "signal" pitches. Collect fanfare examples, and compare them for similar effects. (See Figure 3.14)*

Listen-points
Challenge yourself to hear

- the gradual emergence of a low tonic "home-tone," with its slow crescendo (occurring in the opening 11 seconds of the piece!)
- the "signal" call of the trumpet
- the full symphonic response and its crescendo on the sustained pitch
- the timpani's crescendo and decreasing tempo on pitches 1 and 5

Follow the notation.
 The opening of this symphonic poem is similar to some of the brass fanfares whose function is to call listeners to attention, to introduce dignitaries, or to present an air of foreboding and warning. Can you recall other fanfare compositions? Discuss circumstances in which you have heard one.

ATTENTIVE LISTENING EXPERIENCE 3.18 *CD track 41, "Seki no To" (Japan)*
Possible Use: *Secondary, instrumental*
Instruments: *Syamisen, male voice*
Notable Elements: *"Bending" pitches, nagauta ensemble*

FIGURE 3.16   *Syamisen.*   *(Instrument from* Musical Instruments of the World *[Diagram Group, 1997]. Reprinted with permission by The Diagram Group.)*

Context: *Kabuki is the shining example of musical theatre in Japan. The staged plays are replete with songs, dances, instrumental music, scenery, costumes, refined displays of movements from the martial arts, and of course highly stylized character acting. Kabuki music includes narrative forms performed as commentary on the onstage acting. It sets the scene or explains actions and parts of the plot; it involves long lyrical songs called nagauta, and offstage music called geza that provide moods and musical clues to action. The song here is from a late eighteenth century kabuki play, in which a cross section of Edo-period Japan, including a professional singer, a carpenter, and a sake peddler, meet on a ferry after paying their New Year's visit to a shrine, and each of them perform for one another.*

Teaching Commentary: *Focus listening on the sounds of individual instruments, voices, their techniques, and their collective ensemble performance. Note the expressive nature of vocal and instrumental performance of the nagauta form. (See Figure 3.16)*

Listen-points
Challenge yourself to hear

- the male singer
- the syamisen player

- the sustained pitches of the male singer
- places where the singer's and syamisen player's pitches match
- the moment when the singing voice bends expressively higher
- the sound of the lower male voice of the syamisen player who is softly calling "ho" and "yo" as part of the syamisen's performance practice

Compare this nagauta to examples of vocal music found in other examples of theatrical productions that utilize music as part of their means of expression. What do the vocal styles sound like? How does the sung music relate to the instruments that accompanies it?

ATTENTIVE LISTENING EXPERIENCE 3.19 *CD track 42*, Gender wayang *(Bali), CD track 43*, Orchestra *(U.S.)*
Possible Use: *Elementary or secondary, general, instrumental*
Instruments: *Gender wayang (metallophones), orchestra*
Notable Elements: Pitch
Context: *Tunings vary from one culture to the next, but the act of tuning is a valued process for musicians of vastly different cultures. For the Balinese, it is of prime importance that two paired metallophones are tuned unalike but complementary to one another so that the vibration rate of the sound waves of each, called frequencies, are far enough apart to produce "beats." (Refer to*

FIGURE 3.17 *Gender wayang. (Instrument from* Musical Instruments of the World *[Diagram Group, 1997]. Reprinted with permission by The Diagram Group.)*

CD track 31, as well.) As for the symphonic orchestra, the tuning process begins at the entrance of the concert master (or mistress), who then directs the first-chair oboe player to sound a middle A (440) that is then matched by all the other instruments. Once the musician has matched the A, a musical warm-up ensues in which scales, arpeggios, and parts of the musical passages for the evening are played until called to attention again by the concert master.

Teaching Commentary: *Discover the manner in which tunings occur for instruments of the Balinese gamelan and the Western symphony orchestra. Respond to questions regarding tuning.*

Listen-points
Challenge yourself to hear

- Two approaches to tuning, one from Asia, instruments of the Balinese gender wayang (CD track 42) and one from Europe, instruments of the symphonic orchestra (CD track 43)
- Two bronze bars from two Balinese metallophones (bar 1, bar 2, and then the two bars together)
- Strings, winds, and brass instruments of a Western symphony orchestra

Ask yourself about CD track 42

- Do the two bronze bars sound the same pitch? If not, which is higher, the first bar or the second bar?
- What happens when the two bronze bars are played at the same time?

Ask yourself about CD track 43

- Which instruments sound, when? Is there a lead instrument? Why would it be possible for someone not trained in the tradition of classical symphonic music to hear the tuning as a "piece"? (This has truly been the perception for some who have heard an orchestra tune for the first time, that this tuning period sounds like its own musical piece!)

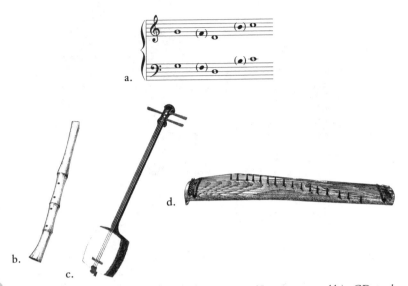

FIGURE 3.18 **a.** *Principal Pitches of Yaegoromo (Japanese ensemble), CD track 51.* **b.** *Syakuhachi;* **c.** *Syamisen;* **d.** *Koto.* *(Instruments from* Musical Instruments of the World *[Diagram Group, 1997]. Reprinted with permission by The Diagram Group.)*

ATTENTIVE LISTENING EXPERIENCE 3.20 *CD track 51,* "Yaegoromo" *(Japanese sankyokn ensemble)*
Possible Use: *Secondary, instrumental*
Instruments: *Syakuhachi (flute), syamisen (lute), koto (zither), male voice*
Notable Elements: *Jiuta ensemble, pitch, melismatic, heterophony*
Context: *"Yaegoromo" was composed in 1804, during Japan's Edo period, and was originally intended for voice and syamisen. The text is based upon five poems, and the title itself translates as "Piles of Eight Robes" thus giving some indication of time and a possible connection to nobility. The syakuhachi and koto may have been added later, and the contemporary jiuta ensemble of the three instruments (plus voice) resulted. The syamisen and koto play the main melody, together, with few variations,*

but the syakuhachi is more melismatic and more individual in its interpretation of the melody. The central pitches of the melody are limited, and the heterophony of the instruments is slight as they stay close to these few pitches.

Teaching Commentary: *Note the timbres, the pitches, and the manner in which they are matched, instrument-to-voice. Sing the key pitches of the melody, slowly and in a sustained manner. (See Figure 3.18)*

Listen-points
Challenge yourself to hear

- the male voice's slow sustained pitches
- syakuhachi (flute)
- syamisen (plucked lute)
- koto (zither)
- the singer's selective pitches ("1," "do," the tonic home-tone; "5," "sol" and the octave "1," "do") and their "lower-neighbor" passing tones ("7," lowered "ti" and "4," "fa")
- the instrumental performance of pitches similar to the singer's
- the ametrical, freely expressive musical "feel"
- a lower-pitched section, brief higher-pitched section, a return to the lower-pitched section

How long can you hold a pitch? Sing it? Play a pitch on a wind instrument for as long as you can.

ATTENTIVE LISTENING EXPERIENCE 3.21 *CD track 52,* Scottish bagpipe drone
Possible Use: *Elementary or secondary, general*
Instruments: *Bagpipe*
Notable Elements: *Drone*
Context: *The bagpipe is widely evident in traditional music throughout Europe, and is heard from Russia to the British Isles. The Scottish Highlands bagpipe is best known, and is played*

mainly outdoors as a solo instrument, or in groups. One or more drone pipes provide the pitches of the drone, which may play octaves and a fifth, and a mouth or chanter pipe brings air from the player to fill the bag and with its five to seven holes is the means for producing the melody. All pipes are fitted with single or double reeds. The repertoire for Scottish piping consists of folk tunes and pibroch, a complex form of theme with variations.
Teaching Commentary: *Follow the pitches of the melody that soar over the drone pitch. Sing or play the drone pitches, adding the florid melody to voices or instruments. Pair two oboes, two voices, two violins, or two trumpets for performing drone and melody parts. (See Figure 3.19)*

approximate
durations

melody pipe

a.

drone-pipes

b.

FIGURE 3.19   a. *Transcription of Scottish bagpipe drone, CD track 52;*   b. *Bagpipe.*   *(Instrument from* Musical Instruments of the World *[Diagram Group, 1997]. Reprinted with permission by The Diagram Group.)*

approximate pitches

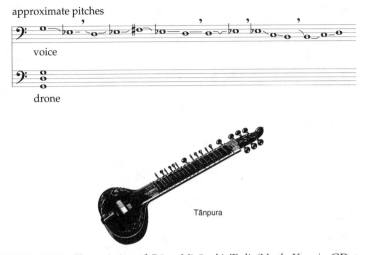

voice

drone

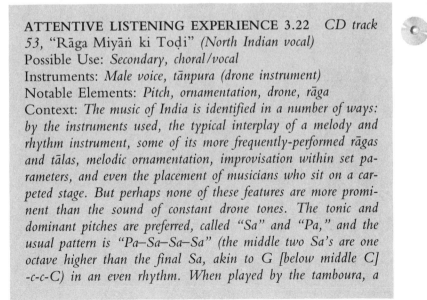

Tānpura

FIGURE 3.20 *Transcription of Rāga Miyān ki Todi (North Korea), CD track 53. (Instrument from* Musical Instruments of the World *[Diagram Group, 1997]. Reprinted with permission by The Diagram Group.)*

ATTENTIVE LISTENING EXPERIENCE 3.22 *CD track 53,* "Rāga Miyān ki Todi" *(North Indian vocal)*
Possible Use: *Secondary, choral/vocal*
Instruments: *Male voice, tānpura (drone instrument)*
Notable Elements: *Pitch, ornamentation, drone, rāga*
Context: *The music of India is identified in a number of ways: by the instruments used, the typical interplay of a melody and rhythm instrument, some of its more frequently-performed rāgas and tālas, melodic ornamentation, improvisation within set parameters, and even the placement of musicians who sit on a carpeted stage. But perhaps none of these features are more prominent than the sound of constant drone tones. The tonic and dominant pitches are preferred, called "Sa" and "Pa," and the usual pattern is "Pa–Sa–Sa–Sa" (the middle two Sa's are one octave higher than the final Sa, akin to G [below middle C] -c-c-C) in an even rhythm. When played by the tamboura, a*

tall lute-zither with four strings and an empty neck as a sound chamber, one pitch blends and dissolves into the next so that it is difficult to aurally identify the separate pitches. The singer (or player) weaves the melody according to the principles of the rāga, ornamentating above, below, and between the pitches.
Teaching Commentary: *During multiple listenings, focus on the ornamental manner in which the melodic pitches are performed. Sing the "Sa" and "Pa" pitches, and play the drone pattern on stringed instruments or a piano (with pedal). (See Figure 3.20)*

ATTENTIVE LISTENING ACTIVITY 3.23 *CD track 54,* Symphony No. 5 *(Ludwig van Beethoven, Germany)*
Possible Use: *Elementary or secondary, instrumental*
Instruments: *Symphonic orchestra, emphasis on strings*
Notable Elements: *Motive*
Context: *Under Beethoven's mastery, the musical form called the symphony achieved its full monumental stature throughout Europe by the early part of the nineteenth century. Several of his*

Symphony No. 5

L. van Beethoven

FIGURE 3.21 *Theme, Symphony No. 5 in c minor (Ludwig van Beethoven), CD track 54.*

symphonies are widely performed as international music, from Berlin to Beijing, and more than a few of his melodies are so popular as to be immediately identifiably even by school children. The manner in which he created a melodic idea and then developed it across the instruments of the orchestra and through the duration of a form are key to his style. As is demonstrated in the opening of the first movement of his Fifth Symphony, Beethoven valued the technique of "putting something significant first."
Teaching Commentary: *Draw attention to the opening motive and its continued presence that emerges throughout the piece. (See Figure 3.21)*

ATTENTIVE LISTENING EXPERIENCE 3.24 *CD track 56,* "The Great Ambush" *(China)*
Possible Use: *Elementary or secondary, general*
Instruments: *Pipa*
Notable Elements: *Pitch, performance technique, program music*

FIGURE 3.22 *Pipa. (Instrument from* Musical Instruments of the World *[Diagram Group, 1997]. Reprinted with permission by The Diagram Group.)*

Context: *The Chinese pipa lute was developed from lutes that arrived as soliders and traders returned from travels to Central Asia and India. For over two millennium, the pipa has figured prominently as a solo and ensemble instrument. It is especially known for its repertoire of through-composed pieces that tell stories of high drama, particularly of military skirmishes and full-blown battles. This program music requires tremdendous technical facility, and a wide variety of tempi, registers, and dynamics. This piece tells the story of the battle in 202 b.c.e. between the emperor of the Ch'u dynasty and his challenger from the Han dynasty.*

Teaching Commentary: *Find some of the performance techniques that set this Chinese lute apart as a highly expressive instrument. Note the storytelling function of pipa, and then listen in order to identify events of "The Great Ambush." (See Figure 3.22)*

Listen-points
Challenge yourself to hear

- the plucking and strumming of individual strings and groups of strings on the pipa
- the rapid tremelo effect of repeatedly plucking the same string
- the lower and higher registers of the pipa
- the variety of dynamics and tempi used
- the programmatic effect of the music to tell the story of "the great ambush"

Imagine the segments of the story of the battle between the emperor of the Ch'u dynasty and his challenger. How is the music moving the story into and out of these segments? While this is the order of events intended, some of them are difficult to discern.

The massing of troops
The line-up
The drum beats
The signals

The artillery barrage
The bugle calls to open a gate
The calling of the generals
The taking of battle stations
The dispatch
The ambush
The skirmish
The cannonade
The shouts
The charge
The siege
The call to retreat
The Ch'u army routed
The suicide of the Ch'u leader

LISTENING FROM NEAR AND FAR

It is a precious privilege to be able to take the time to direct the attention of young people to the explicit features of a musical piece, and school is the likely place for it to happen. There, teachers can open the ears and direct the attention of students as to "what is really going on," in not only a single selection but also in the musical world at large. Granted, a snippet of Korean chamber music or Vedic recitation from North India can seem extremely removed from the lives of young people, and the music of their bands, choirs, and orchestras (to say nothing of the mediated music they listen to beyond school) feature the timbres, tunings, and textures they know far better and which they greatly prefer. By earliest adolescence, students often come to specialize in music—if they specialize at all, as singers or pianists, violinists, saxophone or trombone players, and they may well be of the opinion that much of the world's music is off-limits and irrelevant to them. But not to have the experience of knowing some of these "other" musical cultures through multiple listenings and focused study would appear to miss the mark of a central goal of contemporary music education, to understand music for its multiple manifestations. It is the clever teacher who can convincingly balance students' preferred styles and specialized training, with the need for them to know the wider spectrum of music's possibilities, and who understands that a thorough musical education encompasses far more than the merely familiar styles. Opportunities for attentive listening, even a few minutes' worth of class time once or twice weekly, can reveal to students rich musical perspectives that might otherwise remain a mystery to them.

PROBLEMS TO PROBE

1. Over the course of multiple listenings to an assortment of selections, jot down what you are hearing—of the instruments and elemental features, as well as your thoughts as to the musicians and contexts associated with the music. Compare your first thoughts, from your initial listening, to thoughts that arise through repeated listenings for their depth and breadth. Use your jottings in raising questions for discussion with colleagues.

2. Choose one selection from the CD, and consider its use as an Attentive Listening Experience for students of all ages, backgrounds, and venues. Present an argument for this musical selection as a valuable listening experience for students at multiple levels and instructional settings. Redesign, adjust, or extend the experience to suit particular groups of students.

3. Review your sketch of a sample course schedule, selected in Chapter 1, and insert at least two Attentive Listening Experiences to fit the schedule. Think: Which experiences will be meaningful to developing my students' knowledge of Music with a capital "M"?

CHAPTER 4

Learning through Engaged Listening

∞

By now, the "listen-to-learn" theme is in full swing. It has been centralized in the chapters on Sound Awareness (Chapter 2) and Attentive Listening (Chapter 3) as key in developing our K–12 students' understanding of musical styles, processes, and cultures. No doubt, we would agree that since music is the aural art, it must be engaged in aurally, with graphic devices such as notation used as ancillary techniques for getting to the heart of music's structures and meanings. Yet for many of our students, from the very young to the more seasoned and sophisticated adolescent learners (and even adult learners, for that matter!), listening must be folded into a means of interactive engagement with the music. Some students will do it naturally: They will move and groove to a rhythm from Trinidad, hum along to a melody from Ireland, add a harmony part to a Mexican corrido, or beat out an ostinato pattern for a story-song from Liberia. Many others will need to be invited to do so, and to be led beyond their initial responses to further possibilities for their engaged listening. They may find themselves learning (best) while doing, as they sing, or play an instrument, or move in subtle or elaborate ways. We teachers who can provide multiple means for musically involving our students will succeed in developing their understanding of the music which people make meaningful and useful in their lives.

PARTICIPATORY CONSCIOUSNESS

Engaged Listening is the active participation by a listener in some extent of music-making while the recorded (or live) music is sounding. In fact, participatory experiences with recordings require active musical responses from its listeners, including live music-making. The accompanying CD selections motivate Engaged Listening through multiple encounters which children and youth can have with the music: singing and playing along with the recorded music, and moving eurhythmically to it or in an actual dance pattern. These encounters necessitate the careful and conscious listening that is far beyond the passive, armchair style of consumer listening, which is no wonder, given music's power to activate both the mind and the body into a deeper involvement with it. Music-making activities underscore the presence of elements that are operating within the music, and can bring a thorough analysis of musical structures in the process. As the music surrounds its young listeners, the invitation to them to enter the groove or the flow can stimulate listening to its peak.

Participatory consciousness is a phrase that has emerged in the fields of ethnomusicology and community music (a professional field of training and music facilitation work that is particularly strong in the U.K.) to describe the phenomenon of engaged listeners finding their place in a musical piece through the making of it, and of musicians teaming together to express themselves musically. Engaged Listening can lead to thoughts concerning the use of music by musicians within a culture, and to curiosities concerning individual and collective meaning-making through their musical practice. Noted ethnomusicologist Charles Keil has posited in his contributions to *Music Grooves* (coauthored with Steven Feld in 1994) that the act of musical participation has an impact beyond musical understanding, in that it has the potential to determine self-identity and to define reality. He articulated that participatory consciousness can be achieved through focused listening to the collective whole as well as to the separate and individual parts in live and recorded music, which then can lead engaged listeners into an ecological synchrony with themselves and with the natural world. As elementary and secondary school students find their place in the music, they come to possess it and to develop a personal association with it. They are then engaging with the highly skilled musicians of the recordings as well as with their classmates and colleagues, joining in to respond and contribute to a further realization of the music within their own realities.

For young listeners who engage as music-making participants, musical understanding is assumed, but the bonus is that musical participation may be a conduit to their understanding of the wider musical world. Engaged Listening allows student participants entry-points to the inside of the music as producers rather than as mere consumers, as they listen to themselves and others while singing, playing, and dancing along.

ENGAGED LISTENING EXPERIENCES

Following are found partial notations for CD selections deemed appropriate for the Engaged Listening experiences of K–12 students in choral, general, and instrumental—and any other music-instructional—settings. While they may find it challenging to "engage" on a first listening, when students listen long enough and often enough, they can become increasingly interactive with the essential elements of a musical work or excerpt. They may pick up suggested phrases and patterns aurally, and will do so more quickly as they become familiar with the music. For those who read notation, or who are visually oriented and aided by following the graphic rise and fall, and greater or lesser density, of note-symbols-on-a-page, portions of the selections are given in standard Western staff notation.

The music for the Engaged Listening Experiences is a collective of vocal and instrumental expressions from some of the world's numerous musical cultures to draw students into a musical engagement. From the Americas there is music of Trinidadian steel drum ensembles, a Puerto Rican salsa band, a mariachi ensemble of Mexico and the American southwest as well as Carribean-style calypso and Brazilian berimbau music. There's more too: a classic Louis Armstrong jazz piece based in blues form, jazz standards by Dave Brubeck and Paul Desmond, and even a notable song by rock/pop icon Bruce Springsteen. Out of Africa, there is an epic song of the Kpelle of Liberia, and music in maqam rast from Egypt. Selections from Asia include pieces for a traditional Chinese orchestra, a Japanese percussion ensemble, and a Balinese gamelan. European examples include music for musical theatre by a Belgian song-writer, a waltz for piano, a set of Irish jigs, and music for a Bulgarian circle dance. While the list of genres and traditions is not exhaustive, it does offer occasion for students to open their ears to some examples of the great musical variety that exists here on the planet.

There are suggestions for the "possible use" of the selections and their activities and it will come as no surprise that vocal selections can generally be geared toward choral and general classes while many of the instrumental selections will be relevant to students in band, orchestral, and jazz settings. Still, crossovers can easily occur, too, so that players can sing melodies and singers can play percussive phrases, and all listeners can conduct and respond through movement to some of the tracks. Further, if a musical selection appeals to a teacher, it can find its way into a music class, regardless of what the class is called. When the aim of the instructional experience is to broaden the musical experience of students, then of course any of these selections can be applied to students of any level of experience and instructional setting. The teacher's own flexibility and willingness to adapt these selections and their strategies are of course the keys to successful classroom experiences.

Two instructional approaches, or sets of "teaching tips," are offered for the use of each of the selections. There are "the obvious" suggestions for performing precisely what is heard and/or is notated, on authentic instruments, in as authentic a manner as possible, and "the optional" suggestions for making do with what one has available or extending from the more obvious possibilities. "The optional" tips include using the voice to sing or chant, the body as a "corpophone" or rhythm-maker (for clapping, patting, snapping, stamping, slapping), and an array of standard school instruments. (For several of the activities, a "Challenge" advisory is issued for what may prove challenging to all but the most advanced students.) Students can know and appreciate music as they enter into it as a listening experience, but they are more greatly engaged as they respond to music in active ways through contributions vocally, bodily through movement, and instrumentally.

ENGAGED LISTENING EXPERIENCE 4.1   *CD track 2,* "Gunslingers" *(Trinidad)*
Possible Use: *Steel drum ensemble; Elementary or secondary, instrumental or general*
Context: *It is a remarkable accomplishment, a feat of human ingenuity, for the Trinidadians to have evolved a musical style from the fashioning of fifty-five-gallon oil drums. Many of the melodies and rhythms were already there, played by tamboo-bamboo bands whose members struck, stamped, and scraped lengths of bamboo alongside the sounds of bottles, spoons, and other household items. But when the oil drums washed to shore near the end of World War II, musician and machinist Ellie Manette and others began hammering dents into the metal drums so that each dent had its own pitch. The drums, or pans, come in various sizes and pitch ranges, are often paired (such as in the case of the double tenor or double second pans), and are carried around*

Gunslingers

FIGURE 4.1 *Gunslingers, CD track 2.*

the necks for Carnival parades or mounted on wheeled racks for rolling onto the stage for competition. From December to the time of Carnival (typically in February or early March), steel drum bands are practicing in panyards all over Trinidad to ready themselves for the new arrangements they will play at the national *competition called the Panorama. Anything goes, too, from classical music to Latin popular tunes on the steel drums.*

Teaching Tips *(See Figure 4.1)*

The Obvious: *Play the melody and harmony on steel pans (tenor and double seconds).*
Play the rhythm on shakers (maracas) and cowbell.

The Optional: *Sing the melody.*
Play the melody and harmony on available instruments (for example, on xylophones).
Tap the rhythms on a table, desk, or floor surface.
Pat the rhythms on the body.

ENGAGED LISTENING EXPERIENCE 4.2 *CD track 3,* "Partridges Flying" *(China)*

Possible Use: *Elementary or secondary, instrumental or general*

Context: *The music of China, in China and in Chinese communities like those found in Taiwan, Hong Kong, Singapore, and even cities like San Francisco, is richly varied, and includes traditional arts of opera, vocal narrative songs, folk songs, solo instrumental music, chamber music, and large choral and orchestral pieces. The sound of "silk and bamboo" instruments, including the er hu fiddle, the pipa lute, the qin and zheng zithers, the free-reed sheng mouth organ, and both the vertical notched xiao flute and the horizontal di-tze flute, are linked to the long history of Chinese music-making. One of the principles of traditional Chinese music is the aesthetic of "adding flowers" by embellishing a melody, so that the player of each instrument may follow a melody but also personalize it according to the techniques that are possible on that instrument. In some music, there are occasions for both embellishment as well as straightforward and fairly unison performance by multiple instruments.*

Partridges Flying

FIGURE 4.2   *Partridges Flying, CD track 3.*

Teaching Tips *(See Figure 4.2)*
The Obvious: *(At 0' 18") Play the melody on flute/ recorder and violin.*
Add the low-pitched drum near the end.
The Optional: *Sing the melody, mm. 10–13.*
Play the melody on available instruments.
Practice playing melodic trills.
Complete the melody: create the second phrase in a manner that stylistically matches the first phrase.

ENGAGED LISTENING EXPERIENCE 4.3   *CD track 4,*
"Mi Bajo y Yo" *(Puerto Rico)*
Possible Use: *Percussion ensemble, jazz ensemble; Elementary or secondary, instrumental, general*

Context: *The rhythmic vitality of salsa is key to that genre's identity and beauty. The Puerto Rican concept of ritmo (rhythms) refers to the polyrhythmic organization of the rhythms, and to the timing, volume, and timbre of the instruments that play it. The interlocking rhythmic patterns of the clave, guiro, and congas give listeners cause to dance, as the melody sounds in between accented and unaccented pulses and their subdivisions. Whereas in West Africa, an unchanging rhythm pattern played by a bell functions as a time line, Puerto Rican and pan-Latin salsa and other dance forms are grouped around the clave pattern. Clave has come to refer to not only the instrument but also to the foundational rhythm around which all other instruments are linked. Salsa is grounded in Puerto Rican and Cuban sensibilities, but its vitality has won the hearts of dancers all over the world.*

Teaching Tips (See Figure 4.3)
The Obvious: *Play high and low congas, guiro, clave—by ear or by note.*
Play the melody on piano.
Play the bass line on bass.

Dance the salsa: Say:	"Quick —	Quick —	Slow"
Think:	♩	♩	𝅗𝅥
(Face front) Step:	Back	Forward	Forward
(Feet together)	Forward	Back	Back
	Right	Left	Right
	(Get an attitude in the hips!)		

The Optional: *Clap the clave pattern.*
Play the conga part on available percussion instruments.
Tap the rhythms on a table, desk, or floor surface.
Pat the rhythms on the body.
Play the piano melody and bass line on piano.

FIGURE 4.3   *Mi Bajo y Yo, CD track 4.*

ENGAGED LISTENING EXPERIENCE 4.4 *CD track 16,*
"Festival Music" *(offstage (geza) ensemble, Japan)*
Possible Use: *Percussion ensemble; Elementary or secondary,*
general, instrumental
Context: *In the tradition of Japanese kabuki theatre, there is*
both onstage and offstage music. While the syamisen lute domi-

nates the onstage music, a battery of instruments called geza plays from a concealed room at one side of the stage. The geza musicians play sound effects, signals, and other music not covered by the musicians on stage. Their role is to heighten drama, set the mood, and punctuate the action. Some of the geza music is borrowed, including pieces from the matsuri bayashi ensemble of festival musicians who perform on floats through neighborhoods for holiday processions. For kabuki audiences, this music is a striking aural symbol of local music celebrations they remember from their childhoods.

Teaching Tips

The Obvious: *Play the melody on flute/recorder—by ear (*Challenge* It moves quickly, so pick out discernible phrases).*

Play the rhythms on taiko and o-daiko drums, and gong.

The Optional: *Play the melody on available instruments—by ear.*

On trap set, or snare and bass drums, or conga drums, play rhythms that can be distinguished.

Sing, pat, or chant selected phrases.

ENGAGED LISTENING EXPERIENCE 4.5   *CD track 18,* "Traveling in Soochow" *(China)*
Possible Use: *Secondary, general*
Context: *The di-tze flute is a splendid example of a "bamboo" instrument, one of the eight sounds of the Chinese categorization of instruments by the material from which they were made: earth, stone, metal, skin, wood, gourds, silk, and bamboo. Its unique timbral quality is a result of a paper membrane that is placed near the blow hole, giving it a reedy quality. The pentatonic scale is the basis of the melody, and even a cascading melody and the*

Traveling in Soochow

FIGURE 4.4 *Traveling in Soochow, CD track 18.*

decorative grace notes stay within these pitches. A hammered dulcimer, probably arriving in China from western Asia during the time of the Silk Road, plays the same melody as the di-tze, sustaining its pitches through a rapid wrist motion that produces a tremolo effect.

Teaching Tips *(See Figure 4.4)*

The Obvious: *Play the melody on flute/recorder (and hammered dulcimer), plain pitches or ornamented.*

The Optional: *Sing the melody with careful attention to the durations and the breaths between them.*
Play the melody on available instruments.
Eurhythmically move (hands, arms, whole body) to the sustained and "fluttering" ornamental notes.

ENGAGED LISTENING EXPERIENCE 4.6   *CD track 20,*
Cantonese Opera *(Hong Kong)*
Possible Use: *Elementary or secondary, choral/vocal, general, instrumental*
Context: *Chinese Opera takes its rightful place among the brilliant forms of musical theater that exist in the world. There are*

Cantonese Opera

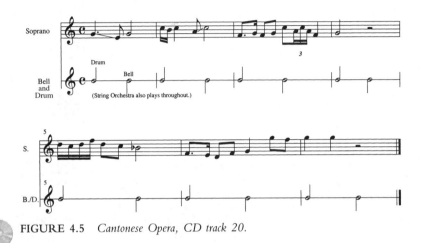

FIGURE 4.5   *Cantonese Opera, CD track 20.*

*over three hundred types of regional forms of theatre in China,
from popular street plays and folk forms to the full-fledged professional productions headquartered in cities such as Beijing,
Shanghai, and Canton. These professional operas were popular
with nobility and common people alike as early as the sixteenth
century. They continue to attract audiences today, due not only
to the exquisitely rendered song and instrumental music but also
the dance, acrobatics, costumes, sparse but effective staging, and
symbolic use of props. Prospective members of the opera troupes
are identified as children, and are put through many years of rig-
orous training in singing, dancing, and gymnastics before they are
readied for the stage.*

Teaching Tips *(See Figure 4.5)*
The Obvious: *Sing the melody (on a neutral syllable).*
       Play drum and bell parts.

The Optional: *Play the melody on available instruments.*
Pat for drum, clap lightly for bell.

ENGAGED LISTENING EXPERIENCE 4.7   *CD track 24,*
Take Five *(Paul Desmond, U.S. Jazz)*
Possible Use: *Jazz ensemble; Elementary or secondary, instrumental, general*
Context: *The history of jazz music is both American and international in scope, and its sound spans a spectrum of instruments and voices, large and small ensembles, influences and fusions. Small jazz combos numbering three, four, and five musicians began to surface in the U.S. in the late 1940s as serious music to be listened to. Beyond the dance music of stage bands, these combos were known for their improvisatory styles and experimentation with modes and meters. Paul Desmond, an award-winning alto saxophonist and jazz composer, joined with pianist and jazz composer Dave Brubeck in 1949 to form the Dave Brubeck Quartet. In 1959, they recorded Desmond's "Take Five," and it became the first jazz instrumental piece to sell a million copies. The melody, instrumentation, and especially its metrical play, have made it a standard for combos and a model of what jazz composition can be.*

Teaching Tips
The Obvious: *Play the drum part throughout—by ear.*
Play the piano vamp—by ear.
The Optional: *Conduct the five-beat meter.*
Move to a five-beat meter, giving accent to beat 1 and a lesser accent to 4; devise a small-group choreography.
Pat or tap out the piano rhythm: ♪♩ ♪♩ ♩ ♩
Sing the melody.
Play on instruments available—by ear.

Aruh li Min
(Maqam Rast)

FIGURE 4.6 *Aruh li Min (Maqam Rast), CD track 25. (Transcription by Scott Marcus.)*

ENGAGED LISTENING EXPERIENCE 4.8 *CD track 25,* "Maqam Rast," "Aruh li min" *(Egypt)*
Possible Use: *Elementary or secondary, choral/vocal, general*
Context: *A typical twentieth century Egyptian instrumental ensemble may consist, as it does in this piece, of kaman (violins), qanun (plucked zither), ud (plucked lute), nay (end-blown reed flute), cellos, double bass, and percussion instruments such as riqq (tambourine) and dombek (goblet-shaped drum). A singer is often at center and up front of such an ensemble, and no singer has ever been more popular than Umm Kulthum. The daughter of a professional musician, she was born with a beautiful voice and a remarkable ear, and by the time she was 10 years old was already performing astonishing renditions of folk and popular songs to great acclaim. She became the featured attraction of live performances to thousands of listeners, in cinema halls and theatres. Her recorded repertoire is known to all Egyptians and is her legacy to others who now emulate her style. Maqam rast, with its half-flatted pitches at the third and seventh degrees, is the framework for the melody that is played heterophonically by the instruments.*

The text of the first verse is "To whom shall I turn? (Aruh li min) And whom shall I call to relieve me from your injustice? You are both my joy and a deep wound. It's all your fault." The piece was composed by Riyad al-Sinbati.

Teaching Tips (See Figure 4.6)

The Obvious: (At 1'28") Play percussion parts on riqq (tambourine)—by ear or by note (see Chapter 5). Follow the notation.
Sing the phrase "Aruh li min" when it occurs.

The Optional: Play percussion parts on available tambourines and drums.
Sing the verse "Aruh li min."
Dance a movement pattern: (In a circle, hands held, arms up, elbows bent)

		Think:	1 - 2 - 3 - 4
(Feet together)		Step:	Right Left Right Hold
(In circle)			"R - L - R - Hold"
			counts to the right
			"R - L - R - Hold"
			counts in
			"R - L - R - Hold"
			counts out

(Refer also to notation, Chapter 5, page 146)

ENGAGED LISTENING EXPERIENCE 4.9   *CD track 29,* "El Gustito" *(Mexico)*
Possible Use: *Mariachi ensemble; Elementary or secondary, choral/vocal, general*
Context: *Mariachi music has been traditional to western Mexico for over a century, and its sounds are now widely heard north of the country's border, particularly in the southwestern U.S. From the barrios of Los Angeles to the chains of burrito and fajita restaurants across North America, the presence of mariachi*

El Gustito

FIGURE 4.7   *El Gustito, CD track 29.*

music is strong and immediately identifiable as "Mexican." Few recognize that mariachi music is further shaped by Mexican-American musicians and others who perform it, and by innovations that are far from Jalisco, the reputed place of its birth. So well known is mariachi that few are aware that it is only one of

FIGURE 4.7 *Continued.*

multiple musical expressions that emanate from Mexico. Mariachi melodies are carried by singing voices and violins, chordal accompaniments by a guitar-like instrument called the vihuela, and bass lines by the guitarron, or "big guitar." A pair, or more, of trumpets play bright and lively interludes for vigorous dance pieces known as sones and jarabes. Common to mariachi music is the strophic form (a song whose melody is repeated with different texts for each repetition), harmonic patterns that feature I, IV, and V chords, a metric feeling that fluctuates between pulses of two and three, and melodies that are harmonized by thirds. Like much of the music of the world, mariachi music is enculturated into the ears of appreciative listeners and dancers and is learned by musicians in the oral-aural way of folk music.

Teaching Tips *(See Figure 4.7)*

The Obvious: *Sing the vocal melody and harmony in thirds (on a neutral syllable like "loo")—by ear or by note.*

Play vilhuela, guitarron, brass parts—by ear or by note.

The Optional: *Conduct the three-beat meter.*

Eurhythmically move, swaying right and then left for three beats in each direction.

Keep a three-beat movement: on "1" pat, on "2" and "3" clap.

Move to a three-beat pattern: (Feet together)

	1	2	3
Think:	1	- 2	- 3
Step:	Right	Left	Right
Then:	Left	Right	Left
(Bend knees):	Down	Up	Up

ENGAGED LISTENING EXPERIENCE 4.10 *CD track 32, "West End Blues" (Louis Armstrong, U.S. Jazz)*
Possible Use: *Jazz ensemble; Secondary, instrumental, general*
Context: *The blues is a song form with its own history, and yet traces of its origin have been found in African folk music. But it is decidedly American in its development, and has also been widely influential in the development and performance style of jazz. It consists of a number of harmonic patterns, the most widely used of which is the 12-bar (or 12, 4-count measures) blues pattern with its fixed chordal progression I–I–I–I, IV–IV–I–I,*

V–V–I–I. It is known for its "blue notes," flattened pitches at the third and seventh degrees, and for the improvisatory manner in which the melody is expressively rendered. While blues is primarily a vocal form (three-line stanzas organized with the same text for lines one and two, and a rhyming third line), the influences of its harmonic pattern, blue notes, and improvised performance style on jazz are legion. Among the best known blues-inspired jazz pieces are W. C. Handy's "St. Louis Blues" (1914) and Louis Armstrong's "West End Blues" (1928). In the latter, there are five "stanzas," all of them wordless, each one featuring an instrument: piano, a trombone solo, scat-singing and clarinet, piano, and trumpet. Louis Armstrong's trumpet starts and completes the piece.

Teaching Tips

The Obvious: *Play the melody on trumpet—by ear.*
Play the chords in quarter note rhythms on piano—by ear.

The Optional: *Pat the steady beat on lap, desk or floor surface, accenting "1."*
On the second round of melody, tap with the "metallic" percussive sound that can be heard.
Play the melody and chords on keyboard—by ear.
Play the melody on available instruments.

ENGAGED LISTENING EXPERIENCE 4.11 *CD track 33, "Marieke" (Jacques Brel, Belgium)*
Possible Use: *Secondary, choral/vocal*
Context: *The theme of loss runs through the text of Jacques Brel's "Marieke": the loss of love, the damage to a nation through war, the devastation of once-flourishing Belgian cities of Bruges and Ghent. The song concerns the march by German soliders*

across the fields of Flanders, Belgium, in World War I on their way to attack Paris. The text obliquely refers to the blood spilled and destruction of everything in their path, and the way in which the poppies later grew out of the leveled land. Several languages appear in the text—English, Flemish, and French. The acceleration of the song toward its close, and the repeating phrase, "the day is done," express the anguish, the helplessness, and the hopelessness of loss. Belgian songwriter Jacques Brel wrote this and other songs in order to vent his social comments and world-weariness in a lyrical manner, many of which are collected into the musical theater, Jacques Brel is Alive and Well and Living in Paris.

Teaching Tips

The Obvious: *Sing the melody—by ear.*
Play the chordal accompaniment on guitar or piano—by ear.

The Optional: *Play the melody on available instruments.*

ENGAGED LISTENING EXPERIENCE 4.12 *CD track 34*, Waltz in C♯ Minor *(Frédéric Chopin, Poland)*
Possible Use: *Elementary or secondary, general*
Context: *The greatest Polish national composer of the nineteenth century, Frédéric Chopin, was a virtuoso pianist with a brilliant concert career in all of the best halls of Europe. He wrote almost exclusively for piano, and even the rare combination of the instrument with strings in a few works nonetheless features the brilliance of the piano's lead. Along with his waltzes, he also composed preludes, ballades, etudes, noctures, and impromptus, all musical gems in their sweet elegance. His waltzes (German, "valse") were not meant to be danced. They were intended as concert pieces, sophisticated musical gems too intricately expressive to dance to, but appropriate for deep listening, as people did*

Waltz in C♯ Minor

Frederic Chopin

FIGURE 4.8 *Waltz in C♯ Minor, CD track 34.*

in the salons where they heard him play. Still, Chopin's elevation of the dance form to concert music does not remove it from the listener feeling the "1-2-3" and wanting to whirl away in waltz style.

Teaching Tips (See Figure 4.8)
The Obvious: *Play on the piano.*
The Optional: *Conduct the three-beat meter.*
(*Challenge*) Try to move in waltz-like fashion, alone or with partner:

	Think:	1	-	2	-	3
(Feet together)	Step:	Right		Left		Right
	Then:	Left		Right		Left
		Down		Up		Up
		(Adjust to tempo changes)				

Compare this 1-2-3 movement to the mariachi movement: Do they feel the same or different? How?

ENGAGED LISTENING EXPERIENCE 4.13 *CD track 35, "Born in the USA" (Bruce Springsteen, U.S.)*
Possible Use: *Elementary or secondary, instrumental, general*
Context: *Before his rise to fame in the late 1970s, the composer of "Born in the USA" had predicted: "I saw rock 'n' roll's future, and its name is Bruce Springsteen." Critics have called Springsteen the greatest living rock 'n' roll star, and he paid his dues as singer, songwriter, and guitarist in a variety of local bands in New Jersey until he gathered the musicians around him that made up his signature E Street Band sound of guitars, keyboards, drums, and a saxophone. His popularity came as a result of his ability to connect with his listeners as a working-class American with a job, a car, a girlfriend, and a hometown. Springsteen's music could be uplifting, brooding, and celebratory, and his "Born*

in the USA" *(recorded in 1984) is his most commercially successful album, with its title song that is known throughout the
world for its positive energy and proud spirit.*

Teaching Tips

The Obvious: *Play the "groove" on keyboard and drums—
by ear.*

The Optional: *Play with mallets on a drum on beats 2
and 4.*

Clap on beats 2 and 4.

Sing the verse—by ear.

ENGAGED LISTENING EXPERIENCE 4.14 *CD track
36,* Three to Get Ready and Four to Go *(Dave Brubeck,
U.S. Jazz)*

Possible Use: *Jazz ensemble; Elementary or secondary, instrumental, general*

Context: *The shifting meters, from 3/4 to 4/4 and back again—
multiple times—are alluded to in the full title of this piece from
a colloquial phrase widely known at the time of its recording in
1960, "Three to get ready, four to go, come on cool cat, go-go-
go!" Dave Brubeck, who called himself "a composer who plays
the piano," wrote the piece for his renown quartet consisting of
piano, bass, drums, and saxophone. Brubeck was fascinated with
meter, and this piece, along with his "Blue Rondo a la Turk"
(written in 9/8 but grouped 2 + 2 + 2 + 3) and Paul
Desmond's "Take Five" (in 5/4 meter), provided fresh material for the Dave Brubeck quartet and other small ensembles of
the time. The muted and subtle sound of individual instruments
combine in Brubeck's pieces to express a rhythmic vitality for
which cool jazz became known. Brubeck received a Lifetime
Achievement award in 1996 from the National Academy of
Recording Arts and Sciences.*

Teaching Tips

The Obvious: *Play the piano, cymbals, drums (first round)—by ear.*

Play melody on sax (second round)—by ear.

The Optional: *Conduct the three-beat meter (first round).*

Pat on 1, clap on 2 (first round).

Conduct the changing meters (continued rounds): Note pattern 1-2-3 (2✗) 1-2-3-4 (2✗)

ENGAGED LISTENING EXPERIENCE 4.15 *CD track 37,* "Tar Road to Sligo" *and* "Paddy Clancy's Mug of Browne Ale" *(Ireland)*

Possible Use: *Elementary or secondary, instrumental, general*

Context: *The time of "the Celtic dragon" has arrived in the world, according to observers of Ireland's recent economic successes, and Irish music has become the country's most sought-after export. The triangular wooden harp, called the clairseach, may be the Irish national instrument, but the sounds of fiddles, flutes, mandolins, tin whistles, bagpipes, and bodhrans have also come to be known as emblematic of Ireland and its traditional music. The fiddle is identical to the modern violin, and often pairs with the cross-blown wooden flute to perform tunes in unison. Add a mandolin, as in the jigs performed here, and the texture is still unison as the melody skips along in compound meter at a lively speed. At sessions in pubs in Ireland, and where players of Irish music gather in North America, jigs, reels, and hornpipes keep the toes tapping and invite many to dance along.*

Teaching Tips

The Obvious: *Play the melody on mandolin, flute, fiddle—by ear or by note (See Chapter 5, page 149).*

The Optional: *Sing the melody.*

Play the melody on available instruments.

> *Pat 6/8 rhythms on a desk, table, or floor surface:*
>
> ♩ ♪♩ ♪ | ♩ ♪♫ | ♫♫
>
> *(Refer to notation: Chapter 5, page 149)*

ENGAGED LISTENING EXPERIENCE 4.16 *CD track 38,* "Makedonsko horo" *(Bulgaria)*
Possible Use: *Elementary or secondary, general*
Context: *Dances in the round, or circle dances, are found in many of the world's regions. In Bulgaria's Pirin region, across the border from Macedonia, the horo is a favorite circle dance that features three uneven "beats" consisting of subunits of 3 + 2 + 2 within a seven-count measure. Pomaks, people who converted to Islam during the Turkish occupation, plucked long-necked lutes called tambura(s). The tambura traditionally has four strings arranged in double courses, and typically plays melody and drone tones together. In response to the music made by Pomaks, both men and women join hands in the circle to dance in the formation that feels united and communal.*

Teaching Tips
The Obvious: *Play the melody on plucked lute (guitar, mandolin). (See Chapter 5, page 151)*
Play the drone on the same (or another) instrument.

Dance the horo: (In a circle, hands held, arms up, elbows bent, facing right)

	1-2-3	4-5	6-7
Think:			
Step:	Right	Left	Right
	Step	Cross	Step
Then:	Left	Left	Right
	Lift	Step	Lift

Then move in opposite direction:

Step:	Left	Right	Left
	Step	Cross	Step
Then:	Right	Left	Right
	Cross	Step	Lift

The Optional: *Sing the melody and drone.*
Pat the rhythm ♫♫ ♩ ♩
Play the rhythm on hand drums.
Pat or play the rhythm ♩. ♩ ♩
(Refer to notation: Chatper 5, page 151)

ENGAGED LISTENING EXPERIENCE 4.17 *CD track 39, "Unnai Nambinen" (South India)*
Possible Use: *Secondary, choral/vocal, general*
Context: *The kriti is a South Indian song form that was developed hundreds of years ago to express bhakti, or devotion to a deity, and which is even now an important part of that musical culture. As in the case of most South Indian art music, there may be a written score, but student musicians may nonetheless learn it through the performance of it by their teacher. Featured with the voice is the drone, performed on a portable organ called a harmonium, and rhythms played percussively by the mridangam drum to an 8-beat tāla called Adi tāla. A violin plays alongside the vocal part, often in unison with the sung melody, although there are idiosyncratic differences between them. There is considerable repetition of the phrases to allow listeners to thoughtfully consider the lines of text. "Unnai Nambinen" addresses the Hindu deity, Naiaraja, in this way: "I trusted you, lord, I prostrated at your feet. Wearing a cobra, aiva Naiaraja, Oh lord who dwells in Cidambaram."*

Teaching Tips

The Obvious: *Sing the drone tonic tone.*

Keep the tāla: 1 (2-3-4)   5 (6)   7 (8)
                Clap   Clap   Wave (silent)

(*Challenge*) Sing the opening phrases of the melody—by ear (to 0' 35").

The Optional: *(*Challenge*) Play the opening phrases on available instruments—by ear.*

ENGAGED LISTENING EXPERIENCE 4.18 *CD track 50*, Kotekan "norot" *(Bali)*

Possible Use: *Metallophone ensemble; Elementary or secondary, general*

Context: *The brilliance of the Balinese gamelan rings through the villages and towns of Bali, where musicians play for dance and puppet theater productions, for their communities, their guests, and themselves. Using hard wooden mallets on bronze keys, each "male" gender and gangsa metallophone is tuned with its paired "female" counterpart (which is tuned slightly lower than the male instrument), and the resultant sound of the beats produced by the intentionally varied tuning is a bright and shimmering quality. The melodies of the metallophones are shared; they are split in the style of the hocket between two players who combine the pitches they alternately play to create their melody of interlocking parts. Each metallophone has its own melodic pattern, but it is their conglomerate melody, along with the sound of gongs punctuating the phrases, that makes for the rich musical experience that Bali can boast.*

Teaching Tips (See Figures 4.9 and 4.10)

The Obvious: *(*Challenge*) Play the two melodies on metallophones.*

Kotekan "norot"

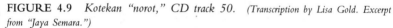

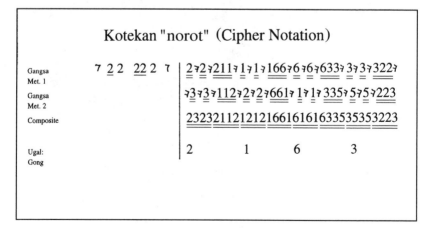

FIGURE 4.9   *Kotekan "norot," CD track 50.*   *(Transcription by Lisa Gold. Excerpt from "Jaya Semara.")*

FIGURE 4.10   *Kotekan "norot" (Cipher notation).*

The Optional: *Pat the constant beat of the single low-pitched gong.*
Sing the sustained gong pattern throughout: 2—1—6—3.
Sing each of the two melodies, using numbers ("1" is home or tonic).

ENGAGED LISTENING EXPERIENCE 4.19   *CD track 55, Episode from* woi-meni-pele *(Kpelle epic, Liberia)*
Possible Use: *Secondary, choral/vocal*
Context: *Among the Kpelle of Liberia, there is an epic genre that involves a lead singer, a chorus of four male voices, and two "bottle tappers." Their music is an interlocking of multiple parts, with the lead singer performing his part and the others supporting it with their musical counterparts. As in much of western and sub-Saharan Africa, this music serves as a component in the telling of a story. The Liberian Kpelle epic-pourer is storyteller, unfolding the events of Womi, the hero and superhuman ritual specialist. The epic-pourer sings Womi's part and the parts of other players in the story, and responds to questions from his listeners who provide the bottle-tapping and the choral phrases. There the interlocking bottles play an ostinato pattern, while the two vocal parts by the four singers form an undulating pattern above which the lead singer improvises his storytelling melody.*

Teaching Tips (See Figure 4.11)
The Obvious: *Sing the voice parts (I & II) on neutral syllables—by ear or by note.*
Play the bottle rhythms on bottles, first one (♫♫) and then the other (| | |), then together—by ear or by note.
Follow the notation of the solo voice.
The Optional: *Pat the bottle rhythms on the lap, desk or floor surface.*

Episode from *woi-meni-pele*

FIGURE 4.11   *Episode from woi-meni-pele, CD track 55.*

ENGAGED LISTENING EXPERIENCE 4.20   *CD track 57, "Iron Duke in the Land" (Julian Whiterose, Trinidad)* Possible Use: *Elementary or secondary, choral/vocal, general* Context: *Calypsos are heard throughout the Carribean, but nowhere more than in Trinidad, where the Creolized genre originated in the late nineteenth century. At Carnival time, drums, dances, processions and stick fighting were gradually replaced by the official endorsement of calypso competitions, where singers accompanied by guitars would offer political commentaries based on*

Iron Duke in the Land

FIGURE 4.12   *Iron Duke in the Land, CD track 57.*

*contemporary events. Julian Whiterose, nicknamed "Iron Duke,"
recorded "Iron Duke in the Land" in 1914, and used the popular Creole phrase "sans humanite" (without pity) as a tag line
to his verses.*

Teaching Tips *(See Figure 4.12)*
The Obvious: *Sing the melody.*
                 Play the chords on guitar.
The Optional: *Tap the rhythm, "Iron Duke in the land, fire
                 brigade" as it occurs.*

ENGAGED LISTENING EXPERIENCE 4.21   *CD track
59, "Riachao" (Brazil)*
Possible Use: *Elementary or secondary, choral/vocal, general*
Context: *Since half of Brazil's population can claim African ancestry, it should come as no surprise to hear Africanisms in the*

Riachao (Begins at 0:03)

FIGURE 4.13   Riachao, CD track 59.

music. Call-and-response forms, polyrhythms, ensembles of drums and other percussion instruments, and the integration of music with dance are manifestations of the influences of the Yoruba, Ewe, Fanti-Ashante, and other groups in Brazil. In the north-eastern coastal state of Bahia, the most African part of the country, the stylized martial art/movement form called capoeira is performed to the accompaniment of voices and instruments. A musical bow called the berimbau is prominent in the music for capoeira, and its single wire string is played with a stick and a basket rattle, while the body of the player serves as a resonating chamber. A solo voice calls to a chorus, and this is the music that inspires the martial art movements of the capoeira.

Teaching Tips (See Figure 4.13)
The Obvious: *Sing the solo and chorus segments.*
Play the percussive rhythm on tambourine.
The Optional: *Add a basic drum rhythm ♩ ♫*

ENGAGING THE DISENGAGED

As surely as students can become engaged in a musical piece, they can also become disengaged. They are likely to lose attention, or never to develop their musical focus in the first place, if they are not appropriately prepared for a thoughtful experience. Even music that may seem more immediately appealing, due to driving rhythms, catchy melodies, or unusual timbres, can fall flat without a teacher's careful facilitation. Students in secondary school as well as elementary school do well when they are ushered into a musical experience with leading questions (for example, "Have you any idea what instrument is playing that high melody?"), with a colorful comment, (for example, "My first impression, on listening to this singing style, was the sound of a mythical— even magical—bird"), or with a story line (for example, "If you only knew about why this music means so much to the people who play it; let me tell you about it.") to trigger their interest. As the experience proceeds to possibilities for student participation, the pace with which the listening is blended with singing, playing, or movement of some sort is important for keeping the students on-task and in-gear. The best results of engaged listening will come from the careful balance of listening time with participation time, with room also for remarks by teacher and students. As in all good teaching, the teacher's reception of student questions and comments, and of course reinforcement of student attempts at musical involvement, will guarantee their engagement in selections from the wide world of music.

PROBLEMS TO PROBE

1. Select an activity to trial-teach to a group of K–12 students as a 10-minute segment or full-fledged 50-minute lesson. Evaluate the impact of the activity at the level and venue of the student group, and discuss with colleagues and classmates any modifications that you might recommend.

2. Choose one selection and activity, and develop it into a study-unit across three sessions for a class of your choice (for example, band, choir, general music, world music culture course). Develop the sessions by extending the strategies for deep listening and participatory experiences, and through contextualization. (See *Thinking Musically* for ideas.)

3. Review your sketch of a sample course schedule, selected in Chapter 1, and insert at least three Engaged Listening Experiences to fit the schedule. Think: Which experiences will be meaningful to developing my students' knowledge of Music with a capital "M"?

CHAPTER 5

Performance as Enactive Listening

∞

What is music, if not wrapped around the performance of it? This may be the perspective of many young students in elementary and secondary school programs who are eager to become maximally involved in the making of it. All forms of cultural circumstances call for the performance of music, as music serves functions ranging from religious and social rituals to celebrations of life, the seasons, and the holidays when people take time to do what they most enjoy. Music-making figures prominently into so many realms of our lives because it is meaningful and useful to us. Composers conceive of music for performance, conductors (directors and teachers) organize for it, singers, players, and dancers practice and prepare to perform it, and listeners bask in the resonance of the performance experience. Many are drawn to perform music, in many cultures, and they learn their repertoires and performance techniques through informal enculturative processes—growing up in the culture—and through arduous hours of listening to their mentors and masters, attempting to perform what they have heard, taking in critical comments, adjusting their further attempts, and practicing until their performance attains a level that is passable, if not a perfect rendering, of the music. For our K–12 classrooms, the cross-cultural phenomenon of learning to perform unfamiliar music that is beyond the experiences of students—from an Andean panpipe piece to the music of xylophones from the Ivory Coast—is musically challenging to us as teachers yet enriching from every angle. The presence of listening at every step of the way toward the performance of these musical expressions is the essence of Enactive Listening, a learning phase and instructional process that is relevant to students of every age and level.

LISTENING AS "MEANS" AND METHOD

Music, such as the pieces contained in this chapter, can be brought to performance level by students through the combined use of notation and continued careful listening to the selections and styles presented. The goal of Enactive Listening, the third and potentially deepest level of listening, is to utilize listening as the guide to stylistically appropriate performance. This oral/aural means of learning is a development from the theoretical notions I set forth in *Lessons from the World* (1991/2001), based upon observations of teaching and learning in various cultures, and which choral educator Mary Goetze moved into pedagogical application with her *Global Voices in Song* CD-ROM project (2002). When a sound recording exists of the musical work or style, intensive listening to every musical nuance of a selection should be possible so that the live student performance can come close to matching the recorded performance of culture-bearers and traditional musicians. Before attempting to perform, students benefit from opportunities to listen to the timbral qualities of instruments and voices, their attacks and decays, the dynamic flow of a piece, its melodic and rhythmic components, and the interplay of multiple parts. Then their singing and playing can begin, but with frequent checkpoints throughout the learning process to listen again and to attempt to approximate what the style requires. The performance of a piece will no doubt be a rendering that is unique to the particular performers—a class of students or members of an instrumental or vocal ensemble. At times, recordings of styles and genres are available, although not of particular pieces, in which cases listening is geared to characteristic musical features that can be transferred to other pieces within the same style. With the recording of an actual piece or a similar one within the genre, there will still be a reckoning by students with the intricacies of the musical culture, and a greater understanding of and appreciation for the music and its makers (and the culture in which it is rooted) will result.

It is inarguably challenging for students to learn music that is new to their ears, and listening alone can be a time-consuming pathway to learning music for performance. At the same time, reading music notation can be frustrating not only to performers who do not read but also because notation can never fully represent the multiple facets of musical sound. Yet driven to perform, musicians in a variety of the world's cultures find notation to be a useful aid, perhaps imperfect, and yet given to graphically guide the re-creation of the essence of a musical work, style, or culture. When coupled with careful and continuous listening, notation can support and enhance the experience of performance as enactive listening. Notation alone does not "get it" ("it" being the stylistically accurate goal of performance)—although it can be helpful to us as teachers, while even the mere act of listening to other works within the same musical tradition can greatly inform our K–12 student musicians of the "gist," the signals and salient features of the style, that should be considered. In this chapter, there are scores for songs and instrumental pieces for selections contained on the accompanying CD ("Straight from the CD"). Some are songs for solo or unison voices, sometimes with suggestions for piano or guitar accompaniment, which can be introduced to classes in elementary and secondary schools. These and the multi-part songs will find a natural place in choral classes in middle and high schools. There are also pieces for secondary school instrumental ensembles. Other selections can be worked into percussion ensemble classes, or classes that are open to explorations of music that have traditionally been beyond the standard school (and collegiate) repertoire. As before, suggestions of "possible use" are offered, but in the end it will be the teacher's personal judgment as to what uses to make of the music, at what levels and in what venues.

Most of the selections are not lengthy, but could be expanded through repeated performance of verses, refrains, and particular sections, or with variations and extensions created by ensemble members (see Chapter 6, Creating "World Music"). The music "straight from the CD" spans a variety of cultures, so that students might seriously learn something of the performance practices of (among the selections) a Ghanian percussion ensemble, the melody and guitar accompaniment of a Mexican-American corrido, the shared melody of two Peruvian panpipes that play in alternating, hocketed fashion, and the exuberant harmony of singers in Kenya who understand the importance of making music communally. Likewise, the challenge is there to learn to perform music "in the style of the CD," and there is again a span of cultures and traditions among the selections, including a traditional Navajo song, percussion pieces associated with Japanese festivals and Chinese performances of their "flower dance," a Xhosa lullaby from South Africa, and the lively music of the Brazilian samba. Three jazz selections are "by invitation only" to listen to the CD recordings, and to learn by ear ("Take Five," "West End Blues," and "Three to Get Ready and Four to Go") for which transcriptions and notations are widely available, but in fact the musical value of playing jazz and blues forms by ear cannot be overestimated. As in previous activities for Attentive Listening and Engaged Listening, included with these experiences in Enactive Listening are suggestions to the instructor for facilitating students' thinking about the qualities of the instruments and voices, the musical elements, and the contexts in which the music is performed by musicians within the culture. "Listening Tips" and "Performance Tips" are just that: Suggestions for us to take forward into our classroom settings.

A further set of scores are provided for vocal and instrumental music for which there is a selection of the style on the accompanying CD but not the exact piece ("In the Style of the CD"). While the notation may be time-effective, it is useful to lead students in learning music from the oral presentation by their teacher of segments and whole pieces, with the aim of furthering their ear-training skills and understanding of music's transmission process within the culture of origin. The songs and instrumental pieces provided here will challenge students to make the transfer of stylistic features from a recorded selection to a different notated selection, compelling them to apply higher order skills of musicianship to do so. That ability to transfer features from known to "new" and unfamiliar music is the ultimate demonstration of musical learning. Of course, additional recorded examples of the style for students to hear and analyze, across many lessons and sessions, would prove effective in the course of learning how to perform the style and would serve to musically enculturate students into the tradition. Recordings from the culture-cases within this Global Music series are particularly useful for offering students an earful of styles and their nuances.

ENACTIVE LISTENING EXPERIENCES I: STRAIGHT FROM THE CD

ENACTIVE LISTENING EXPERIENCE 5.1 *CD track 5,* Atsiagbeko *(Ghana)*
Possible Use: *Percussion ensemble; Elementary or secondary, general*

Listening Tips
Instruments: *Iron double bell (agogo), shaker (axatse), master and supporting drums, male voices (solo call and group response)*
Notable Elements: *Layered texture, open-ended form with instruments entering and exiting at varied times*
Context: *Africa, and West Africa, and even the country of Ghana by itself constitute numerous cultural and linguistic groups,*

Atsiagbeko

FIGURE 5.1 *Atsiagbeko, CD track 5.*

each with musical genres and instruments that define and distinguish them. Yet there is throughout much of sub-Saharan Africa a tendency toward percussive sounds, including percussion instruments such as drums, rattles, and bells, and percussive techniques for performing wind and string instruments. There is also widespread use of polyrhythmic performance, where short rhythmic, timbral, and/or meloldic motifs interact together to form a musical whole, an improvisatory "in the now" process of music unfolding, and an association of music with dance. The narrative dance music, Atsiagbeko, demonstrates all of these characteristics in an open-ended form that features common instruments of Ghanian peoples and the call-and-response technique of vocal music.

Performance Tips (See Figure 5.1)
- Begin with vocal call-and-response. Chant with great speed.
- Play the time line on agogo bell, slowly at first and gradually faster.
- Layer in the axatse part.
- Shift between listening and note-reading to learn tenor and bass drum parts.
- Play for as long as it is mutually agreeable to do so, adding in and removing parts with flexibility. The call-and-response can initiate the performance.

ENACTIVE LISTENING EXPERIENCE 5.2 *CD track 6,* "Calypso Freedom" *(African American, U.S.)*
Possible Use: *Secondary, choral/vocal*

Listening Tips
Instruments: *Claves, hand claps, female voices (solo and chorus, sounding simultaneously)—full and bright*
Notable Elements: *Homophonic vocal harmony, improvised vocal interjections by solo singer*
Context: *The protest song is alive and well in the world, from Santiago to St. Louis to the cities of South Africa. Among African Americans, vocal music has served well to communicate directly or indirectly (often through Biblical texts) the sadness and pain of inequitable treatment and also the hope of change to come. The cause of freedom is central to the purpose of many protest songs, as it was in the African-American protest songs popular during*

Calypso Freedom

FIGURE 5.2 *Calypso Freedom, CD track 6.*

(continued)

the Civil Rights Movement of the 1960s, which was renewed in this 1989 rendition by the women's ensemble, Sweet Honey in the Rock. The calypso style heard here, with clave accompaniment, may be linked to the West African work songs sung by plantation slaves in the Carribean.

FIGURE 5.2 *Continued.*

Performance Tips (See Figure 5.2)
- Sing the solo part in unison, noting the vocal slides, drags, and subtle holds.
- Sing the chorus part in harmony, gradually adding a soloist.
- Clap hands on the off-beats 2 and 4.
- Add the clave pattern.
- Move: on beat 1, step right foot to right, and on beat 3, step left foot to right.

- In the second measure of a two-measure sequence, reverse feet, moving left.
- Move: loosen up the torso, free the hips, shoulders, and head to sway; bend knees and dip on beats 2 and 4.
- Beyond the notation of one verse, add the solo interjections: "Yay, but I ain't scared of nobody's . . . They can wear blue shirts or black shirts . . .")
- Create additional verses about relevant causes.

ENACTIVE LISTENING EXPERIENCE 5.3   *CD track 7,* "The Ballad of César Chávez" *(Mexico)* Possible Use: *Guitar ensemble; Elementary or secondary, choral/ vocal, general*

Listening Tips Instruments: *Guitar, male and female voices—slightly nasal in quality* Notable Elements: *Strophic verse-by-verse form* Context: *The narrative ballad of Mexicans and Mexican Americans known as* corrido *has remained popular for more than a century. Accompanied by one or two guitars, singers tell the stories of bandits, sheriffs, soldiers, and liberators. Corridos are prevalent along the Texas-Mexico border, and in California where migrant workers live. The corrido featured here tells of the struggle of César Chávez, the Mexican-American leader who led the struggle in the 1960s for fair treatment of grape growers and other Chicano farm workers. The text describes the march from Delano, California, to Sacramento, to speak to Governor Edmund "Pat" Brown about injustices done to migrant workers.*

Performance Tips (See Figure 5.3)
- Sing the melody (upper voice) with guitar chordal accompaniment.
- Experiment with comfortable keys, as E may be too high (or at an octave lower, too low). Try singing in keys of D, C, or G.

The Ballad of César Chávez

*Words separated by ' are sung as an elision.

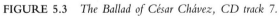

FIGURE 5.3 *The Ballad of César Chávez, CD track 7.*

Additional Lyrics

2. Compañeros campesinos
   este va a* ser un ejemplo
   esta marcha la llevamos
   hasta mero Sacramento.

3. Cuando llegamos a Fresno
   toda la gente gritaba
   y que viva César Chávez
   y la gente que llevaba.

4. Nos despedimos de Fresno
   nos despedimos con fe
   para llegar muy contentos
   hasta el pueblo de Merced.

5. Ya vamos llegando a Stockton
   ya mero la luz se fue
   pero mi gente gritaba
   sigan con bastante fe.

6. Cuando llegamos a Stockton
   los mariachis nos cantaban
   que viva César Chávez
   y la Virgen que llevaba.

2. Companion farmers
   This is going to be an example
   This (protest) march we'll take
   To Sacramento itself.

3. When we arrived in Fresno
   All the people chanted
   Long live César Chávez
   And the people that accompany him.

4. We bid good-bye to Fresno
   We bid good-bye with faith
   So we would arrive safely
   To the town of Merced.

5. We are almost in Stockton
   Sunlight is almost gone
   But the people shouted
   Keep on with lots of faith.

6. When we arrived at Stockton
   The mariachis were singing
   Long live César Chávez
   And the Virgin of Guadalupe.

(The selection on track 7 ends here; following is the remainder of the *corrido*.)

7. Contratistas y esquiroles
   ésta va a ser una historia
   usteded van al infierno
   y nosostros a la gloria.

8. Ese Señor César Chávez
   él es un hombre cabal
   quería verse cara a cara
   con el gobernador Brown.

9. Oiga, Señor César Chávez,
   su nombre que se pronuncia
   en su pecho usted merece
   la Virgen de Guadalupe.

7. Contractors and scabs
   This is going to be your story
   You will all go to hell
   And we will go to heaven.

8. That Mr. César Chávez
   Is a very strong man
   He wanted to speak face to face
   With Govenor Brown.

9. Listen, Mr. César Chávez,
   Your name is well known
   On your chest you well deserve
   The Virgin of Guadalupe.

*Underlined words indicate elisions.

FIGURE 5.3 *Continued.*

- Add the harmony (lower voice), which is a third lower than the melody.
- For a fuller harmony, add a third higher than the melody (although this harmony does not sound on the recording).
- Discuss the song text translation, and ways in which the text relays the details of a current event.
- Using the same chords (and even the same melody, if desirable), create a corrido on a current event.

ENACTIVE LISTENING EXPERIENCE 5.4 *CD track 9,* "Navajo Corn-Grinding Song" *(Joe Lee, Arizona, Navajo)* Possible Use: *Elementary or secondary, choral/vocal, general*

Navajo Corn Grinding Song

FIGURE 5.4 *Navajo Corn Grinding Song, CD track 9.*

Listening Tips (See Chapter 3)
(Listen repeatedly and follow the "Attentive Listening" suggestions in Chapter 3)
Performance Tips (See Figure 5.4)
• Sing the song while reading the notation and text.
• Sing the song without reading the notation and text.
• Sing the song, with attention to the elisions of syllables, varied pronunciation (such as "hi" for "hay"), and the nasal quality.
• In a circle facing left, step to the beat.
• Repeat the verse at various dynamic levels.

ENACTIVE LISTENING EXPERIENCE 5.5   *CD track 19, Music from the* "Kiembara xylophone orchestra" *(Ivory Coast)*
Possible Use: *Marimba ensemble; Elementary or secondary general*

Listening Tips
Instruments: *Xylophones (4), bowl-shaped drums (3), rattles attached to players' wrists*
Notable Elements: *Timbre, melodic and rhythmic motifs*
Context: *The Senufo people live in the Ivory Coast, Mali, and Burkino Faso, and share a culture similar to that of other West Africans. Musical instruments include mirlitrons held in front of the mouth, iron scrapers, gourd rattles, trumpets, whistles, and the harp lute, along with the xylophones and bowl-drums featured in this selection. For each wooden bar of their xylophones, there is a gourd resonator. These gourds have membranes made from spiders' webs which cover holes drilled especially to allow the vibration of the membranes to create the buzz-like timbre. The sounds of the players' wrist rattles and the jingles on the drums make for the ensemble's unique conglomerate timbre.*

Music from the Kiembara xylphone orchestra

FIGURE 5.5   *Music from the Kiembara xylophone orchestra, CD track 19.*

Performance Tips (See Figure 5.5)
- Sing and then play the melody for xylophone 1.
- Sing and then play the melody for xylophone 2.
- Combine the two xylophone parts.

- Play the high drum part, starting with the left hand and chanting "Left—Right—Left—Right (break) Right—Left—Right," play the high drum.
- Add the low drum with the high drum.
- Play all xylophone and drum parts together.
- Extend the piece by featuring just the drums, or just the xylophones, then combining them.

ENACTIVE LISTENING EXPERIENCE 5.6 *CD track 21,* "Habanera" *from* Carmen *(George Bizet, France)* Possible Use: *Secondary, choral/vocal*

Listening Tips
Instruments: *Symphonic orchestra, male chorus, female (soprano) voice*
Notable Elements: *Vocal timbre, chromatic melody, ostinato*
Context: *One of the most celebrated operas of all time is Georges Bizet's "Carmen," and the aria that follows the male chorus and freely sung recitative is one of the most familiar. At the moment of the aria, the stage is filled with soldiers and female factory workers, among them the flirtatious Carmen. While the soldiers are entranced with Carmen's beauty and coquettish ways, she teasingly sings of love that is wild and free, looking for the one soldier who earlier caught her eye but is not among the troops. The resonant soprano voice is featured in the twisting descent of the chromatic melody, and the use of an ostinato in the accompaniment has a trance-like effect on the listener. The habanera is an Afro-Cuban dance and song form that may have served as a basis for the aria, and the syncopated rhythm in slow duple meter produces an entrancing musical flavor.*

Performance Tips (See Figure 5.6)
- At 1'02", past the male chorus and recitative on the recording, pat the habanera rhythm softly on available percussion instruments.

Habanera (Begins at 1'02")
from "Carmen"

Georges Bizet

L'a-mour est un oi-seau re-

bel - le que nul ne peut— ap - pri - voi - ser, et c'est bien en vain qu'on l'ap-

pel - le, s'il lui - con - vien — de _ re - fu - ser! Rien n'y fait, me - nace ou pri-

FIGURE 5.6 *Habanera, CD track 21.*

FIGURE 5.6 *Continued.*

(continued)

FIGURE 5.6 *Continued.*

- Hum or sing the melody on a neutral syllable (for example, "loo").

- Learn-by-listening to the French text, and sing it; note the repeated and varied phrases within the three sections (A, B, C; "B" is quite brief).

- Divide the class into three groups to sing sections A, B, and C.

- Play the piano accompaniment.

ENACTIVE LISTENING EXPERIENCE 5.7 *CD track 22,*
Andean panpipes: three cortes *(Peru)*
Possible Use: *Recorder ensemble; Elementary or secondary, instrumental*

Listening Tips
Instruments: *Panpipes (sikuri)*
Notable Elements: *Hocket (interlocking melodies)*
Context: *In the Andean highlands, the panpipes known as* sikuri *are always performed communally. Tuned to the diatonic scale, the panpipes are performed in pairs, called the* arca *(leader) and* ira *(follower). No conductor is needed, not even in large ensembles, but the key to the performance is the shared manner in which two or more instruments give-and-take their alternating turns in creating the holistic melody. Panpipes are performed at fiestas associated with various holidays, at weddings, and even during life-cycle events like the child's first haircut* (corte de pelo). *It is common for players to stand loosely in a circle facing one another, where they move gently and freely while playing.*

Performance Tips (See Figure 5.7)
- Sing the melodies of sections A and B.

- In two groups, sing the arca and ira parts; the arca begins on "b" followed by the ira on "c," then arca again on "d" and ira on "e," and so on, in alternating fashion (for repeated notes, the same player performs both).

- In two groups, play the arca and ira parts of section A and B.
- Combine sections A and B, playing them together at an interval of a fourth apart. (This will require four players, or four groups, as the hocketing continues.)
- There is a third section, C, which can be learned by ear.

Andean Panpipes: Three cortes

Parts A, B, (and C, on recording) alone and then together

FIGURE 5.7 *Andean panpipes: Three cortes, CD track 22.*

ENACTIVE LISTENING EXPERIENCE 5.8 *CD track 24,*
"Take Five" *(Dave Desmond, U.S.)*
Possible Use: *Jazz ensemble*

Listening Tips (See Chapter 4)
• Listen repeatedly, and follow the "Engaged Listening" suggestions in Chapter 4.

Performance Tips
• In a jazz combo featuring alto saxophone, piano, bass, and drums, play by ear.

• Access published copies of the piece (which typically may include the melody and chords only).

• Encourage improvisation.

ENACTIVE LISTENING EXPERIENCE 5.9 *CD track 25,*
"Maqam Rast," "Aruh li Min" *(Egypt)*
Possible Use: *Secondary, instrumental (orchestral)*

Listening Tips (See Chapter 4)
• Listen repeatedly, and follow the "Engaged Listening" suggestions in Chapter 4.

Performance Tips (See Figure 5.8)
• Follow the notation for the rhythmically free introduction and the metered section which follows.

• Play the dombek and riqq rhythms.

• Sing and then play the melody of the metered section, observing the half-flatted third (e) and seventh (b) degrees.

• Distribute the melody to flute and violin (and violas), while cellos and basses play lines three and four.

• While the piece is more suited to a string ensemble, with flutes and percussion, the parts can be shared among a larger ensemble of band or orchestral instruments as well.

Maqam Rast (Aruh li Min)

Riyad al-Sinbati

FIGURE 5.8 *Maqam Rast (Aruh li Min), CD track 25.*

FIGURE 5.8 *Continued.*

- Sing the "Aruh li Min" phrases; instruments can play—by ear—in unison the "Aruh li Min" melody and the parenthetical phrases in between the vocal sections.

- To extend this piece, the following design is possible: Introduction, (A) Metered section, (B) Vocal passage (repeated), (A) Metered section.

ENACTIVE LISTENING EXPERIENCE 5.10 *CD track 32,* "West End Blues" *(Louis Armstrong, U.S.)*
Possible Use: *Jazz ensemble*

Listening Tips (See Chapter 4)
• Listen repeatedly, and follow the "Engaged Listening" suggestions in Chapter 4.

Performance Tips
• In a jazz combo featuring trumpet, trombone, piano, "metallic" percussion, clarinet, scat-singer.

• Access published transcriptions of the piece.

• Improvise on the 12-bar blues, but keep in mind the flavor of this early jazz piece.

ENACTIVE LISTENING EXPERIENCE 5.11 *CD track 36,* "Three to Get Ready and Four to Go" *(Dave Brubeck, U.S. jazz)*
Possible Use: *Jazz ensemble*

Listening Tips (See Chapter 4)
• Listen repeatedly, and follow the "Engaged Listening" suggestions in Chapter 4.

Performance Tips
• In a jazz combo featuring alto saxophone, piano, bass, and drums, play by ear.

• Access published copies of the piece (which typically include the melody and chords only).

• Encourage improvisation.

ENACTIVE LISTENING EXPERIENCE 5.12 *CD track 37,* "Tar Road to Sligo" *and* "Paddy Clancy's Mug of Brown Ale" *(Ireland)*

Tar Road to Sligo
and Paddy Clancy's Mug of Brown Ale

FIGURE 5.9 *Tar Road to Sligo and Paddy Clancy's Mug of Brown Ale, CD track 37.*

Possible Use: *String ensemble; Secondary, instrumental (orchestral)*

Listening Tips *(See Chapter 4)*
• Listen repeatedly, and follow the "Engaged Listening" suggestions in Chapter 4.

Performance Tips (See Figure 5.9)
- Ideal for fiddle, flute, and mandolin, but also for string ensemble; play the melody by ear.
- Extend to performance by band or orchestral instruments, in unison.
- Follow the score, playing the melody in unison.
- To extend this piece, the following design is possible: (A) Tar Road, 3 times, (B) Paddy Clancy, 3 times, (A) Tar Road, 3 times. (With each time, another instrumental timbre can be added)
- A percussion part can perform any of the rhythm patterns noted in Chapter 4.

ENACTIVE LISTENING EXPERIENCE 5.13 *CD track 38*, "Makedonsko horo" *(Bulgaria)*
Possible Use: *Guitar ensemble; Secondary, instrumental*

Listening Tips (See Chapter 4)
- Listen repeatedly, and follow the "Engaged Listening" suggestions in Chapter 4.

Performance Tips (See Figure 5.10)
- Ideally for guitar ensemble, play the melody and drone by ear.
- Extend to performance by band or orchestral instruments, in unison.
- Follow the score, playing the melody in unison.
- Add drum for the rhythm: ♫♪ ♩ ♩

ENACTIVE LISTENING EXPERIENCE 5.14 *CD track 49*, "Sumer is Icumen In" *(England)*
Possible Use: *Elementary or secondary, choral/vocal*

Listening Tips
Instruments: *Male and female voices*
Notable Elements: *Choral sound, polyphony, canon*

Makedonsko Horo

Traditional
Transcribed by
Timothy Rice

FIGURE 5.10 *Makedonsko Horo, CD track 38.*

Sumer is Icumen In

FIGURE 5.11 *Sumer is Icumen In, CD track 49.*

Context: *Strongly rhythmic and joyous vocal music characterized thirteenth century England, and the rota (or "round") was a prominent form of the true canon during this time, in which voices enter successively with the same melody. "Sumer is Icumen In" is the most famous rota and one of the most celebrated medieval compositions of all time. Its dance rhythms are undeniable, and were reflective of instrumental music of the time. The Middle English text refers to signs of summer, from seeds growing to animals with their young, and the sound of the cuckoo bird is also clearly noted.*

Performance Tips (See Figure 5.11)
- Listen to the light and "pure," vibrato-less, choral blend and balance of the voices.
- Sing in unison on a neutral syllable ("loo").
- Listen for the old English sound of the text.
- Sing in four groups adding a new group with each repeat of the melody.
- When all parts are entered, end by either staggering out or releasing altogether on cue after the fourth group has completed its round.

ENACTIVE LISTENING EXPERIENCE 5.15 *CD track 58, "Kumbaya" (Kenya)*
Possible Use: *Elementary or secondary, choral/vocal, general*

Listening Tips
Instruments: *Male and female voices, drums*
Notable Elements: *Choral singing, unison and harmony*
Context: *Kumbaya became popular in North America during the folk music revival of the late 1950s and 1960s, and its catchy melody was suitable to the creation of new verses in churches and in gatherings associated with the Civil Rights Movement. It has been sung across sub-Saharan Africa for devotional purposes and at other communal gatherings. The recording of the church congregation in Kenya is yet another rendition of the song, performed by churchgoers who have just paid tribute to a family who has lost a loved one. The pastor draws together members of the congregation, emotional through their bereavement ritual, to sing into a generator-powered microphone.*

Performance Tips (See Figure 5.12)
- Sing the song in the style in which it may be familiar to the group. Compare the familiar style with the rendition on the CD.

- Sing the melody with full and exuberant vocal quality.
- Add the harmony, as noted in the score.
- Select a leader to sing the "call" ("Kumbaya my Lord").
- Add the drum part.
- Move: On beat 1 (after upbeat), step right foot to right, on beats 2-3, step left foot to right and hold.
- In the second measure of the two-measure sequence, reverse direction, stepping to the left.
- Move: Loosen up the torso, free the hips, shoulders and head to sway.
- Sing further versions, and create new verses, for example: "Kumbaya, we're praying, Kumbaya" or "Kumbaya, we're coming, Kumbaya".

Kumbaya

2. Someone's laughing, Lord, Kumbaya
3. Someone's crying, Lord, Kumbaya
4. Someone's dying, Lord, Kumbaya
5. Someone's born, my Lord, Kumbaya

FIGURE 5.12 *Kumbaya, CD track 58.*

ENACTIVE LISTENING EXPERIENCES II:
IN THE STYLE OF THE CD

ENACTIVE LISTENING EXPERIENCE 5.16 "Back Line" *(Trinidad) (Refer to CD track 2)*
Possible Use: *Steel drum ensemble*

Performance Tips (See Figure 5.13)
• Sing the melody of the tenor several times to get the feel of the piece.

• Encourage movement while singing (and playing).

• Add the bass line, which provides the steady pulse; allow time for the tenor and bass parts to fit together in ensemble.

• Add the double second and cello parts; note their slow, sustained character.

• Experiment with shakers (maracas) and cowbell (similar to "Gunslingers," Chapter 4).

• Perform multiple times, and encourage improvisatory interludes, so long as the harmonic scheme and characteristic groove is maintained.

ENACTIVE LISTENING EXPERIENCE 5.17 "Salsa Rhythm" *(Puerto Rico) (Refer to CD track 4)*
Possible Use: *Percussion ensemble, jazz ensemble*

Performance Tips (See Figure 5.14)
• Examine the six lines of rhythms, noting their points of coincidence and complements, and the dense rhythms versus the lines of low activity.

• Consider chanting the rhythms, using any set or system of syllables, with student imitation of the teacher's oral modeling.

• Play at a moderate tempo throughout.

• Play the conga part; note the higher and lower notes and find places on the drum that will represent them well.

• Layer the bongos in over the conga, again finding higher- and lower-pitched timbres to play.

Back Line

Len "Boogie" Sharpe

Transcription and
arrangement by Shannon Dudley

FIGURE 5.13   *Back Line, CD track 2.*

- Add the low drum (a bass drum, or a low conga sound), and rehearse the three drum parts until they are in tight ensemble with one another.
- Play the claves in their ostinato rhythm; note the slight variation of the tied eighth-quarter at the end of the second measure.
- Add the cymbals (or triangles, or cowbell), and notice how this rhythm complements and fits between much of the claves' rhythm.
- Finish this trio of rhythms with the guiro playing up and down, adding it to the claves and cymbals.
- Play all six lines together—multiple times.
- Experiment with a performance arrangement that gradually layers in instruments, and that allows instruments to "rest" at their own discretion, coming back in as they choose.
- Use this rhythm as the foundation for melodic improvisation; invite a pianist, brass players, guitarists and bass players to join in.

Salsa Rhythm

Traditional

FIGURE 5.14   *Salsa Rhythm, CD track 4.*

ENACTIVE LISTENING EXPERIENCE 5.18 "Banjaran" *(Java) (Refer to CD track 8)*
Possible Use: *Metallophone ensemble (Orff or other)*

Performance Tips (See Figure 5.15)

• Sing the numbers of the melody depicted in the cipher notation, where "1" is tonic; note that there are two phrases of 16-beats each and that each phrase can be sung twice before going on to the next in a-a-b-b form.

• Sing the a-a-b-b form several times, and experiment with singing loud and fast, and slow and soft.

• Chant the gong cycle, noting that it is the same for both melodic phrases. (See Chapter 6, "colotomic structure," and *Thinking Musically*, pp. 64–66, for details of the gong names and "nicknames."

• Combine singing and chanting, and perform multiple times in loud/fast and soft/slow styles.

• Play the melody on metallophones (ideally, or other instruments), and use percussion instruments for the sound of the four gongs.

• Add a drum (in Java, a double-headed drum called kendang performs the lead role in cueing loud/fast and soft/slow styles), suggesting that it play a steady pulse, subdivisions, and occasional flourishes.

• Determine in advance or allow the drummer to determine the length of the piece in performance.

ENACTIVE LISTENING EXPERIENCE 5.19 "Shí Naashá *(Navajo) (Refer to CD track 9)*
Possible Use: *Elementary or secondary, choral/vocal, general*

Performance Tips (See Figure 5.16)

• Discuss the significance of this song to the Navajo who created it: "Shí Naashá" translates "I am going," referring to the Long Walk period of 1863–64, when the Navajo were ordered to walk up to 400 miles (depending on the point of origin) from as far as Fort Defiance, Arizona to Fort Sumner in southeastern New

Banjaran

```
5 1 5 2
t * t N
5 1 5 2
t P t N
5 1 2 3
t P t N
1 2 3 4
t P t N
      G

2 3 2 4
t * t N
2 3 2 4
t P t N
2 3 2 1
t P t N
3 4 3 2
t P t N
      G
```

FIGURE 5.15   *Banjaran, CD track 8.*

Mexico, so as to be assimilated into American society. Many perished as not only the walk, but also conditions at Fort Sumner were abhorrent, and the U.S. government permitted the Navajo to return to their homelands five years later.

- The song text translates as "I am going. Beauty is all around me. I am going in freedom."
- Sing the melody of the song on a neutral syllable to appreciate its flow.
- Sing the melody phrase-by-phrase, with the teacher modeling and students imitating the phrases; note that "ei" and "hei" sound as "ay" and "hay" while all other syllables are as transliterated.
- A hand drum can be used to keep a quarter-note pulse, including playing an introduction of the song (and dance).
- While singing the song, dance a round dance: In circle formation, move to the beat, clockwise, stepping long (for beats one and two), then short (beat three).

Shí Naashá

Traditional

FIGURE 5.16 *Shí Naashá, CD track 9.*

ENACTIVE LISTENING EXPERIENCE 5.20 "Matsuri Bayashi" *Japanese Festival Music (Japan) (Refer to CD track 16)*
Possible Use: *Percussion ensemble; Elementary or secondary, general*

Performance Tips (See Figure 5.17)

- Chant the rhythm of the piece, saying the syllables; drop the pitch of the voice for the "to ro" and "to ro ro" segments (student imitation of the teacher's modeling is an appropriate technique).

- On the lap, pat with the right or left hand, as indicated, while chanting; note that "tsu" is always left and "tan" of "tan tek-ka" is always right.

- After repeated chanting and patting, take mallets to the drums (if not taiko drums, then available drums: djembes, snare [with snare muted], congas, Orff timpani) and play; hard mallets rather than soft are stylistically appropriate.

- Play the melody on flute or recorder.

- Chant, then play, gong part on a high-pitched gong or cymbal, with a hard wood mallet.

- Repeat pattern five times, with gradually increasing speed.

FIGURE 5.17 *Matsuri Bayashi, Japanese Festival Music, CD track 16.* *(Transcription by William P. Malm.)*

ENACTIVE LISTENING EXPERIENCE 5.21 "Caiqiu Wu" *(China) (Refer to CD track 18)*
Possible Use: *Percussion ensemble; Elementary or secondary, general*

Performance Tips (See Figure 5.18)
• Play the woodblock rhythm with the bell (or triangle); note the syncopated surprise in measure 7.

• Play the melody on recorder or flute; note the increasing complexity of the melodic variation in versions II and III.

• Perform the three parts with repeats and no breaks between versions.

Caiqiu Wu
Chinese Festival Music

Traditional,
As arranged by Han Kuo-huang

FIGURE 5.18 *Caiqui Wu, Chinese Festival Music, CD track 18.* *(From* The Lion's Roar: Chinese Luogu Percussion Ensembles, Second Edition, *by Han Kuo-huang and Patricia Shehan Campbell. © 1996 World Music Press.)*

- The piece accompanies a folk dance called "Flower-ball Dance," in which the dancer holds a large silk flower in both hands; create graceful and flowing dance movements.

ENACTIVE LISTENING EXPERIENCE 5.22 "Feng Yang Hua Ge" *(China) (Refer to CD track 20)*
Possible Use: *Elementary or secondary, choral/vocal*

Performance Tips (See Figure 5.19)
- Sing the melody of the song on a neutral syllable, but change to singing the percussion syllables in the "fast" section; note that "drrr" is a rolled "r" and that "piao" is pronounced "pee-ow."
- Sing with the Chinese text; note the following pronunciation hints: "uo" (Zuo, luo) sounds as "oh"; "ou" (shou, you) sounds as "ow"; "u" or "uh" sound as short "u" ("uh"); "bie" sounds as "bee"; "i" (di, zih) sounds as short "i" ("ih"); "ui" (hui) sounds as "wee."
- The translation of "Feng Yang Hua Ge," or "Flower Drum Song," is "Left hand gong, right hand drum—with drum and gong in hand I come to sing; Other tunes I do not know but Feng Yang song" (the syllables that follow in the "fast" section are intended to sound onamatapoeically like drums and gongs.
- Experiment with a drum and gong accompaniment to the melody; consider also playing the melody on a glockenspiel to simulate the sound of a Chinese cloud gong.
- "Feng Yang Hua Ge" can be paired with "Caiqiu Wu," preceding or following it in a program performance (although their origins differ).

ENACTIVE LISTENING EXPERIENCE 5.23 "Segáh Sarki" *(Turkey) (Refer to CD track 25)*
Possible Use: *Secondary, choral/vocal*

Performance Tips (See Figure 5.20)
- This popular Turkish song is derived from a seventeenth century poem by Karacoaglan, with the current melody (stemming

Left hang gong, right hand drum—
With drum and gong in hand
I come to sing;
Other tunes I do not know
But *Feng Yang* song . . .

 FIGURE 5.19   *Feng Yang Hua Ge, CD track 20.*

from the 1940s) by S. Kaynak. It addresses a girl named "Elif." The first verse given here speaks to "a crazy heart which so admires Elif" even as a thin snow falls and flows outside. The refrain (beginning in the third line) expresses the man's admiration for Elif, and how his heart will turn as cold as stone if he is not accepted (and "a cure is not found for the problem of love") by her.

- Pat a 10-beat pattern so to become familiar with the song's meter; count and pat 1 (2) (3) 4 (5) 6 (7) 8 (9) (10) [the beats in parentheses are silent].
- Play the 10-beat pattern on hand drums, dombek (goblet drum), and finger cymbals.
- Sing the melody on neutral syllables.
- Learn to sing the song's text; principal pronunciation advisories are these: all "c" sound as "ch" (ce, cik, can); the "e" sounds as a long "a"; the "a" sounds as "ah"; the "i" sounds as "e"; the German umlauts over the vowels in "gönül" are spoken and sung with a rounded mouth and pursed lips.
- Add the percussion instruments to the sung melody.

Segáh Sarki

Traditional

FIGURE 5.20 *Segáh Sarki, CD track 25.*

ENACTIVE LISTENING EXPERIENCE 5.24 "Ata, Ata Mai Pe'a E Fiafia" *(Samoan) (Refer to CD track 27)*
Possible Use: *Elementary or secondary, choral/vocal*

Performance Tips (See Figure 5.21)
- The song is popular among Samoans as a communal song to express the joy of being together. It is sung with children, too, in schools and even preschool settings. "Pe'a e fiafia" means "if you're happy," and each verse begins with a suggestion for demonstrating that happiness: "ata" (smile), "oso" (jump), "pati" (clap), "siva" (dance).
- Sing the song in unison; the middle note in each chord is the melody.
- Sing the higher harmony part, which is consistently a third above the melody.
- Add the third vocal part, which frequently sits on middle "C" or is progressing there (f-e-d-c).
- Sit in a circle on the floor while singing, legs crossed and hands at the ready to perform this four-beat ostinato: pat lap on "1," clap on "2," slap right hand to left upper chest on "3," pat lap on "4" (for timbral variation, substitute floor pats for beats "1 and "4."
- With two wood sticks for each student, practice this ostinato: tap stick ends on floor for "1," tap wood sticks together on "2," reverse sticks and tap together again on "3," tap stick ends on floor for "4."
- Practice singing in harmony with the ostinato patterns, gradually increasing speed with each repetition.

ENACTIVE LISTENING EXPERIENCE 5.25 "Haere Mai" *(Maori) (Refer to CD track 27)*
Possible Use: *Secondary, choral/vocal*

Performance Tips (See Figure 5.22)
- "Haere Mai" is a welcome song of the Maori of New Zealand, sung in the exhuberance of the four-part choral style, the bass

Ata, Ata Mai Pe'a E Fiafia

Traditional

1. A - ta, a - ta mai, pe - 'a e fi - a - fi - a

A - ta, a - ta mai, pe - 'a e fi - a - fi - a

A - ta, a - ta mai, pe - 'a e fi - a - fi - a

A - ta, a - ta mai, pe - 'a fi - a fi - a

Additional Verses

2. Oso, oso mai, pe'a e fiafia.

3. Pati, pati mai, pe'a e fiafia.

4. Siva, siva mai, pe'a e fiafia.

5. Fa'atalofa mai, pe'a e fiafia.

FIGURE 5.21 *Ata, Ata Mai Pe'a E Fiafia, CD track 27.*

line of which is chanted in a low-pitched, punctuated and percussive style. The women typically stand with arms at their side,
shaking their hands to represent the spirit within and surrounding them as they sing; they may also utilize various gestures to express the text. The men stand behind the women, and
the bass chanters may stamp and show strong, if even fierce,
facial expressions.

FIGURE 5.22 *Haere Mai, CD track 27.*

FIGURE 5.22 *Continued.*

- The text is roughly translated: "Welcome (haere mai) to our family (e nga iwi e) into the house of the marae (ki runga o te marae). We are all together (Hui, ai tatou katoa), the men (e hine ma), the women (e tama ma)." The song is sung as an invitation for people to come into their communal gathering place, the marae, to join in with the extended Maori family on their land.

- Sing the song in separate parts and then together; note these pronunciation hints: All vowels sound as they would in Italian (for example, "a" is "ah," "e" is long "a," "i" is long "e"); the "ng" is a nasalized sound that typically precedes a vowel; "ae" sounds the "ah-ay" elision.

- The chanted bass line can emphasize the "h," exhaling ample breath in a vigorous manner, coming from low in the abdomen and quickly expelled.

- Sing while gently swaying, shifting the weight from one foot to the other; the bass chanters may stamp the rhythms that they chant.

ENACTIVE LISTENING EXPERIENCE 5.26 "Las Mañanitas" *(Mexico) (Refer to CD track 29)*
Possible Use: *Elementary or secondary, choral/vocal, general*

Performance Tips (See Figure 5.23)
- This "Happy Birthday" song of Mexico is sung and/or played; the text translates:

There are the songs sung at daybreak that King David used to sing.
The girls who are so pretty also sing them this way:
"Wake up, my dear, wake up!
Look, it has dawned already!
The little birds are now singing,
The moon has already disappeared."

- Play the melody and harmony (mostly a third higher) on trumpets and violins (preferably both instruments on both parts).
- Play chords on guitar (or vilhuela), strumming ♩ ♫ ♫ in each measure.

Las Mañanitas

Traditional

FIGURE 5.23 *Las Mañanitas, CD track 29.*

- Add a bass to play either chord roots or the notated bass line.
- Alternate between singing (with guitar and bass) and the instrumental rendition described.
- Encourage the trumpets and violin to create an interlude to perform with the guitar and bass.

ENACTIVE LISTENING EXPERIENCE 5.27 "The Flower of Sweet Strabane" *(Ireland) (Refer to CD track 37)* Possible Use: *Elementary or secondary, choral/vocal*

Performance Tips (See Figure 5.24)
- Sing the melody of this love song to the accompaniment of a guitar (or accordian, harp—or piano, if it is an "Irish-American" sound that is preferred); a dotted-quarter rhythm for the accompaniment is appropriate, as are arpeggiated chord-pitches at six per measure
- Play on bodhran (or hand drum) an ostinato rhythm: ♩. ♫♩

ENACTIVE LISTENING EXPERIENCE 5.28 "Drowsy Maggie" *(Reel)*, "Dierdre's Fancy" *(Jig) (Ireland) (Refer to CD track 37)* Possible Use: *Recorder ensemble; Elementary or secondary, instrumental*

Performance Tips (See Figures 5.25 and 5.26)
- Play on flute or fiddle (or other instrument) the melody of the reel and jig; all instruments should sound monophonically in unison on the melody.
- Play the chords on guitar (or accordian, harp, or piano).
- Consider these two melodies together, with bodhran as introduction to each and thus setting the differing meters in place; the previous song can be added to a performance in this order: "Drowsy Maggie," "Sweet Strabane," "Diedre's Fancy"—with each melody faster than the one before it.

The Flower of Sweet Strabane

Traditional

If I were king of Ire - land and all things at my will I'd roam for re - cre - a - tion, no com - forts to find still, Of com - forts I would like the best as you might un - der - stand is to win the heart of Mar - tha the flo - wer of sweet Stra - bane.

Her cheeks they are a rosy red, her hair golden brown
And o'er her lily white shoulders it carelessly falls down
She's one of the loveliest creatures of the whole creation planned
And my heart is captivated by the Flower of Sweet Strabane.

If I had you lovely Martha away in Innishowen
Or in some lonesome valley in the wild woods of Tyrone
I would use my whole endeavour and I'd try to work my plan
For to gain my prize and to feast my eyes on the Flower of Sweet Strabane.

Oh, I'll go o'er the Lagan down by the steam ships tall
I'm sailing for Amerikay across the briny foam
My boat is bound for Liverpool down by the Isle of Man
So I'll say farewell, God bless you, my Flower of Sweet Strabane.

FIGURE 5.24 *The Flower of Sweet Strabane, CD track 37.*

ENACTIVE LISTENING EXPERIENCE 5.29 "Bitola"
(Macedonia) (Refer to CD track 38)
Possible Use: *Secondary, choral/vocal*

Drowsy Maggie (Reel)

Traditional

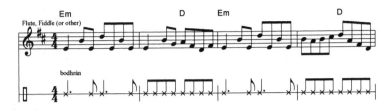

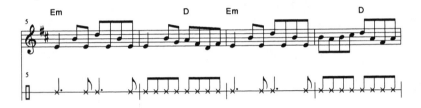

FIGURE 5.25 *Drowsy Maggie (Reel), CD track 37.*

Deirdre's Fancy (Slip Jig)

Traditional

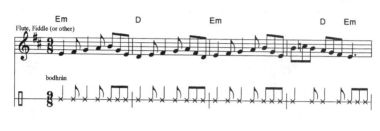

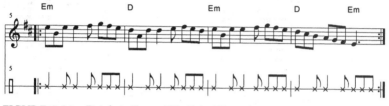

FIGURE 5.26 *Deirdre's Fancy (Slip Jig), CD track 37.*

Performance Tips (See Figure 5.27)

- Read the translation of the nostalgic song, a tribute to the town of Bitola in Macedonia (part of which overlaps into Bulgaria where it is known as the Pirin region).

- Pat the underlying rhythm: 1 (2) (3) 1 (2) 1 (2), with the beats in parentheses felt but not heard.

- In the typical fashion of a choral rehearsal, learn the top line melody together; pronunciation hints include these: vowels sound as they do in Italian, "j" sounds as "y," "z" sounds as "zh."

- Sing the harmony parts, noting that where there are only three rather than four parts, the male voices double that lowest part (also, that the lowest parts can be sung an octave lower than written).

- The vocal technique requires a face-frontal style, nazalized; a tingling in the face may even be felt, so forward is the style.

Bitola

*Violins, accordion, brass, bass

Translation

Verse 1

Bitola, my birthplace
I was born in you, you are dear to me.

Verse 2

I have passed through many towns and cities
I have nowhere found one more beautiful than you.

Verse 3

Hey, birthplace, who could possibly
Say goodbye to you and not cry?

Chorus 1

Bitola my birthplace
Know that I love you from the heart.

Chorus 2

Bitola my birthplace
I love you, I sing of you.

FIGURE 5.27   *Bitola, CD track 38.*

- Chords can be played by accordian, with bass on the chord roots; violins alone or with brass instruments (particularly trumpet) can play alongside the voices, and for the instrumental interlude.

- A lesno (slow) dance accompanies this song; in circle formation with hands held up and elbows down, the movement is as follows; Facing forward, stepping to right

Think: 1 (2-3) 1 (2-1-2)   1 (2-3) 1 (2-1-2)
          1 (2-3) 1 (2-1-2)

Step:	Right	Left	Right	Left	Left	Right
	Step	Cross	Step	Lift	Step	Lift

ENACTIVE LISTENING EXPERIENCE 5.30 *Rāga-Malavi, Tāla-Adi,* "Nennarunchinanu Annidiki" *(South India) (Refer to CD track 39)*
Possible Use: *Secondary, choral/vocal*

Performance Tips (See Figure 5.28)
- Examine the transcription of this orally-transmitted South Indian vocal form; note the ornamentation of the melody and its variations over the course of repeated phrases, the major tonality of the rāga, the strict 8-beat tāla cycle despite the highly decorated melody, the chitaswara section that features the solfege (sargam) syllables, the melodic sections of pallavi, anupallavi, and charanam that comprise the kriti (song form).
- This kriti is attributed to the esteemed eighteenth century composer, Tyagaraja, a contemporary of Beethoven. The translation of the text is as follows: "I have fixed my mind on you, on your holy feet, as you are the sole upholder of the universe. Oh, you the wind that sweeps away the cloud of heinous sins! For the sake of maintaining my family and children, I cannot bring myself to be so hard-hearted as to learn and adopt the deceitful modes and talks [speech] of this wicked age." Despite its sacred text, it is performed at house concerts and concert halls (as well as in Hindu temples).

Rāga-Malavi, Tāla-Adi

FIGURE 5.28   *Rāga-Malavi, Tāla-Adi, CD track 39.*

FIGURE 5.28 *Continued.*

• While the drone pitches are sounding (on tamboura, piano with pedal, cello, harmonium or sruti box), slowly sing a section of the kriti; the vowels are prounounced as they would be in Italian (except for "nee" which sounds as written).

• Over a period of sessions, learn the remaining sections of the kriti, which can be performed as a solo or in unison.

ENACTIVE LISTENING EXPERIENCE 5.31 "Music for Legong Dance" *(Bali) (Refer to CD track 50)*
Possible Use: *Metallophone ensemble (as in Orff or secondary school instrumental)*

Performance Tips (See Figures 5.29 and 5.30)
• Sing the numbers for each of the metallophone lines as they appear in cipher notation.

Music for the Legong Dance

Traditional

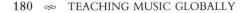

FIGURE 5.29 *Music for the Legong Dance, CD track 50.*

Legong Music in (Cipher Notation)

Soprano Metallophone	3 3̲4 3 4̲	3 3̲4 3̲4̲5	7 7̲5 7 5̲	7 7̲5̲ 7̲5̲4	3
	5 4̲5̲5̲4	5 4̲5 4̲5	4 5̲4 4̲5	4 5̲4 5̲4	3
Alto Metallophone	3 1 3 4	3 1 7 5	7 5 7 5	7 1 3 4	3
	3 1	4 1	7 1	4 1	3
Bass Metallophone	3	1	7	4	3

FIGURE 5.30   *Legong Music (Cipher Notation).*

- Sing and then play the third, fourth, and fifth lines together, and observe the varied durations of the melodic pitches.
- Sing and then play the hocketed melody of lines one and two, separately and then together.
- Play all five parts of the music for the legong dance of Bali, together; play repeatedly.

ENACTIVE LISTENING EXPERIENCE 5.32 "Chawe Chidyo Chem'chero" *(Zimbabwe) (Refer to CD track 55)* Possible Use: *Elementary or secondary, choral/vocal*

Performance Tips (See Figure 5.31)
- Sing each of the three lines, students in imitation of the teacher; note that the vowels sound as they would in Italian, and that double consonants are quickly elided ("dy," "mw").
- Layer in the phrases one at a time, singing four times altogether.
- Note that this is the sung response to a story about the kudu antelope of southern Africa, and translates as "It is the sound (of me) eating the food of the forest."

Chawe Chidyo Chem'chero

Traditional
After the sung version of
Dumisani Maraire

FIGURE 5.31   *Chawe Chidyo Chem'chero, CD track 55.*

- Tell the story (or assign others to tell it), with pauses for the sung response; improvise upon this version and tell it dramatically.

  Once there was a family with a big farm-field in which they grew maize, wheat, yams, millet, and other crops. There was also a kudu, a wild antelope with grey fur and curly horns, who was lately infringing upon the family's fields and eating the food they were cultivating. The family—father, mother, and little boy, met to discuss what might be done with kudu to prevent him from eating their mainstay, the very food they ate and took to market in exchange for other goods. They agreed that the boy should be delegated to go deep into the field to chase the kudu away. And so he went, far into the fields, where he waited, crouching in the high grasses with an assemblage of metal pots and pans, looking for kudu. At sunset, who should slip out of the forest and into the family's field but a proud and hungry kudu. As the boy raised his pots and pans to frighten away kudu, the clever kudu—who knew how much people enjoy music—began to sing. The boy was stunned, entranced, and stood frozen in air as he listened to the kudu's song: "Chawe chidyo chem'chero." (sing) He went home to his family, happy to have heard the music, but with the news that he could not chase kudu away. Again the family gathered to discuss what might be done with kudu. (At this point—and much more can be made of this in the telling of the story, the mother goes to the field with sticks to clack together, hides, hears the song (sing), is entranced, returns home. The father follows the same sequence, but has a spear instead, hears the song (insert), returns home unable to use it on the singing kudu. The moral of the story is clear: The kudu sings for his supper, as he understands the power and magic of song, and the family learns to live alongside of—but not superior to—the kudu. (The response is sung three times in all, once at each musical "entrancement" by the kudu.)

ENACTIVE LISTENING EXPERIENCE 5.33 "Thula Mama Thula" *(South Africa) (Refer to CD track 58)*
Possible Use: *Elementary or secondary, choral/vocal*

Performance Tips (See Figure 5.32)
- Discuss the translation of this Xhosa lullaby: "Mother, the baboon took away the baby; the baby cried and said 'iyo.' Be quiet mother, be quiet. the baboon put the baby over its shoulder; the baby cried and said 'iyo'."
- Pat the rhythm of the melody, and chant the text rhythmically.
- Learn the song's melody (the top line of the three voices).
- Add the two harmony parts, which move in parallel motion to the melody.
- Gently rock or sway to the pulse while singing.

Thula Mama Thula

Traditional

| 1. | Im - fe | ne | mam' im - fe - | ne | Yam tha bath' um |
| 2. | Kwa - thu - la | ma - ma Thu | la | thu - la ma - ma - |

| ntwa na | wa - su - ke | wa - kha - la | wa - thi i - yo. |
| thu - la | thu - la | ma - ma thu - la | thu - la yi - thi tu. |

FIGURE 5.32 *Thula Mama Thula, CD track 58.* *(Transcription by Alvin Peterson.)*

ENACTIVE LISTENING EXPERIENCE 5.34 "Kwaheri"
(Kenya) (Refer to CD track 58)
Possible Use: *Elementary or secondary, choral/vocal*

Performance Tips (See Figure 5.33)
- Discuss this Swahili song's use as a farewell at the close of social gatherings.

- In modeling and imitation fashion, learn the melody (top line) and three harmony parts of the song, with students imitating the teacher; note these pronunciation points: (the vowels sound as they do in Italian; "m" as its own syllable sounds as "im"; "j" sounds as "j")

- Pat and clap the rhythm of the first measure as an ostinato: ♩. ♩. ♩ pat clap clap

- Sing while keeping the rhythmic ostinato; as an alternative, step the ostinato.

ENACTIVE LISTENING EXPERIENCE 5.35 "Water Come a Me Eye" *(Jamaica) (Refer to CD track 57)*
Possible Use: *Percussion ensemble; Elementary or secondary, choral/vocal, general*

Kwaheri

Traditional

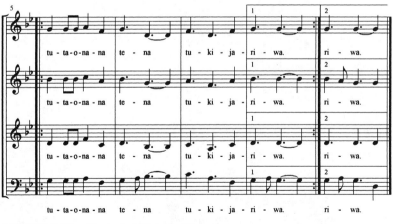

FIGURE 5.33 *Kwaheri, CD track 58.*

Water Come a Me Eye

FIGURE 5.34   *Water Come a Me Eye, CD track 57.*

Performance Tips (See Figure 5.34)
- Sing this familiar calypso tune, adding one percussion part as accompaniment with each repetition.
- Play the guiro and maracas together, noting that the ostinatos are of different lengths (guiro is one measure, while maracas is two measures).

FIGURE 5.34 *Continued.*

- Play the cowbell and claves together, noting that the first is just a two-beat ostinato (played open and bright [O] and closed and muted [+] while the claves' standard pattern spans two measures.
- Play all of the ostinato rhythms together, and add the singing.

ENACTIVE LISTENING EXPERIENCE 5.36 "Samba Batucada" *(Brazil) (Refer to CD track 59)*
Possible Use: *Percussion ensemble; Elementary or secondary, general*

Performance Tips (See Figure 5.35)
• In step with the oral tradition, students can learn individual parts by imitating their teacher's modeling of them.

Samba Batucada

FIGURE 5.35 *Samba Batucada, CD track 59.*

- The bass drum (surdo) is played open [O] by bouncing off the skin and thus allowing the sound to "ring"; if not indicated as such, then no bounce should follow the strike of the drumhead.
- For the ganza part, any shaker is possible, from maracas to cans or cups filled with dried beans or rice; the reco-reco, or scraper, is similar to a guiro; the tambourin part can be played on hand drum held at chest level and struck by a hard mallet.
- Layer in parts one at a time, always beginning with the surdo but varying the order of the other instruments.
- Play repeatedly, allowing certain instruments to rest and then enter again.

THE ENACTIVE *ACT* OF LISTENING

One way to achieve the performance of songs, percussion pieces, and instrumental selections is to perform directly from notation. After all, if the music is laid out graphically to see, and the notational symbols comprise their own logical system for the conversion from sight to sound (which indeed they do), then why not just sing (or play) it straight from the notes? Many do. However, when the style of a particular composer or collective culture is not familiar, it becomes clear that the notation alone is simply not sufficient and that an aural image of the music is critical to conveying the essence of the style. Notation is compact and convenient, but it is not possible for it to be entirely precise. For student performers of a Mexican corrido or a Chinese luogu percussion piece to hope to approximate an acceptable sound, their listening will be necessary to take them in that direction. Teachers are well aware that Enactive Listening is costly in the instructional time that is expended to allow students to catch "the spirit" of a musical selection as well as the musical details (as it is also time-intensive in teachers' own listening route in preparation for teaching). But the benefits exceed the cost, in that students who apply listening to their learning will not only perform well but will also be more deeply informed. The enactive *act* of listening is certain to raise stronger performers who, through the careful study of one or a small handful of unfamiliar musical selections, may grow more sensitive to musical subtleties of cultures across the globe.

PROBLEMS TO PROBE

1. Select a musical activity to trial-teach to a group of K–12 students. Note any modifications that you might make in teaching the activity "the next time," in the margins of the description and/or score. Compare notes with the experiences of other trial-teaching colleagues.

2. Expand upon a musical selections, converting it from a single one-shot musical experience to a series of three class lessons or sessions, by accumulating additional recorded selections, further cultural/contextual information, and at least one more performance experience. Consider the series of lessons or sessions as an instructional unit centered on one musical culture.

3. Review your sketch of a sample course schedule, selected in Chapter 1, and insert three Enactive Listening Experiences to fit the schedule. Think: Which experiences will be meaningful to developing my students' knowledge of Music with a capital "M"?

CHAPTER 6

Creating "World Music"

∞

People make music meaningful and useful in their lives when they are at liberty to express themselves in original ways. At various points in the progression of musical learning, our K–12 students move beyond the need to sing and play precisely "what's there" on the recording and in the notation. The goal of re-creating musical works is a noble one, yet the goal of creating new musical expressions has been underestimated by some who teach music, or has been relegated by them to only those students with the most advanced of music training. I argue here that students are capable of creative musical work early on in their training, and find this view harmonizing well with the pedagogical approach of Emile Jacques-Dalcroze, the practical implications of Keith Swanwick's *Teaching Music Musically* (1999), and the creative curricular ideas of John Paynter in his *Music in the Secondary School* (1982) and Jackie Wiggins in her *Teaching Music for Understanding* (2000). Further, students actually learn *through* such musically creative activity. As Mihalyi Czikszentimihalyi has posited in his *Creativity: Flow and the Psychology of Creative Discovery and Invention* (1996), children and adolescents have the inherent potential for chanelling their thoughts forward into a flow of original expressions, and their own personal music-making is certainly one of the repositories of this flow.

While the re-creation of music in participation and performance experiences is an excellent outcome of careful listening, the creation of new music allows the dual aims of listening and the intellectual internalization of sonic structures to be achieved and demonstrated. Creating "world music" is yet another means towards understanding the concept of people making music meaningful and useful in their lives, as students are in a sense placed inside the music and its sonic structures. Composition, improvisation, songwriting, and even the act of extending a piece beyond what is represented of it on a recording or in a score are avenues of creative expression that are informed by attentive, engaged, and enactive levels of music listening. Creating (and performing) music is a solid measure of musical understanding, a highwater mark in the global music education of our students.

CREATING, RE-CREATING, AND CONSERVING

Two perspectives exist among those who teach and perform some of the world's great musical traditions regarding the creation and re-creation (performance) of music. There are those who hold firm to the belief that any performance of music should stay close to its source, so that a reproduction of it can be had that pays tribute to the manner in which it was conceived by those from the culture. This view allows that music should sound in every venue outside the culture as it sounds within the culture, or at least as closely approximate to that sound as is feasible. The preservation of the musical practice or piece intact and unvaried is key to the view of these conservationists, so that the tradition can be continued precisely as is. Careful listening and constant practice, often with culture-bearers mentoring and modeling, are the likely techniques employed in this pathway to re-creating the music as it has sounded in particular circumstances on specific recordings. The experiences in Chapter 5 are described from such a vantage point, and listening, modeling, and imitation are maintained as critical means by which to preserve and conserve the music.

Yet another stance regarding creation and re-creation is taken by those musicians who are drawn to music because of its very nature as an expressive artistic form. They value the potential for new musical expressions that can emerge as an outgrowth of experience and training in a wide variety of musical traditions. The point of listening, performance, and analysis of the music of, for example, Bali or Bulgaria, they contend, is to provide ideas that lead to the making of new songs and musical pieces. This view stands at the far end of conserving music through the precise re-creation of it, and may be seen as "expressionist" in that creating "original music," or even music "in the style of" a particular genre or tradition, is the ultimate outcome of a rock-solid musical education. Through this expressionist mode, students have come so far in knowing music as to have developed the analytical tools and techniques for making new music.

In fact, one approach may lead to another, and teachers may have reason to act as both conservationists and expressionists in their design of curricular experiences for their students. The study of music in order to perform it in a close replication of the original requires keen aural training, which is in fact a precursor to the ability to compose and improvise music. Music, the aural art, is very much aligned with its use as an expressive art. Yet when any one of the world's musical traditions are concerned, we teachers have tended to feel uncertainty and nervous caution about creative compositional and improvisational experiences. We may have worried that we might be seen as "tampering" with the music should we attempt to change it, rearrange, or allow our students to create new music in the style of a given tradition. We have leaned toward the safety of re-creating music in as authentic a performance as is possible, and then have grown frustrated when the resultant sound is not nearly close enough to the cultural ideal. Such sensitivity is commendable, and yet it would be reasonable for us to do the best we can in performance experiences we shape for our students, compare them to recordings of "the real thing," and then allow our students to play with the possibilities of creating pieces in the style of the traditions they have studied. Like two overlapping circles in a Venn diagram, where one circle represents the original music and the other is the students' recreation of it, or "them" and "us," there is the overlap of same rhythms, melodies, and forms where the circles intersect while there are also the distinctive differences of tunings, timbres, and melodic and linguistic nuances that fit in each of the two circles outside the intersection.

Straight from the mouths of culture-bearers, the message to teachers is that "It's OK to create and re-create 'world music.'" Particularly for educational purposes, the performance and composition (and improvisation) of songs and instrumental pieces that are associated with various musical cultures other than the mainstream are successful strategies for developing students' further understanding of music, musicians, and culture. When music is treated respectfully, with ample time given to its study, it is often a source of pride for people from a culture to hear their traditions—or new expressions reminiscent of their traditions—performed by those who have given their time and energy to it. When students can launch their creative work from recorded examples, and then return to them in making comparisons between the musical source and their newly minted music, they are paying tribute to the inspirations and origins of their musical creations. A completely authentic rendering of a piece may not be possible, but when elementary and secondary school students possess a music as their own, whether it be a re-creation or a new piece, that music becomes genuine to them as listeners and performers. These experiences can touch both cultural insiders and students in ways that are deeply fulfilling.

EXTENDING WHAT'S ALREADY THERE

The CD selections that accompany *Thinking Musically* and this text are typically brief, but they do offer glimpses of musical cultures, genres, and styles. The scores that appear in Chapter 5 are transcriptions of these selections, and they are thus just the length of a minute or two (or even a half-minute) of the listening cuts with which they are associated. They are of appropriate length for instructional purposes alone, but as program pieces for public performance, some of them may require an extension to a length that is satisfying to performers and their listening audiences. (Program-length extensions for some selections are already described in Chapter 5.) The re-creation of music in enactive listening experiences can turn the corner to a kind of creative experience through collective, student-oriented activities for designing in advance, and even in the act of performance, extensions of the style, song or instrumental piece.

Musical extensions by elementary and secondary school students, guided by teachers with a sense of how musical pieces each have their own architectural shape, can bring about an understanding of smaller and larger musical structures that comprise segments and complete selections. Through the Socratic method of questions-and-answers to students, further listening, and models and illustrative examples which the teacher may provide, and through a system of trial-and-error sequences that require both teacher and student assessment, experiences in extending music into an appropriate program length are likely to be successful and satisfying. A percussion piece, a folk song, and a jazz improvisation can be lengthened through repetition, variation, embellishment, and the addition of new sections. Pieces suitable for performance by an ensemble of band or orchestral instruments, or by a full-sized choir, can be realized through the same application of techniques for extending "what's already there."

Following are examples of ways in which performance pieces can be extended. Refer to Chapter 5 for scores and discussion of these selections.

Extending "Atsiagbeko," CD track 5. As in the case of much of the music of sub-Saharan Africa, and of music of the African diaspora (such as some forms of Afro-Latin and Afro-American music), the open-ended nature of this percussion music invites extension through the manner in which instruments may be layered in (and out), the combinations of textures in partial or full ensemble, and the use of the vocal call-and-response as introduction and interlude in the music. This is improvisatory music, to be sure, and while the rhythm of the agogo bells and axatse shaker needs to stay constant, one or the other can "rest" and then return again. The tenor and bass drums play the notated rhythms multiple times, as these are fundamental patterns, but they may also take turns exploring other rhythms not too distant from these patterns. If there are two or more tenor and bass drummers, the constant pattern can be maintained while one or the other improvises upon that pattern. This music can easily extend to three minutes or more, and even the audience can join in the music-making experience by responding "Yah!" to the vocal call, by clapping the double bell (agogo) or shaker (axatse) part (assisted by the teacher or a designated student), or through an invitation to dance.

Extending "All for Freedom," CD track 6. This protest song just gets going before it fades away on the recording, and yet the critical stylistic components are laid out for a choral performance. Extensions of the piece can happen in several ways: by performing just the chorus (with claves and hand-claps) first and last, with the solo verse added in between, by repeating the chorus, and by adding verses which students can create to fit the solo melody. Possible verses to add might be these (the dash indicates two eighth notes where the notated melody is a quarter note, and the italicized words and syllables indicate lower pitches in the second undulating melodic phrase):

2. We're marching for our freedom and-we won't take "no." We'll *take* it to *the* people, *to* the *peo*ple we will go.

3. Our freedom is a precious gift-for which we aim. The *world* deserves *some* freedom, *treat*ing *peo*ple all the same.

Students can be guided to work together in small groups to write rhyming couplets that fit the rhythm of the melody. This is a rousing song that may entice audience participation, so be ready to "bring it on"!

Extending "Music of the Kiembara xylophone orchestra," CD track 19. The melody of the first xylophone repeats its motive four times in the score, and the second xylophone plays three phrases on a constant "e" pitch, spinning out a variation on the melody in only the third (of four) phrases. Meanwhile, higher- and lower-pitched drums "ground" the music in their continuing ostinati. Turn a group of students loose on wooden xylophones (and/or marimbas), and then divide them into two xylophone groups. While the groups play on, designated students can improvise eight measures of melody, using the pitch set (B, d, e, g, a, b). A likely design for a longer work might begin with the original eight bars repeated four times, followed by solo improvisations (with ensemble) that alternate with the ensemble itself (no solo). Six to ten solos make for a piece that appeals to listeners, and four more playings of the original eight bars could produce a strong musical conclusion.

Of course, the extensions of these and other selections are most likely to unfold in classes where the climate is rich with occasions for listening and which foster an open give-and-take dialogue between students and their teacher. A warm and caring environment, set by the receptive teacher with the ability to gently but clearly offer constructive criticism, will draw out the possibilities for music-making that the public will enjoy.

FULL-FLEDGED COMPOSING AND IMPROVISING

The art of creating new and original musical expressions is enveloped in the processes of composing and improvising. The music section of *The National Standards for Arts Education* (1994) recommends the meeting of two separate standards, improvisation (#3) and composition and arrangement (#4), calling for students to create embellishments, variations, melodies with consistent style, and finished compositions that demonstrate unity and variety, and tension and release. Composition and improvisation exist on a continuum of sorts, and they may also appear to overlap, since what distinguishes them is the extent to which the new music is planned and prearranged as opposed to the spontaneity of its generation in the moment of performance. Of the two processes, the more deliberate process is composition which entails the crafting of pieces, reflection upon them and their subsequent revision, while improvisation consists of the simultaneous invention and performance of music. Some have referred to improvisation as the playful exploration of musical possibilities, and yet composition can also be exploratory in its early drafts and "playful," that is, satisfying and even joyful in its process of tweaking and revising, from its early to finished-product stages. On the other hand, improvisation can be serious business, with performers intent and driven in the creation of their musical expression. Some have defined composition by the use of notation, and yet there are traditions where no notation exists, but where composers are nonetheless certain that every musical nuance they have conceived can be orally transmitted and preserved intact.

It is fair to say that composing and improvising are important processes in all the musical world. J. S. Bach, Mozart, and Beethoven are better known for their composed works, and yet all were brilliant improvisers. Composer-pianist Franz Liszt took his musical fantasies, many of them which began as improvisations at the keyboard, and set them to notation that could be performed by others. The great European instrumentalists of the last several centuries made their names at least in part for the cadenzas that they could perform, including those they worked out in advance, those that were composed for them, and those they spontaneously created. In India and in much of southwestern Asia, improvisation of extraordinary complexity is central to vocal and instrumental forms that unfold in performances that can last several hours, while preplanned composition is rare to nil. The cultures of sub-Saharan Africa prize improvisation as the essence of solo and communal music-making, as do African-based musical cultures in North, Central, and South America, and in the Caribbean. There are also composers from these world regions who have carefully considered, crafted, reflected, and revised works in their compositional process, directing performers to follow their plan, and sometimes even committing their music to notation. Bruno Nettl's collected essays, *In the Course of Performance* (1998), illustrate some of the rich variety of improvisatory processes that exist in the world, from the purely exploratory to the more intentional and even preplanned expressions, and is a valuable read for those who wish to know more of the global spectrum of expressive musical possibilities.

Students can compose and improvise from a very early age and with even limited training. Clearly, a violin student with ten years of lessons or a trumpet player with continuous lessons and band experiences from fourth grade through secondary school, is at a unique advantage to have developed the facility to perform well, as opposed to students who have opted out of (or were not exposed to) a formal musical education. Those students with substantial training will know a battery of performance techniques for engaging in musical expression, while those without such training may not. Still, all students have ears, and even younger students or those without musical training have listened with interest and earnest to music in their family and social environments; they have a stockpile of informal musical experiences that have enriched them. Many students may have the urge to write songs, to play with sounds, to "vent" their personal feelings in musical ways, and need the invitation and professional guidance to know how. Full-fledged composing and improvising may be right around the corner for students, a means and an end for their musical learning. Their involvement may begin in elementary ways, and yet the creative reserve may be waiting to be activated. Teachers who can tap into students' creativity may find that the flow is greater than they could ever have imagined.

TECHNIQUES FOR CREATING "WORLD MUSIC"

Sensitivity is a given, both cultural and musical, in approaches to creating music that utilizes techniques and stylistic features belonging to music-makers and their music. One would wish that no one in this age of cultural awareness would bulldoze into a musical culture, take music without permission, and perform it without a sincere effort to understand its meaning and value within the culture. Yet it happens, when in fact a basic ethical stance for those working as musicians, teachers, conductors, and arrangers is to honor the intellectual property rights of performers and creators, to seek their permission, to offer recompense, and to attribute the source of the music in all of its possible uses. Others have ventured into creating new music based upon the elemental traits and forms of a tradition, and have naively believed it to be precisely equivalent in value, function, and style to the music of culture-bearers—when it is not nearly parallel. As teachers we must proceed with caution, listening and learning all we can of a musical tradition, using sources (like the Global Music Series) whose music has been given by permission from traditional musicians, talking further when possible with culture-bearers about their music, and creating new pieces in full knowledge of the fact that the resultant sound may only approximate the tradition. The principal aim of creating "world music" is to allow students to engage in the process of listening, analysis, and planned and spontaneous performances of musical elements and compositional (and improvisational) techniques. It is an instructional aim, where the creative process is a means to the ultimate goal of understanding the musical expressions of the world's cultures.

Suggestions for creating "world musics" from melodic, rhythmic, and formal structures follow. Some are recommendations for pieces "in the style of" particular genres and recorded excerpts, while others describe possibilities for creating "brand new" music through the application of noted compositional techniques. Some require the use of elements found in many musical cultures, while others invite creative experiences associated with elements that are uniquely found in a single culture. They are intended for K–12 students in various choral, general, and instrumental settings, where 15-minutes here or a full class there of the sort of creative activities described can greatly benefit their developing musicianship. Processes and resultant pieces may feature instruments or sound sources that are significant to given cultures, while timbral possibilities also include classroom instruments, "found sound" instruments, and other instruments that are easily accessible by the teacher but which may be foreign to the musical culture. Strategies for creating "world musics" run the gamut of processes in improvisation and composition, with the intent of producing new but stylistically appropriate pieces that fit a particular musical culture, or world music fusion pieces that combine instruments and techniques. All of these "world music creations" are inspired by genres and styles that do exist, so that they are produced with reference to music that has come before.

Using the terms of compositional techniques as organizers, these terms are defined, CD selections on which they are heard are noted, and steps for the realization of creative composition and improvisation processes and their products are delineated. These creative "events" are not necessarily to be taken in sequential order, but should be viewed as prompting some of the possible experiences that might occur in the classroom for achieving a fuller understanding of music's sonic structures. Their possible use is dependent upon the needs and interests of both students and teachers, and levels of difficulty (initial, intermediate, advanced) are advisory only—particularly in that these experiences can be adjusted to greater or lesser complexity by the perceptive teacher. One event alone may be sufficient in some cases, while all may be taken together to comprise a unit of experiences across several class sessions. These events are intended as models (rather than as an inclusive collection of musical experiences) for what might be done with students in creating world music.

CREATIVE "WORLD MUSIC" EXPERIENCE 6.1
Call-and-response *(The juxtaposition of solo with group)*
(Initial)
Refer to *CD tracks 5* (Atsiagbeko), *58* ("Kumbaya"), *59* ("Riachao")

Events:

1. Choose a 4-beat rhythm that can be played on percussion instruments by a group in response to 8-beat solo "calls." Change soloists every 4 calls. Do the same with rhythmically chanted phrases, deciding together on a 4-beat response to the chanted 8-beat solo calls.

2. Search for and collect songs with call-and-response forms, and develop (for performance) a medley of single verses of these songs.

3. Design an instrumental piece that is anchored in call-and-response form.

4. Write a solo-and-response song, selecting a theme such as peace, freedom, friendship, solidarity, and developing several verses. Prepare for performance, with or without an instrumental interlude that uses the same technique.

CREATIVE "WORLD MUSIC" EXPERIENCE 6.2
Drone *(One or more pitches sounding persistently)*
(Initial)
Refer to *CD tracks 11 ("Rāga Purvi-Kalyan"), 38 ("Makedonsko horo"), 52 (Scottish bagpipe drone)*
Events:

1. Experiment with instruments with the capacity to play a drone (bagpipes, dulcimers, various lutes and fiddles, keyboards). Explore techniques for sustaining a tonic and/or dominant drone pitch while improvising a melody above it.

2. Experiment with drone and melody possibilities by pairing instruments such as two clarinets, two trumpets, saxophone and baritone, flute and oboe, violin and guitar, cello and violin. In a partnership of two players, change roles from "drone-keeper" on tonic and/or dominant pitch to "melody-maker." Set time periods (for example, one minute each) or beats (16 beats) for maintaining the drone and melodic improvisation before switching to the other role.

3. Over a tonic and/or dominant pitch drone, improvise a melody based upon a set of pitches (within a diatonic major scale, a harmonic minor scale, Dorian mode, a tetratonic set of four pitches, a chromatic pentachord, for example). Select a meter and develop an eight-measure piece.

4. Develop an improvisation for voices similar to the previous event.

CREATIVE "WORLD MUSIC" EXPERIENCE 6.3
Groove *(The way ensemble musicians interact during performance) (Initial)*
Refer to *CD tracks 4 ("Mi Bajo y Yo"), 5 (Atsiagbeko), 59 ("Riachao")*
Events:

1. Using a selection of percussion instruments (for example, djembes, congas, double bells, cowbells, shakers [gourds with beads inside or outside], claves, sticks), designate someone to improvise a rhythmic phrase of 8 beats. As the player repeatedly plays, guide the entry of a new instrument on another improvised rhythm every two phrases of 8 beats (that is, every 16 beats), Once players are entered into the music-making, encourage them to listen to the music and to find their individual groove in rhythmic interaction with the others. The playing can continue through many cycles until someone tires and takes time out, or when all decide to end the music.

2. Try a similar plan for other instruments: brass mixed with percussion can take the course of a Latin groove, but any combination of instruments has the potential for its players to develop a "groove." Percussion instruments add that rhythmic dimension that works players into their groove, but playing percussively (pizzicato strings, sharp brass and wind attacks) can enhance the groove potential, too.

3. Invite singers to join in the improvisatory "groove music," singing (or scat-singing) their own or others' poetic verse, or melodic inventions on a neutral syllable.

4. Encourage performers to find their own rhythm or melodic phrase by listening to others in the ensemble, and to design their contribution to the groove as complementary to those of others in the ensemble.

CREATIVE "WORLD MUSIC" EXPERIENCE 6.4

Hocket, Interlocking Parts *(Texture of one musical part subdivided among several musicians)*
(Initial)
Refer to *CD tracks 22 (Andean panpipes: three cortes), 50* (Kotekan "norot"), *5* (Atsiagbeko)
Events:

1. Choose a familiar melody, such as "Frere Jacques." In hocket fashion, split the melody between two singers, two players, or two groups of singers or players, and perform alternating pitches of the melody. Start slowly and play several times, increasing the performance speed with each repetition.

2. Create a melody, setting parameters such as "16 notes in 16 beats," "in a moderate tempo," "using five (or four) pitches." Sing or play the melody in hocket fashion.

3. Compose a melody of interlocking parts. On recorders, xylophones, or wind, brass, or string instruments, play the first part and then the second part, and then interlock the two parts into the composite melody. Discuss the characteristics of the individual parts that make for a satisfying composite melody of interlocking parts.

4. Improvise percussion music consisting of interlocking parts. In small groups of 5 or 6 players, each with his or her own drum, bell, shaker, or other percussion instrument, designate an order of entry for the instruments. Select a phrase length of 12 beats, during which one, then two, then three instruments (and so on) play together, listening and determining how to interlock and complement their fellow musicians. Note that the result of a strong interlocking rhythm is a "groove."

CREATIVE "WORLD MUSIC" EXPERIENCE 6.5 Motive, Theme *(Melodic or rhythmic fragment used to construct a larger musical entity)*
(Initial)
Refer to *CD tracks* 29 *("El Gustito")*, 40 (Also Sprach Zarathustra), 49 ("Sumer is Icumen In"), 54 (Symphony No. 5, Beethoven)
Events:

1. Sing or play themes from known instrumental and vocal works. In game-like fashion, try to entice others to "name that theme" in two, three, four (or more) pitches. (Perform the theme fragments with rhythm intact). Notice how themes not only tend to come first, but also repeat immediately and/or later in the music.

2. Discover features of a memorable motive or theme. Note their phrase length, their pitches (intervals between them, repeated or not), their rhythmic features, the articulation and dynamics of them. Find examples of them in various styles. (In rock/pop music, they are referred to as a "riff" or "lick.")

3. Compose a motive, which is typically shorter than a theme (about 4–5 pitches in an interesting rhythm). Play the motive on a variety of instruments. Play it at several pitch levels. Encourage development of the motive into a small composition.

4. Compose a theme of two measures, and use it as the foundation of an improvisation. Repeat the theme, vary it, extend it, contrast it with a different melody, return to it.

CREATIVE "WORLD MUSIC" EXPERIENCE 6.6 Ostinato *(Constantly recurring melodic, rhythmic, or harmonic motive)*
(Initial)
Refer to *CD tracks* 5 (Atsiagbeko), 50 (Kotekan "norot"), 59 ("Riachao")

Events:

1. Create an ostinato rhythm to accompany the singing or playing of scales. Use body sounds (patting or clapping, for example) or percussion instruments in performing the ostinato. Stylize the scale to fit the swing of the ostinato rhythm.

2. Identify familiar melodies or songs for which rhythmic or melodic ostinati can be created and performed.

3. Create a melodic or rhythmic ostinato of one or two measures first, and layer in improvisations to fit it.

4. Create a harmonic ostinato for undergirding melodic improvisations. Consider chordal progressions (for example, I–I–IV–IV–ii–ii–V–I) or bass lines that respond to modal pitches (such as Dorian or Lydian modes). Once the harmonic ostinato is set, take turns improvising melodically above it.

CREATIVE "WORLD MUSIC" EXPERIENCE 6.7
Part-counterpart *(Structure in which one part is responded to by one or more supporting parts)*
(Initial)
Refer to *CD track 55 (Episode from* woi-meni-pele*)*
Events:

1. Designate a lead singer or player within a group, and encourage the individual to create a principal melody.

2. Select players who can offer a complementary counterpart rhythm to the principal melody.

3. Invite players to provide a melodic counterpart to the principal melody.

4. Encourage singers to provide a melodic counterpart to the principal melody.

CREATIVE "WORLD MUSIC" EXPERIENCE 6.8 **Colotomic structure** *(In Southeast Asia, articulation of the metric grouping, or cycle, of one or more instruments in an ensemble)*

(Intermediate)
Refer to *CD track 8 ("Ketawang Puspawarna")*
Events:

1. Using a 16-count cycle, and using mnemonic-like syllables ("gong" and "nong," for examples), chant the occurrence of four different gongs that appear in a Javanese gamelan (gong ageng [G for "gong"], kenong [N for "nong"], kempul [P for "pul"], kethuk [t for "tuk"]):

16	1	2	3	4	5	6	7	8	9	10	11	12	13	14	15	16
G/N	t		t	N	t	P	t	N	t	P	t	N	t	P	t	G/N

(Note that the cycle begins and ends on count 16, and that both the gong ageng and kenong sound on that count.)

2. Divide into four groups of gong-chanters, and chant slowly and evenly the gong syllables as they occur. (See *Thinking Musically*, pages 64–66, for further explanation of colotomic structure.)

3. In the event that gamelan gongs are unavailable, convert the chanted cycle to the sounds of four distinct timbral qualities; percussion instruments such as gongs, cymbals, bells, even woodblocks are examples. Play the cycle repeatedly until the colotomic structure is familiar and comfortable to the ear.

4. Compose a "fixed melody" of 32 beats for melody instruments that will sound over two gong cycles. Assign instruments to play it (xylophones are a natural, but string and wind instruments will make an innovative sound). Add a drum that can play a basic rhythm pattern alongside the melody and gong cycle, and that can signal by its own performance the loud- and fast-playing, and soft- and slow-playing, sections of the piece. Repeat the gong cycle at least eight times (and the fixed melody at least four times), or until the drummer signals for the group to slow its tempo at the end of a cycle to the ending.

CREATIVE "WORLD MUSIC" EXPERIENCE 6.9 Corrido *(Narrative song genre in Mexico and Mexican American culture)*

(Intermediate)
Refer to *CD track 7 (The Ballad of César Chávez)*
Events:

1. Choose a figure of local or national interest, and write four or five descriptive strophic verses about him or her. Follow the a b c b rhyme scheme found in the strophes of "The Ballad of César Chávez."

2. Speak the text several times to find a rhythm in triple meter that fits the words. Using notation, sketch (in 3/4 meter) the rhythm of a first verse.

3. Using the same tonic and dominant chords that accompany the melody of "The Ballad of César Chávez," play a harmonic accompaniment on guitar. In the key of E major, play an introduction, then follow this scheme:

E (2 mm) B (2 mm)

B (2 mm) E (1 m) B (1 m)

E (2 mm) B (4 mm)

E (1 m) B (1 m)

Transpose down to D major (D and A chords) or C major (C and G chords) if the vocal range requires that adjustment of key.

4. Allow the rhythm of the words to flow into a melody, which can parody the melody of "The Ballad of César Chavez" or become something quite new.

CREATIVE "WORLD MUSIC" EXPERIENCE 6.10   Jig:
(In Ireland, dance genre in compound meter)
(Intermediate)
Refer to *CD track 37 ("Tar Road to Sligo" and "Paddy Clancy's Mug of Browne Ale")*
Events:

1. Improvise rhythms of the jig. Pat (on the lap, various surfaces, drumheads) possible rhythms of the single jig (6/8), slip jig (9/8), and double jig (12/8).

2. Improvise jig melodies in 6/8/, 9/8, and 12/8. In a group, select a jig meter, agree upon a key (e natural minor, for example), and determine a two-measure melody that everyone can play. Play that group melody together as a response to individual two-measure improvisations.

3. Choose one of the jig meters and create a jig melody of two four-measure phrases. Each melody can be set in the key of e minor, shifting the harmony to D Major, and returning to e minor (or play in an a minor-G major-a minor scheme). Perform them in a-a-b-b order. Add a drone to accompany the melody, even if it is only a bass line shifting between e and d (or a and g), and create an ostinato rhythm to coincide with it.

4. Explore playing the jig on instruments close and far from the tradition, from fiddles and flutes (close) to saxophones and trumpets (far). Listen to the sound of the jig played in unison by same instruments (all guitars, or oboes) and by a heterogenous group (such as a concert band).

CREATIVE "WORLD MUSIC" EXPERIENCE 6.11
"Oriental" scale *(Non-diatonic scale with interval arrangement of H–m3–H–W–H–m3–H; "H" is half-step, "m3" is minor third, "W" is whole step)*
(Intermediate)
Refer to CD track 46 *("Oriental" scale)*
Events:

1. Sing and play the (first) five pitches of the "Oriental" scale, as notated. *(See Figure 6.1)*

2. Play a tonic or tonic-dominant drone while taking turns singing and playing the "Oriental" scale in various tempi.

"Oriental" scale

FIGURE 6.1 *"Oriental" Scale*

3. Divide into small groups of singers and instrumentalists of various timbres, and perform the "Oriental" scale.

4. With repeated emphasis on the augmented second between e and f♯, create an eigh-measure piece based on the "Oriental" scale.

CREATING "WORLD MUSIC" EXPERIENCE 6.12
Changdan *(In Korea, rhythm patterns drummed or otherwise articulated)*
(Advanced)
Refer to *CD track 17 (Komungo Sanjo)*
Events:

1. Speak the strokes of the chang-gu drum of Korea:

<u>1 2 3</u>	<u>4 5 6</u>	<u>7 8 9</u>	<u>10 11 12</u>
Dong dak	Kung(da da)dak	Kung dak	Kung dak

2. Play the strokes on a double-headed drum, or on two drums. (Refer to *Thinking Musically*, page 72, for performance techniques of the strokes.) Accompany the melody, "Ahrirang."

3. In the style of the Korean instrumental piece, select one instrument to play a slow melody, improvised, that fits the changdan. Attention to the first and fifth pitches, and the flatted third degree, in a pentatonic arrangement, would enhance the possibilities for the improvisatory piece to sound like "Komungo Sanjo."

4. While a melody instrument (any zither or guitar to violin or saxophone) and drum are all that is necessary in this chamber music, listeners can practice the "hohup" breath rhythm, exhaling on beat 1 and inhaling on beat 2 and 3.

CREATIVE "WORLD MUSIC" EXPERIENCE 6.13
Maqam *(In the Middle East, term for melodic mode)*
(Advanced)
Refer to *CD track 25 ("Maqam Rast")*

Maqam Rast

FIGURE 6.2   *Maqam Rast*

Events:

1. Play a maqam called "rast" from C to c, half-flatting the third (e) and seventh (b) degrees. Work with a tuner, striving to play midway between the e and e♭ and b and b♭ degrees. Play the maqam slowly, then twice as fast (two times). (Note that fixed-key instruments, such as piano, are not able to play maqam accurately, as the mode pitches fall in quarter-tones—in between the cracks of the keys.)

2. In 4/4 meter, create brief melodic phrases (no longer than 7–8 beats) for the lower tetrachord (c–d– e♭–f) and the upper tetrachord (g–a–b♭–c). Practice them together, playing them repeatedly over several sessions until they become familiar and fluid. Then in timed, one-minute improvisations, allow various players to play melodically while integrating the set phrases and finding transitions between them.

3. Create a melodic piece in maqam rast by ordering the melodic phrases (of event (2) in a logical development. The length of the piece may run eight to ten measures of 4/4. Play the composition together in unison on available instruments, and repeat.

4. Experiment with the use of tambourine to accompany the composite melody. See the riqq (tambourine) ostinato of Maqam Rast ("Aruh li min," CD track 25) as an example.

CREATIVE "WORLD MUSIC" EXPERIENCE 6.14
Quarter-tone interval *(Intervals between the Western major and minor seconds, or major and minor thirds; in Arab music, half-flat)*

(Advanced)
Refer to *CD track 11 ("Rāga Purvi-Kalyan")*, *17 (Komungo Sanjo)*,
Events:

1. Explore the performance of pitches outside of Western tuning by singing or playing along with recordings that feature melodies in different tuning systems.
2. Examine on a fretless stringed instrument the visible and audible adjustments that can made to play quarter-tones. For woodwind and brass instruments, determine what techniques assist in performing quarter-tones accurately. What, if any, modifications are possible for setting xylophones or keyboards into another tuning?
3. Sing or play a "chromatic-plus" scale of quarter-tones, slowly, with time to think about and listen to the discrete differences of pitch between C and C♯, C♯ and C♯♯ (D♭), C♯♯ (D♭) and D, and so on. Try also a "sliding scale," slowly ascending by sliding from one pitch to the next higher one, scooping upwards.
4. Improvise melodically, fluctuating between discrete and sliding pitches, playing slowly enough to distinguish the quarter-tones.

MUSIC'S ARTISTIC INSPIRATIONS

There are other avenues of creativity that are inspired by the world's musical cultures, and elementary and secondary students may find themselves growing through listening and performance experiences into other expressive forms. It may well be the power of the musical sound—its timbral quality, or haunting melody, hypnotic rhythm, or its entire sonic envelope—that draws them to their need to respond outside the realm of the purely musical. Perhaps they will spontaneously move to the music, or want to pat out or clap a rhythm of their own invention, or add a harmony they are able to conjure up. But they may also be inspired by what they hear to want to describe it in colorful prose, to tell a story—real or imagined, about the music and its makers, or even to "wax poetically," literally writing poetry that raises images of the music and the culture from which it springs. It is not unheard of, either, for young people to be prone to paint what they hear, realistically or surrealistically, selecting colors and textures to express visually what they have experienced by listening. Others may take photographs (their own, or clipped from magazines) as visual representation of what they hear in the music, or use crayons, markers, fabrics, and various other found-objects on paper or cardboard. Music inspires and motivates thoughts that may well lead students to expressive actions that spread across the arts, which may emerge spontaneously and on a voluntary basis, or which are developed through the guidance and support of thoughtful teachers.

For teachers of elementary school children, the possibilities for nurturing and motivating their artistic responses and inventions are frequently wide open for development. Music teachers, in consultation with teachers of art, dance, drama, language arts, and physical education, can launch from a single song or selection any number of possibilities for children to interpret, expand, and express in their own personal ways the power and meaning of the music. As they open their ears to a Maori song or a Japanese percussion piece, and as they understand the music's elemental features and cultural context, children can be led into expressive experiences that have them drawing, painting, dancing, storytelling, and acting. "Writing-across-the-curriculum," a curricular practice in both elementary and secondary schools, is a pursuit likely to be inspired by the musical experience and that can be developed further through the teacher's modeling, shaping, and reinforcing behaviors. Secondary school classes in art, including specialized courses in painting, sculpture, photography, and the media arts, may be prime venues for developing students' artistic inspirations from the music they hear. In some schools, a student's senior project may begin with a musical selection from some locale in Africa or Asia and then catapult to any of a number of artistic expressions that explore in depth the music's power and meaning to the student and to the performers and their listening audiences within the culture of origin.

Students make the music their own through their continued involvement with it. However, sometimes their artistic inspirations may not match the original intent or function of the music as it was conceived and created within a culture. For example, young children may find themselves compelled to move in dance-like fashion to a musical selection, while adolescents might well groove to it in their low-keyed subtle ways. For music that is so closely linked to movement by the people of a given culture, this may be entirely fitting, and yet if dance was not associated with it during its inception, is it appropriate for students nonetheless to express themselves through their creative movement? Particularly if the music was intended for solemn prayerful occasions, this movement could prove problematic and even offensive to those within the culture. In most cases, and for the sake of the creative impulses of our students, it is pedagogically sound to allow students some freedom of personal response and artistic expression. When in doubt, we find ourselves consulting as we can with culture-bearers, comparing student responses and inventions with the role of music within its original culture, and leading them in discussions about music's meanings to cultural insiders and outsiders as well.

WORLDS OF CREATIVE MUSIC

A creative musical expression can be a highpoint in the musical life of a student. Whether an actual piece that gels into a fixed—even notated—composition, or rather, the process of making split second decisions in the act of improvisation, personally expressive music is extremely gratifying. The inside intricacies of a musical work from any part of the world can be known when the techniques of the piece become the basis for exploration, extension, and development in new ways. Further, the techniques that comprise genres and styles, if fully understood through listening, performance, and creative experiences, can become the basis for further music-making of a personally expressive nature. Making music in the style of a call-and-response technique as it appears in a Ghanian percussive piece, and in hocketed fashion according to its use by Andean panpipes, are means of knowing the particular musical selections as well as music at large for its variety of component structures. These opportunities call students to problem-solve, to practice and play out skills and concepts they have begun to acquire, and to personalize their understanding of musical structures through applications that are meaningful to them. When teachers provide opportunities to make decisions on melodic and rhythmic contents of a piece, and in its formal organization, the growth potential of their students' musicianship is considerable. Their musical manipulations of maqams and motives are certain to bring them more fully into new worlds of creative music.

PROBLEMS TO PROBE

1. Select an event, or set of events, to trial-teach to a group of K–12 students, and be conscious of your role as facilitator rather than

director of the creative experience. Evaluate the effectiveness of the process by which the students improvise or compose, noting the instructional steps that were useful guides for the students. Notate in the margins of this book any modifications that you might recommend.

2. Of the techniques and their suggested events, discuss with colleagues which ones are more likely to invite improvisational or compositional processes, and reasons why.

3. Review your sketch of a sample course schedule, selected in Chapter 1, and insert three events to fit the schedule. Think: Which experiences will be meaningful to developing my students' knowledge of Music with a capital "M"?

CHAPTER 7

Music, Cultural Context, and Curricular Integration

∞

Questions of context regarding music could fill reams, but answers to even a handful of them will enable our students to understand reasons why and processes by which people make music meaningful and useful in their lives. Music as musical sound is a critical dimension by which it can be known by our students, and yet a fuller awareness of music is possible through knowledge of its instruments (and voices), elements, and contexts. When they study issues surrounding the creation and performance of music, and consider music as cultural thought and behavior, they can be adding layers of meaning to the sonic experience. Since music lies at the intersection of cultural, historical, social, and linguistic studies, it is a springboard for developing these realms of knowledge. The curricular designs we conceive, and from which we deliver instructional experiences, may sweep across conceptions of music alone to music within its cultural contexts, including the sources of its expressions, its traditions and changes, and its meanings to its makers and listening audiences. Our K–12 students may find it highly stimulating to probe the music of their listening, participation, or performance for the circumstances of its origins, the means of its transmission, the functions it fulfills, the settings of its creation and re-creation, and the interpretations which performers give to its textual and expressive features. Due to the variance across student motivations and styles of learning, some may find themselves greatly intrigued with contextual circumstances surrounding the music, such that knowing its cultural context will in fact deepen their understanding and appreciation of the music itself. Both through music classes, and in classes that integrate music across subjects and disciplines, we teachers of choral, general, and instrumental classes can do much to lead our students to a more comprehensive understanding of music's role and purpose in the lives of cultural insiders and outsiders alike.

MUSIC-AS-MUSIC

For teachers whose course subject is music, the aim of their professional efforts may seem obvious and as straight as an arrow. "But of course," we smugly say, "the mission of music teachers is to teach music." Teachers are often charged with teaching a particular style, genre, or tradition of music, or they may teach music in its many stylistic manifestations (or at least those which they can successfully select and schedule into their classes). Yet they will teach music-as-music, for the sheer sound of it, and for its sonic structures, and all of the strategies for developing listening, performance, and creative expressive skills will fill their classroom time with students. Music will be sung, played, danced, listened to, analyzed and created anew, all in a discovery of what makes it tick.

The traditions of music instruction are embedded in descriptions of school and university degree programs, courses, and curricular statements. In secondary school band programs, the repertoire and performance skills of wind, brass, and percussion instruments as they comprise the ensemble's wall of sound are the point of daily class meetings. Likewise, in the choral ensembles of secondary schools, the emphasis is on vocal technique, choral blend, and the preparation of repertoire for performances within the school community and interscholastically. In music classes for children, skill-building and concept formation are the hoped-for outcomes of performance-based lessons. Even in academic music courses at the university, the greatest weight traditionally has been given to a strictly musical analysis of phrases, forms, and components of melody, rhythm, and texture. There are curricular competencies to attain, all-district proficiencies to develop, and state and national standards to meet, so that students will sing or play accurately and expressively, improvise, compose, and arrange with ease, read and write music in various meters and keys, describe and analyze music for its constituent features, and evaluate their own and others' performances and creative musical endeavors. Teaching music-as-music is more than a full-time endeavor.

The ultimate goal for efforts in music-as-music instruction is a keen musical understanding, and the strategies for attaining it are through the development of performance and listening analysis skills. It is no wonder, given the commitment by teachers of energy and ideas to raising up musically competent students, that many choose the conservatory-styled pathway of staying enveloped in the sonic features of the music. This route has proven highly successful at all levels, too, for teachers know that "practice makes perfect" the skills and understandings of a solid musicianship. Time is of the essence in the growth of musical skills, so that class time is devoted to their development, and performance dates loom overhead to press teachers to keep the focus on music-as-music. For teachers who follow this time-honored approach, everything else that surrounds the music may seem like "icing-on-the-cake," "window-dressing," and peripheral to the point of music's sonic self.

MUSIC-AS-CULTURE

As stellar as are the notable successes of music-as-music instruction, something is missing in the scenario. To know music is to know also *about* music, and to study it in as thorough and comprehensive a manner as possible. The study of music "close-up," in all of the cultural details that surround its sound, and to draw back in consideration of its broader implications, is a certain way of knowing it fully. Rather than to detach music from the contextual issues that surround it, a study of its connections to the past and the present add depth to musical understanding while also allowing music to function in its natural way as an important piece in study of the world and its people. For as ethnomusicologist Bruno Nettl ensures us once again in his *Encounters in Ethnomusicology: A Memoir* (2002), music is not separated from culture: it *is* culture. Musical study is both an end and a means through which cultural understanding may result. Furthermore, knowledge of music's role and meaning within culture can lead to enhanced understanding of the musical sound.

The ninth, of nine music standards within *The National Standards for Arts Education* (1994), underscores the aim of relating music to history and culture. The subpoints recommend that teachers facilitate not only the description of characteristics of music genres and styles from a variety of cultures but also the classification of works by genre, style, historical period, composer, and title. Implicit within this standard is the need for students to know something of the circumstantial surroundings of the music they listen to and perform, because music is certainly reflective of people's thoughts and behaviors.

In a music-as-culture approach to instruction, stories and histories of music are offered to students so that they might understand the circumstances of the music, its composition, its performance, and its reception by listening audiences—then and now, here and there. Knowledge of how performers (and listeners) think and behave is useful information, as is how music is transmitted and learned, interpreted, and changed over the course of time and place. Music-as-culture teaching is related to contextualizing the music, coming to terms with a song or instrumental piece for the ideas and associations that have given it meaning. Band directors and choral conductors teach music-as-culture when they lead students in knowing, for example, who composed the piece, and for what reasons. At the university, academic music courses become embedded in the principles of music-as-culture when attention is given to the cultural, historical, and social issues associated with the composition, performance, and critical and popular reception of a work. When teachers of music in elementary schools "storytell" to children a song's meaning to the song-bearers, music-as-culture is very much in operation. These perspectives catch the imagination of our students, and they are drawn to the frameworks that explain away music's uses and meanings.

Music can be listened to in attentive, engaged, and enactive ways, and still it is possible to follow tenets of the music-as-culture approach. Teachers can offer lessons in listening analysis, participatory and performance experiences, and creative composition (and improvisation), and still manage to discuss with students the time and place of the music's origin, the rationale behind its acceptance as popular or artistic expression, or the role it plays in people's lives. One approach does not negate the other, and a thoughtful and well-organized teacher can manage to balance the two.

MUSIC IN CONTEXT

Music does not exist in a vacuum, and courses and curricular programs that pay tribute to its connections to the stories behind it increase its relevance to students. Knowledge of music's context helps to further humanize it, personalize it, and associate it with students' interests, and to provide for them an understanding of its cultural, historical, and social meanings. Students who listen to or perform "Take Five" are further informed and personally connected to it on hearing about the life and works of Paul Desmond, its composer, and Dave Brubeck, leader of the quartet that recorded it. Students who discover the significance of the conch shell to Buddhism, that it symbolizes the sound of the Buddha's penetrating voice, listen differently to its sound than those who have had only the aural experience. Students who understand the tradition of corn-growing and corn-grinding among the Navajo and their Pueblo neighbors will hear the Corn-Grinding Song of Joe Lee and his friend for its historical and cultural meaning, rather than as a melody, a rhythm, and a set of "nonsense syllables" (which it is decidedly not). Context adds substance to the musical experience, and enriches it for students who deserve to know its connections to the lives of its makers.

In an effort to connect a musical work to its context, teachers are well advised to examine its connections to time and place. Increasingly, authors and editors are providing this for songs, song collections, choral pieces, and band and orchestral pieces they publish, where the opening pages of a score or textbook may contain descriptions of the composer, inspirations for the work, its premiere performances and recordings of the work, its use and reception by performers and listeners, and (for vocal works) text translations. The recent turn of scholars toward the integration of social and cultural issues in their musicological research has begun to affect the scholarship of their teaching, as academic course textbooks and lectures have begun to shift emphases from fundamental analysis of music to contextual matters as well. Still, as teachers we will find that our own research, the discussions we lead in our classes, and the student projects we assign, may be warranted, in order to bring maximal meaning to the music we feature in our courses and programs.

One model for the provision of musical context to our students, the Cultural Prism Model, is anchored in a series of journalistic who-what-when-where-how questions. These questions help to shed splinters of light from the multiple sides of a crystal prism, turning the music into a veritable treasure-load of cultural information. Culture-bearers who are musicians (as well as those who may not call themselves musicians) living locally, and scholars, too, may be key to providing answers to fundamental questions of context, and teachers and students can work alone, together, and in tandem with those living in or familiar with the culture and its music to seek out responses. These questions can provide a template for filling-in-as-you-go items and issues for contemplation and classroom projects, with each information-byte adding meaning to the music in study. A similar approach to integrated instruction, an "Extended Facets Model," was independently developed by Janet Barrett, Claire McCoy, and Kari Veblen in *Sound Ways of Knowing* (1996), and is worthy of study and comparison for ways in which music's cultural context may be probed by students with the guidance of their teachers.

CULTURAL PRISM MODEL

Musical Beginnings: *Who created the music? How old was the creator at the time the piece was created? When was it created? Where? What inspired the creation of the piece? Who first performed it? How was it performed: as music with expectations for quiet listening, dancing, marching (including processionals), or as "background" to social conversations?*

Musical Continuities: *Who performs it now? What qualifications do performers of the music have? Does it always sound the same, or is there flexibility within the tradition to personally interpret it, vary it, transform it? Are there recordings of the piece? Who teaches it? How is it learned? How do audiences respond to the music? Are there social norms for these responses?*

Musical Meanings: *Are there particular social or cultural themes to the music? What use or function does it fulfill? Do historical and contemporary performances of it demonstrate different meanings? Do particular groups of people, as defined by age, gender, ethnicity, religion, socioeconomic status, nation or region, identify with this music?*

Two illustrations of the Cultural Prism Model are offered next, in order to clarify how musical beginnings, continuities, and meanings can be known through the contextual information provided within published material (such as through the contents of this Global Musics series). Further insights can be derived from culture-bearers and scholars, made relevant through classroom discussions, and otherwise researched by us and our students in advance or as part of the learning process. In particular, culture-bearers—who may well be staff workers, parents and grandparents of students, people living and working in the neighborhood of the school, and musicians in the local community— can reveal all sorts of stories behind the music. Even their single visit to a classroom of students can be an occasion for making the human connection to the music, and for allowing students to recognize its use and value by people within a particular segment of society. Music in which students are unlikely to have had previous experience are brought to greater relevance by these information-bytes, and for students who are drawn as much or more to details of music's history and culture as to its sound, this information will not be marginal but of central interest.

CULTURAL PRISM MODEL: APPLIED EXAMPLE 1
"Unnai Nambinen" (CD track 39). (from research by ethnomusicologists Matthew Allen and T. Viswanathan)

Musical Beginnings:
- "Unnai Nambinen" was composed by Muttuttandavar, a temple musician who lived near the coastal city of Cidambaram, in seventeenth-century South India. The composer was "in residence" at the Nataraja temple, one of the most famous Siva temples in India, and an important pilgrimage site for dancers.

- Muttuttandavar performed in an ensemble that included nagasvaram, a long double-reed instrument, and tavil, a double-headed drum. He was deeply familiar with the use of music for worship purposes.

- Muttuttandavar dedicated the song, "Unnai Nambinen," to his personal deity, Nataraja, a manifestation of Siva, to whom he paid tribute with the text, "I trusted you lord, I prostrated myself at your feet."

Musical Continuities:
- Many of Muttuttandavar's melodies, including the one to "Unnai Nambinen," were lost (although his texts were saved and available in print). The melody now used was composed by flutist T. N. Swaminatha Pillai in 1941, and was passed down to his student, T. Viswanathan.

- Kritis like "Unnai Nambinen" were once performed in temples and private homes. They have developed outward from their devotional contexts to concert pieces performed by vocal virtuosos in public halls. Theatres and concert halls in museums and at universities are common settings in North America for performances of South Indian kriti.

- Professionally trained singers of kriti record CDs of favorite kritis and tour internationally. They work closely with their ensemble, typically a double-headed drum called mridangam, a violin (or other melodic accompanying instrument), and a supporting drone instrument such as the tambura.

• Although there are texts that are preserved in print, and many of the melodies are preserved in solfege-style notation, kritis are typically learned orally: the teacher sings and the student follows in imitation, phrase by phrase, and in lengthening phrases and sections, until it is known.

Musical Meanings:

• Nataraja is the "Lord of the Dance," and is the subject of many bronze sculptures that depicts him dancing inside an arc of fire, holding an hourglass drum, his other pair of hands in the shape of gestures for surrendering and protecting, one leg uplifted in a dance pose, and the other pinning down Muyalakan, the dwarf of ignorance.

• Nataraja is known to wear a cobra and a flower garland, as the text describes him, and holds fire embers in his hand. He is widely worshipped, according to the Muttuttandavar's kriti text, "throughout the seven continents."

CULTURAL PRISM MODEL: APPLIED EXAMPLE 2

"Kumbaya" (CD track 58) (from research by ethnomusicologist Gregory Barz, folklorist and folksinger Joe Hickerson, and the oral lore surrounding this song)

Musical Beginnings:

• The origin of "Kumbaya" is unknown, although documents of "hearings" of it date to the mid-1950s, in South Africa and Southwest-Africa (now Namibia). Its presence in the Carribean and in North America by the late 1950s has been noted by singers and folklorists.

• No composer is known. It appears to have been communally-created, passed on in the oral tradition, and learned in the context of Christian worship services.

Musical Continuities:
- "Kumbaya" became popular by the early 1960s, a central song in the repertoire of activists in the Civil Rights movement. It was performed a capella and with guitars, in unison and in harmony, and with new verses created to suit the purpose (for example, "Someone's marching, Lord"). "Kumbaya" is associated with Dr. Martin Luther King, as it was often heard at rallies at which he preached and presided.

- In its continuing life on the African continent as a song intended for community participation, it is performed in Kenya, where it can be heard in an open-air prayer meeting at the Power of Jesus Around the World Church in Kisumu. Following a bereavement ceremony leading to the family's speaking-in-tongues and the congregation laying-hands upon them and waving their hands in gestures of praise, the church pastor began singing the solo call of the "Kumbaya" chorus into a generator-powered microphone. The sung English-language responses of the congregation ensued as they found their way back to their seats.

Musical Meanings:
- "Kumbaya" meaningful in its use in communal worship services and as a vehicle for social justice and solidarity. In its use in the church service in Kisumu, Kenya, it was useful in giving back to members of the congregation their language, and cooling them down from the emotionally charged period of speaking-in-tongues and gesturing in praise.

- The literal meaning of "Kumbaya" requires knowing the original language of the piece, but since the origin of the song is unclear, the phrase has instead been interpreted as "Come, my Lord," in reference to Jesus Christ.

As an exercise for observing one's own perceptual change, it is instructive to initially approach a musical selection primarily for its sonic features and later come to know it as it can be contextualized. Students can be guided to follow a course that begins by listening to the music, then to participate in its making, working it up to performance level, creating other music akin to the piece they have studied, and finally they can come the point whereby they question their own curiosities regarding its origin, development and change, and cultural role. In this way, they can see their perspective shifting from music-as-music to music-as-culture, and they can determine just how knowledge of the beginnings and continuities of the music they study may shape and alter its meaning to them. Of course, the reverse course is also possible, whereby, students examine all the descriptive information available on a musical culture, its uses and functions, instruments, performers, composers, and so on—prior to the musical experience. The build up to hearing the music, and "trying it on for size" through participatory and perfomance experiences, might pique the interest of students and sharpen the musical experience. It may be useful to approach several musical cultures in opposing ways, and allow students to discuss the effects and influences of each. Ultimately, it may be that students recognize that studies in music and its cultural context together are more enriching than to study music as sound (or to study music-as-culture without reference to its sound!)

MUSIC, INTEGRATED

While universities pride themselves for the specialized studies they can provide through the array of departments with their expert faculties, associated research scholars to extend the departmental specialization, and library holdings that span the breadth and depth of departmental discipline, many students—particularly young students—require educational provisions that cut across subjects and disciplines in an integrative fashion. It is not unusual for music specialists in elementary schools to be called upon to use music as a vehicle to teach language arts, social studies, social skills, and (more rarely) science and math. As well, all-subject elementary school teachers are increasingly charged with teaching music alongside these subjects. In middle and high schools, district- and school-wide mandates occasionally organize staff "teams" where music teachers join with other teachers in the arts, humanities, or social studies arenas to design and deliver a coherent course (or courses) for students. Some K–12 teachers fear the loss of potential for developing their students' specialized skills in such programmatic trends, but others see that beneficial interdisciplinary goals can be established and realized through the integration of music across subjects.

"Global" has been used in this volume to refer to the international phenomenon of music, and the importance of teaching music in its vastly varied forms and flavors. The word is also used to refer to educational programs that are comprehensive in scope, which then fit the learning style of children and other students who learn their world experientially—and initially without categorizing it. Through experiences that cross aural, visual, and kinesthetic modalities, a global approach to learning and instruction blurs subjects that have too often been separated by adults who tend to classify, categorize, and compartmentalize their encounters. Global and comprehensive curricular plans may center upon an experience (a book, a museum trip, a performance, an art or construction project) and allow students to follow the themes, strands, and splinterings individually and collectively to satisfy their questions and to become fully informed of the composite experience. These plans may also seemingly start with a concept, for example "clouds" or "repetition," and explore it through experiences in the arts, language arts, social studies, and math and science. Global plans for educational lessons and programs require thoughtful teachers to organize them, but are in fact fitting to the flexibility and flow of the manner by which students learn.

The integration of music with the arts is a common phenomenon in elementary and secondary schools. Particularly in districts and schools where the music teacher may be the only full-time paid teacher of the arts on the faculty, it is not unusual for administrators and teachers alike to expect the music teacher to coordinate efforts for the winter pageant, the school musical, the spring arts festival, athletic events, civic gatherings, parent meetings, and all-school assemblies in commemoration of historical figures, national and regional events. Each art form is unique, and yet the band, choir, orchestra, or "all-music" teacher may be responsible for integrating music with the visual arts, theater, literature, and media arts. Teachers who can act as facilitators are typically successful in music-arts integration programs and projects, as they learn to acquire the "know-how" and the network of individuals with expertise to assemble events that show the uniqueness and integrity of each of the various art forms.

The integration of the arts may appear to be a daunting task, and yet when one considers the blending of the arts in other cultures, it is more natural than not for the arts to overlap. Chinese opera, Kabuki theatre in Japan, and Western opera are examples of performance forms where vocal music, instrumental music, dance, and the theatrical components of acting, scenery, and costumes (the last two of which cross into the visual arts) all come together to form a conglomerate whole. The puppetry of Java, Bali, and other parts of Southeast Asia likewise infuses music within its dramatic presentations. In many of the world's cultures, and particularly in sub-Saharan African cultures, across the Pacific islands, and in Carribean, Central, and South American nations, music and dance are inseparable. The performance of popular music, as well as of art and traditional music, are intended to be enjoyed for the visual aspects of the performance—the dance and sometimes theatrical effects—as well as for its musical sound. The compartmentalization of the arts is a phenomenon of Western culture, while in much of the rest of the world the arts are meant to be a blended experience.

Music and the arts can hold their own even as they are integrated into the study of other subject areas, where a conglomerate and global experience encompassing multiple disciplines can serve multiple goals of learning. Further, the arts may even serve to entice and motivate students who enjoy learning through song, poetry, dance music, stories, or dramatic presentations about medieval Europe, the Mexican Revolution, tenets of Zen Buddhism, scientific properties of tuning systems, social customs in the Balkans, cross-cultural calendrical celebrations, and contemporary political views in South Africa. There is the occasional use by secondary school teachers of history of Tchaikovsky's 1812 Overture within the unit on nineteenth-century America, or of Prokofiev's Romeo and Juliet suite by high school English teachers as they study Shakespeare's play. It would seem as reasonable to listen to "Yaegoromo" in a study of Japan's Edo period, or to consider the "Vedic recitation" of North India in a "world literature" class as an example of the way that text syllables and patterns organized in committing important oral literature to memory. The "grind" of knowing mathematical principles, geographic concepts, and language constructions can seem less so when artistic experiences envelop and present this knowledge for students to learn.

Following are illustrations of music's role in integrated, interdisciplinary learning. Using a sampling of CD selections, the music can serve as a launch to integrated studies and even at times as a centerpiece for knowing a set of understandings that emanate from the musical sound experience. In fact, as it has been said, music may function as the gateway to understanding their world—and ours. Note how the subjects and fields vary somewhat from one example to the next, but how each musical tradition makes pathways beyond itself. Suggestions for integrating music into these subjects are included. They may appear at first to be geared toward elementary school students, partly because of the frequency of integrated curricular studies at that level. However, many of the suggestions are suited to secondary school students, who may be stimulated to engage in class and out-of-class projects, including those that can be accomplished independently, with partners, or in small working teams.

INTEGRATED INTERDISCIPLINARY ACTIVITY 7.1
CD track 2, "Gunslingers" (Trinidad)
Geography: *To many, steel drum music sounds "tropical," since they associate it with cruise ships that travel through the Caribbean—from Port-of-Spain (Trinidad) to Port-Au-Prince (Haiti). Locate Caribbean nations on a map, and plan an imaginary cruise route where steel drum music might be heard.*
Language: *The title of the piece is English, since this is the official language of Trinidad. Explore other languages spoken in the Caribbean, from French and Spanish to Dutch, Garifuna (Black Carib), Hindi, Urdu, and Creole, and locate the nations where they are spoken.*
Dance: *Trinidad and its neighbors have helped to define popular music and its dance forms, many of which have gone international. While "Gunslingers" prompts calypso-style dancing, there are others: Cuban son, rumba, mambo, Puerto Rican (and Cuban) salsa, Jamaican reggae, and Dominican merengue. Find film clips of these dances, and identify people who might teach the dances to you.*
History: *Columbus landed on Trinidad on his third voyage, and named the country for its three major mountains. The Carib Indians lived on the island, and then it was settled by the Spaniards in 1592 until the French became prominent soon after its revolution in 1789. The British arrived in Trinidad in 1797 to overtake the French and their Creole culture. The majority of the population traced their ancestry to enslaved Africans, but were joined in the nineteenth century by South Asians (who now constitute 40 percent of all Trinidadians). The language of Trinidad today reflects both the British and French influence in the Creolized English, called "Patois." Examine the events of the various ruling nations, and also ascertain their influences in Trinidad today.*

Science: *Examine the dents inside a pan associated with individual pitches, all of them purposefully dented by a pan-maker. Talk with a pan-maker, or pan-tuner, about how the placement, shape, and size of the dent of a fifty-five gallon oil drum can affect its pitch. Take a metal lid (to a pot or pan), a hub cap, or some other discarded metal piece (look for possibilities at garage sales or junkyards), and hammer dents into it to produce the pitches of a pentatonic or diatonic scale.*

INTEGRATED INTERDISCIPLINARY ACTIVITY 7.2
CD track 7, "The Ballad of César Chávez" (Mexico)
Geography: *The corrido (of the Texas-Mexico border region) is a song form that is used to tell the story of a current event. Like the Trinidadian calypso and the Chilean Nueva Cancion, the corrido may reveal local situations, portray particular figures of renown within a community, or provide political commentary. On a map find towns along the Tex-Mex border where corridos are likely to be performed. Then study the text of the ballad and locate on a map of California the cities (Fresno, Merced, Stockton, and Sacramento) of which the singers sing.*
Economics: *Migrant workers live hard lives, following the routes that differentiate the growing seasons for strawberries, corn, apples, and the like, sometimes living out of their cars and trucks, and engaging young and old family members in the work on farms and in orchards. Explore the duties of migrant farmers, and the wages earned. What were conditions like for migrant farmers in the 1930s, the 1960s, and now? What are contractors and scabs mentioned in the text?*
History: *Identify key figures in the corrido text and trace their historical contributions: César Chávez, Governor Edumund "Pat" Brown, the Virgin of Guadelupe.*
Language: *Some of the text may be immediately known to bilingual students, or those who are studying Spanish. Select*

words and phrases that can be easily translated: "toda la gente" (all the people), "viva" (long live), "sigan con bastante fe" (keep on with much faith), "nosotros a la gloria" (we will go to heaven), "un hombre cabal" (very strong man), "oiga" (listen), "su nombre que se pronuncia" (your name is well known).

INTEGRATED INTERDISCIPLINARY ACTIVITY 7.3
CD track 15, "Hifumi no Shirabe Hachigaeshi" (Japan)
Geography: *The shakuhachi was brought to Japan from China, although it may be traceable all the way through India and Iran to Egypt, traveling east along the trade routes of the Mohammedan Empire.*
History: *The growth of the modern shakuhachi can be attributed to the komuso, the priest dressed in basket-hats who wandered the streets of Japanese cities, playing the instrument. These priests were believed to be samurai who had lost their privileges during clan struggles beginning in the late sixteenth century. They were granted the opportunity to play melodies for donations, and so their shakuhachi became central to their economic well-being. Because these former samurai warriors were denied the use of their double swords, they redesigned the shakuhachi into the shape and strength of a club to defend themselves against any violence that might come to them. Look to paintings of the Edo period for images of these shakuhachi-playing priests, and read further about the komuso and their fall from samurai power and rise again as priest-musicians.*
Science: *The shakuhachi's five holes produce the tones D, F, G, A, D, and also other tones by half-holing and changing the embouchure. Listen to shakuhachi music to hear sometimes very slight changes of a quarter tone or less. Using a recorder or other wind instrument, experiment with playing pitches less than a semitone apart.*

INTEGRATED INTERDISCIPLINARY ACTIVITY 7.4
CD track 20, Cantonese Opera (China)
Geography: *China's area is greater than that of Europe or the continental United States, stretching from subarctic to subtropical regions. Bordering countries include Korea, Mongolian People's Republic, Russia, Afghanistan, Pakistan, India, Bhutan, Nepal, Burma, Laos, Vietnam, Macao, and Hong Kong. Find China on a map, and note its expansive latitude, its neighbors, its mountains, plateaus, deserts, rivers, and bordering seas. Find Guangdong (formerly Canton), the home of Cantonese Opera.*
History: *The Chinese trace their recorded history through dynasty names. While most of the many regional opera traditions developed in the Qing dynasty (1644–1911), earlier forms of musical theatre in the Ming dynasty (1368–1644) were developing. Of course, instrumental and vocal music in various forms, and dance, theatre, puppetry, and a wide array of visual arts were evident much earlier. Explore the Tang and Sung dynasties (618–979 and 960–1279, respectively) for the rich artistic expressions that developed during those periods.*
Visual Arts: *Within Cantonese Opera, there are four main characters: a scholar or statesman, a warrior or bandit, a principal female character, and a clown or jester. Each of these characters are highly stylized in their mannerisms, speech, costumes, headdresses and hairstyles, and makeup. As to this last character component, look for photos that depict characters close-up for their painted facial designs. Sketch, draw, and paint these designs on paper or cardboard, and wear them as masks.*
Poetry: *The texts of almost all the arias in Cantonese (and Beijing) Opera are based on a series of rhymed couplets with seven or ten syllables in each line. These lines may be divided between two singers or split up by dialogue, too, but are set to two basic types of melodies, one each for feminine roles or military leaders. Take a familiar story and create Cantonese Opera poetry to tell it.*

INTEGRATED INTERDISCIPLINARY ACTIVITY 7.5
CD track 32, "West End Blues" (U.S.)
Geography: *The blues, and the folk forms that preceded it such as work songs, field hollers, and spirituals, were prominent in African-American communities across the South by the end of the nineteenth century. On a map, preferably one from this period, locate the southern states (Mississippi in particular) and cities where African-American communities could be found.*
History: *The sociocultural climate of the period of Reconstruction following the Civil War, and the post-Reconstruction period of the 1890s, was one of bitter feelings by southern white Americans toward the black community. Segregation laws developed, and African Americans came to recognize and express their own identity, so that black sacred and secular music, including the blues, blossomed. Ballads that told of black heroes like Po' Lazarus and John Hardy had a blues-style to them, and the wailing of field hollers poured into the blues form to allow a more expressive and more certain musical identity. Explore this period of U.S. history for people and events that were likely influences of the formation and growth of the blues.*
Poetry: *The blues were known for texts that could express frustration, hope, and anxiety, occasionally disasters or accidents, love-gone-bad, or various vices that men and women were drawn to when hope seemed dim and release from sadness and oppression a distant dream. Collect blues texts, and examine their themes, as well as the language used to convey them.*

INTEGRATED INTERDISCIPLINARY ACTIVITY 7.6
CD track 53, "Rāga Miyān ki Toḍi" (North India)
Geography: *India is its own subcontinent that hangs from the highest mountains in the world, the Himalayas, southward to the Arabian Sea, Bay of Bengal, and Indian Ocean. Its indigenous*

Dravidian peoples live in the south, whereas the northern and central areas have received migrants from parts of Asia to the west and north. The north is frequently called Hindustani. Study a map to find key northern cities of New Delhi, Bombay, and Calcutta, and Karnatic centers like Madras and Bangalore. Find also India's rivers, topographic features, and the oceans and countries which border it.

Visual Arts: *Indian art and sculpture is primarily of a religious nature, so that a study of basic precepts Hinduism, Buddhism, and Islam, minimally, can inform knowledge of and appreciation for the visual arts. The Gupta period (320–600 a.d.) was a golden age for the creation of Buddha images in stone and metal cast. Temples and walls were ornately decorated with Hindu figures and heavenly maidens during the medieval period. Indian Muslim culture is best known from the Mughal period (the sixteenth through the nineteenth centuries), through architectural splendors such as the Taj Mahal, and miniature paintings that flourished alongside the popular Rajasthan school known for the scenes from Krishna's life and escapades (these are the paintings in which Krishna's face is always painted blue). Visit an art museum and find examples of Indian sculpture and painting.*

History: *The dhrupad is one of the oldest Hindustani classical vocal genres, and is typically performed by one or two male singers, accompanied on tamboura and pakhavaj (double-headed drum). It was a common form of temple music in fourteenth-century North India, and by the reign of the Mughal emperor Akbar, was the most important genre of music performed in the Muslim courts. Research the Muslims in India, the Mughal courts, and the life and works of Akbar. In a presentation (and possible simulation of this place and time), play a recording of dhrupad music to truly set the scene.*

Science: *A dhrupad singer needs to have a well-developed control of the breath. Time your ability to hold your breath while sustaining a single tone (on a neutral syllable). Then time how* *long you can hold your breath while singing a moving passage with pitch variation, for example, by singing descending and ascending scales. Compare the two timings and postulate reasons for any differences in singing sustained versus moving passages.*

ETHNOMUSICOLOGICAL ISSUES, CONSIDERED

A consideration of ethnomusicological issues can help to clarify for students the meaning of music locally and cross-culturally, as it has existed historically within a culture and in its contemporary practice. These "issues" are lively topics of considerable interest in the research of those ethnomusicologists (who have at various times been referred to also as musical anthropologists and comparative musicologists) who study music as culture, and music in culture. These issues are defined and discussed in some detail in *Thinking Musically,* and illustrations of their occurrence are given notable attention. The issues may be used as discussion-points in classes of students enrolled in elementary and secondary schools (and also among university students), as appropriate, and as the inspiration for library projects, fieldwork studies, oral histories, and cross-curricular projects. Several of them are noted next, with questions or challenges posed to motivate student activity. The use of the familiar pronouns (you, yours) are intentional, so as to personalize the issues and make the projects fully relevant to lift out and use with young students. They will require the guidance and supervision of teachers, who can set up and facilitate the possibilities for these projects with the potential to enlighten students of the sorts of issues that concern ethnomusicologists.

Global-Local Interests. In the last decade or so, ethnomusicologists have been probing music as a global phenomenon, seeking information as to how it is produced, distributed, and consumed by international audiences, while they also continue to pursue their long-held interests in the local performance aesthetic of music and its situatedness in the lives of people residing in their neighborhoods, villages, regions, or other community arrangement. Tuvan throat-singers from Central Asia and Afro-pop bands from Ghana and Nigeria are examples of musicians whose musical cultures have been raised out of their local expressions to the sort of global phenomena they have become. The international interest in Irish traditional music, and in the more encompassing set of Celtic traditions from Ireland, Scotland, and Wales, are further illustrations of how "home-grown music" can become a commodity, a successful product-for-export that people far from the culture or origin are drawn to listen to and to want to perform. With the rise of "world-beat" (also called "world-pop," and in some commercial circles, just "world music"), there seems to be few musical traditions that have not been recorded on location and packaged for listeners across the globe to know. The concept of globalization is directly relevant to music, and the concept of the global village is made possible through the travel and technology that has enabled us to experience music of coastal and mountain villages, and of the bush and the royal courts.

Project: Local–to–Global Music. *Select a musical tradition originating elsewhere in the world—some distance from your home culture—for which recordings are available (for example, Bulgarian women's songs, West African drumming, Chinese Opera, Irish dance music, Brazilian samba). Contact and correspond with people in the place of the music's origin, or who have migrated from the source-place of this music, to determine the level of continued local interest and use of this music, even as it has spread internationally to your record store, library, or home collection. Consider visiting communities of immigrants, refugees, and asylum-seekers, through their restaurants and cafes, and places of worship, to find people who are knowledgeable of the local music of their homelands and who may wish to discuss its past and current status. See also about visiting their websites, chat rooms, and e-lists, to enter into a dialogue of how music that is now widely available (i.e., globalized) may continue to be valued and used by people living locally.*

Acculturation. The process of musical change has stimulated ethnomusicologists to study individual performers and composers who have come into contact with music and musicians from other cultures, and have crafted their musical expressions to reflect certain features of these cultural contacts. Many Afro-pop bands have embraced the instruments of western pop and rock bands, while continuing their traditional features such as polyrhythmic textures, call-and-response forms, short iterative melodic phrases, and the inclusion of traditional instruments. The gospel music of South Africans is a result of their historical interactions with African Americans, their shared commitment to civil rights and freedom for all citizens of their nations, and their similar affinity to the communal nature of participatory music-making experiences. The bhangra music of the South Asian club scene in the U.K. has emerged as a blend of older bhangra folk music of India with techno-pop textures, evidencing an acculturated style that is more popular in Birmingham (England) than it is in Mumbai (India). Japanese traditional music of the gagaku court developed its own distinctive identity at least a millennium ago, and yet the contacts between people living in China, Korea, and Japan brought about cultural, artistic, and specific musical influences of lasting import. Still other examples of acculturation can be found along the route of the Silk Road, where from Turkey through central Asia all the way east through China, musical instruments, melodies, rhythms, and song texts were shared by merchants, explorers, and travelers, and incorporated into the contemporary musical expressions of urban and rural communities. These and multiple other musical expressions are the results of people-to-people interactions, such that musical changes happen through the influences which people give and take to one another's traditions.

Project: Musical Acculturation. *Scan the radio, TV, MTV, and record store collections for examples of acculturated music. Some may be popular genres of the "world beat" sort, while others may be much older genres that resulted from historical exchanges. Consult the history books to determine what cultural contacts would have happened, and how, to produce these musical forms. Chart these people-to-people interactions, and note which musical features were maintained and which were "borrowed" as a result of the acculturation process. Keep in mind your own music-making, too, and how the songs you write or the improvisations you may produce may be influenced by the music you have heard through live interactions with other musicians.*

Gender 1. Much of the early research of ethnomusicologists focused on musical practices of male musicians, partially because most of the early ethnomusicologists were male. Only since the early 1980s has music associated with females been regularly investigated, and the veils lifted on rich vocal and instrumental traditions that had been long hidden from view. Now women musicians—and the role of music in women's lives—are widely studied by both male and female ethnomusicologists. Vast repertoires of songs and instrumental music performed by women have been revealed, and dance and theater forms in which music is integral are now studied for the contributions which both women and men make to them. Today there is no question that women across the world are musically involved as singers, instrumentalists, conductors, composers, improvisers, arrangers, sound technicians, recording engineers, and music scholars, and the prospects for studying their lives and works are open for exploration.

Project: Women–in–Music. *Select a woman musician (for example, Umm Kulthum, Egyptian singer; Lakshmi Shankar, Indian sitarist; Sarah Caldwell, American conductor; Evelyn Glennie, Scottish percussionist; Celia Cruz, Puerto Rican salsa singer; Pauline Hillaire, Native American (Lummi) storyteller and singer; Midori, Japanese violinist; Nina Simone, jazz singer; Eva Ybarra, Tex-Mex conjunto player; Libby Larsen, American composer; Sangeeta, Indian bhangra star) and trace her training, experience, and contributions to the musical world. Listen to her music, find out about more about the genre of her expertise, her recordings, key performances, and training.*

Gender 2. Male and female roles in music vary from one culture to the next, and may be historically distinguished from contemporary practice. While the feminization of teaching in American public schools has evolved from a nearly all-male profession at the end of the nineteenth century to positions filled greatly by women today, some musical cultures, genres, and instruments are still male-dominated. In India, most teachers of musical sitar, sarod, and sarāngī continue to be men. Thai teachers of pi phat instruments are more male than female, although women are more frequently the teachers of the kim (hammered dulcimer). Sikuri teachers and ensemble leaders of Peru are typically male, as are teachers and directors of samba schools. Yet women appear to be in the majority as teachers of piano in its many world venues, koto (of Japan), Appalachian mountain dulcimer, saung kauk (Burmese harp), and of dance forms like the Indian bharata natyam and kathak, and the Balinese legong.

Project: Teaching-Roles-by-Gender. *Research instruments and musical traditions across the world to determine which ones are decidedly in the hands of men or women to transmit and teach. Arrange for interviews with men and women teachers of several different musical (and dance) forms, and determine how they themselves were trained. Ask about the techniques that these teachers practice, and sort out which ones may be associated with gender or with the musical (dance) form.*

Nationalism and Musical Identity. Music defines us personally and as members of social groups, and our personal musical interests and identities may well be shared by those of similar age, ethnicity, or socioeconomic class, and in particular by citizens of a country or members of an autonomous cultural region. Ethnomusicologists have been intrigued with the manner in which nation-states construct their identity as an outgrowth of shared language, beliefs, and customs. The case of music as an expression of nationalism is found in the nation's choice of "national" instrument, dance, genre, and song or instrumental piece. The national instrument of Ireland is the Celtic harp, while the people of Scotland identify with its highland bagpipes. The Lao of Laos and northeast Thailand call the kaen, a free-reed instrument, the instrument of their musical identity. The Yoruba of Nigeria are culturally linked to their dundun, or talking drum, while people of South Korea identify with their kayagum (zither). Dance and its music are expressions of nationalism, too: for Hawaiians, the hula; for Serbs and Croatians, the kolo; for Hindustani people of North India, the bharata natyam; for the Sioux of the north central part of the United States, the round dance; for Argentinians, the tango. Genres can also be nationalist in expression, such as the symphony's association with Western Europe, as well as their identification with those nations that have embraced certain European ideals. Even particular songs and instrumental pieces are linked to nation-states, not only through patriotic hymns and national anthems, but also through folk and popular songs.

Project: Music-as-National-Identity. *Survey people you know for the instruments, dances, genres, and songs that they believe represents them as a citizen of their nation. Talk with people living locally, and connect with people in other countries by e-mail or through links on the Internet. Look for examples of people who mention multiple musical identities, or who describe changes in their musical identities as a result of maturation or shifts in citizenship, lifestyle, and socioeconomic class.*

PUTTING IT ALL TOGETHER

"People make music meaningful and useful in their lives." Woven through the chapters, this theme has been a guide to the educational experiences in music which teachers can provide to their students in elementary and secondary schools. The rationales are "in" for teaching music musically and globally, that in this time of cultural democracy, it is fair and fitting for students to learn music as the human phenomenon that it is, in its diversity of forms and functions, components and contexts, and stylistic subtleties across cultures. We know that students grow to understand the splendors of music through a sound awareness of its features and functions, starting with the music of their local surroundings and continuing to a discovery of less familiar styles found in the far reaches of the globe. With our facilitation, students can "listen-to-learn" some of the vast array of vocal and instrumental expressions that exist, so that through attentive, engaged, and enactive listening, students will know music for its global and cross-cultural manifestations. Their participation and performance in the music-making, learned largely by listening with care and frequency, can take them ever deeper into the music. Students can be musically playful, too, launching new musical expressions from the broader musical world to which they have become attuned. With the integrated study of subjects and disciplines that surround the music, they can learn its meanings within the context of its creation and use. These experiences bring their attention to ways in which people the world over make meaningful music. With the rationales in place, and the suggested activities running the gamut from exploratory projects to polished performances, the teaching challenge is to configure these thoughts and experiences into a curricular plan that works. This configuration process is hardly new, for we teachers consistently draw from their experiences and studies the materials and methods they will transmit to their students, adding this, deleting that, and sometimes pulling up the carpet to scatter all that was so, as to begin brand new again. We know best our students, the schedules of their school day, the curricular goals set by their districts to be met. Through careful observations, we become aware of the learning styles of students of particular ages, grades, and developmental levels, and the expectations of teachers, administrators, parents and community members. Most importantly, we know now and through our continued teaching pursuits how to reach our children and youth, and how to turn a musical segment into a meaningful experience. We know what students want, and what they need, in order to develop their musical selves to the fullest possible extent.

The schedules of the first chapter, for classes and class units in elementary and secondary school, and for several university-level courses, were intended to provide hypothetical possibilities for teaching music globally. No curricular context was left untouched, for the premise of the book is that music of the world's cultures are appropriate to be taught in choral, general, and instrumental settings for all ages, and in nontraditional venues as well. I have argued that the time has passed for the elementary school-only approach of "songs-of-many-lands," and that the possibilities have never been stronger for bringing the varied genres of the world's peoples to secondary students of band, choir, orchestra, and into nonstandard arrangements for the academic and performance study of music. The schedules were offered as frameworks for teaching some of the world's musical cultures, while the substance for fleshing them out were contained within the chapter-by-chapter suggestions for repertoire and instructional strategies. One of the key and continuing "Problems to Probe" at each chapter's end was a challenge to teachers to evaluate the suggested activities for their practical application within real and imagined instructional settings. Now, at the close of this volume, with thoughtful consideration of and experience in these activities, teachers can sort through and evaluate those of varying levels of difficulty, and assign those of greatest interest and relevance to the classes, courses, and curricular schedules for which they are charged to teach.

Teaching music globally is more than a fleeting flash-in-the-pan trend that will soon dissipate and dissolve. It is a movement already several generations in development, and one which coincides with the internationalism that has emerged across nations and cultures in business, commerce, politics, the sciences, and the intellectual disciplines. Those working in education at large have come to embrace the goal of developing their students' cultural understanding, seeking to achieve it through approaches that allow them a conscious consideration of perspectives on the subject that are beyond the most familiar. Within music, we as teachers cannot help but recognize our responsibility in guiding students to know the beauty and logic of musical cultures here and there, both near and far, in its multiple guise. Such an effort would take us toward the common goal of a thorough-going musical education, as our students grow to know music as Music, with a capital "M."

PROBLEMS TO PROBE

1. Choose a musical selection and develop ideas to respond to the questions of the "cultural prism" model, on its beginnings, continuities, and meanings. Before embarking on the project, ascertain that you have access to information—through printed sources, liner notes, websites, and if possible, culture-bearers and scholars who may shed further light on past and present uses of the music.

2. Read further on ethnomusicological issues in *Thinking Musically* so as to be fully informed of the suggested instructional projects that address these issues. Choose another issue of concern to ethnomusicologists, and design an activity or project that can be applied to students in elementary and secondary classrooms.

3. Review your sketch of a sample course schedule, selected in Chapter 1, and insert one or more integrated learning projects to fit the schedule. Think: Which experiences will be meaningful to developing my students' knowledge of Music with a capital "M"?

Resources

Readings

Further Readings in Education and Ethnomusicology

Anderson, William M. and Patricia Shehan Campbell. *Multicultural Perspectives in Music Education*. Reston, VA: Music Educators National Conference, 1989/1996.

Bachman, Marie-Laure. *Dalcroze Today: An Education Through and Into Music*. Translated by David Parlett. Oxford: Clarendon Press, 1991.

Banks, James. *Multiethnic Education: Theory and Practice*. Boston: Allyn and Bacon, 1995.

Banks, James and Cheryl McGee Banks. *Handbook of Research in Multicultural Education*. New York: Macmillan, 1995/2001.

Barrett, Janet, Claire McCoy, and Kari Veblen. *Sound Ways of Knowing*. New York: Schirmer Books, 1996.

Blacking, John. *How Musical is Man?* Seattle: University of Washington Press, 1973.

Bohlman, Philip V. *World Music: A Short Introduction*. Oxford and New York: Oxford University Press, 2002.

Campbell, Patricia Shehan. *Lessons from the World*. New York: Schirmer Books, 1991. Reprint, New York: McGraw-Hill, 2001.

Campbell, Patricia Shehan, Ed., *Music in Cultural Context*. Reston, VA: Music Educators National Conference, 1996.

Campbell, Patricia Shehan. *Songs in Their Heads*. New York: Oxford University Press, 1998.

Crafts, Susan D, Dan Cavicchi, and Charles Keil. *My Music*. Hanover, NH: Wesleyan University Press, 1994.

Czikszentimihalyi, Mihaly. *Creativity: Flow and the Psychology of Discovery and Invention*. New York: Harper Collins Publishers, 1996.

Delpit, Lisa. *Other People's Children*. New York: Basic Books, 1996.

DeNora, Tia. *Music in Everyday Life*. Cambridge, U.K.: Cambridge University Press, 2000.

Diagram, Group. *Musical Instruments of the World*. New York: Facts on File, Inc., 1976.

Dresser, Norrine. *Multicultural Manners*. New York: Holt, 1996.

Everitt, Anthony. *Joining In: An Investigation into Participatory Music*. London: Calouste Gulbenkian Foundation, 1997.

Floyd, Malcolm, ed. *World Musics in Education*. Hants, U.K.: Scolar Press, 1995.

Freire, Paolo. *Pedagogy of the Oppressed*. Translated by Myra Bergman Ramos. New York: Continuum Press, 1990.

Giroux, Henry A. *Border Crossings: Cultural Workers and the Politics of Education*. New York and London: Routledge, 1992.

Goetze, Mary. *Global Voices in Song: An Interactive Multicultural Experience*. New Palestine, IN: Mj & Associates, Inc., 2002.

Hood, Mantle. "The Challenge of Bi-musicality." *Ethnomusicology* 4(1960):2, 55–59.

Jaques-Dalcroze, Emile. *Rhythm, Music, and Education*. Translated by Harold F. Rubinstein. New York: Arno Press, 1921.

Jorgensen, Estelle R. *In Search of Music Education*. Urbana: University of Illinois Press, 1997.

Jorgensen, Estelle, R. *Transforming Music Education*. Bloomington, IN: Indiana University Press, 2002.

Keene, James A. *A History of Music Education the United States*. Hanover, NH: University Press of New England, 1982.

Keil, Charles and Steven Feld. *Music Grooves*. Chicago: University of Chicago Press, 1994.

Leith-Phillip, Margot and Andreas Gurtzwiler. Eds., *Teaching Musics of the World*. Affalterbach, Germany: Phillip Verlag, 1993.

Lundquist, Barbara, and K. Szego. Eds., *Music of the World's Cultures*. Perth, Australia: Callaway International Research Centre for Music Education, 1998.

Mark, Michael. *Contemporary Music Education*. 3rd ed. New York: Schirmer Books, 1996.

McAllester, David P., ed. *Becoming Human through Music*. Proceedings of the Wesleyan Conference. Philadelphia: Theodor Presser Foundation, 1984.

Merriam, Alan P. *The Anthropology of Music*. Evanston, IL: Northwestern University Press, 1964.

The National Standards for Arts Education. Reston, VA: Music Educators National Conference, 1994.

Nettl, Bruno. *Encounters in Ethnomusicology: A Memoir*. Warren, MI: Harmonic Park Press, 2002.

Nettl, Bruno. *In the Course of Performance*. Urbana-Champaign, IL: University of Illinois Press, 1998.

Paynter, John. *Music in the Secondary School Curriculum.* Cambridge, U.K.: Cambridge University Press, 1982.

Reimer, Bennett. Ed., *World Musics and Music Education: Facing the Music.* Reston, VA: Music Educators National Conference, 2002.

Schaefer, R. Murray. *The Thinking Ear: Complete Writings on Music Education.* Toronto: Arcana Editions, 1986.

Small, Christopher. *Musicking: The Meanings of Performing and Listening.* Hanover, NH: University Press of New England, 1998.

Swanwick, Keith. *Teaching Music Musically.* New York: Routledge, 1999.

Stock, Jonathan. *World Sound Matters.* London: Schott, 1995.

Volk, Terese M. *Music, Education, and Multiculturalism.* New York: Oxford University Press, 1998.

Wiggins, Jackie. *Teaching for Musical Understanding.* New York: McGraw-Hill, 2000.

Reading and Listening

Teaching Materials with Recordings and/or Notated Scores

Adzinyah, Abraham K., Dumisani Maraire, and Judith Cook Tucker. *Let Your Voice Be Heard! Songs of Ghana and Zimbabwe.* Danbury, CT: World Music Press, 1986. (2nd edition, 1996)

Amoaku, W. K. *African Songs and Rhythms for Children.* New York: Schott Music Corp., 1971.

Barnwell, Ysaye M., and Geroge Brandon. *Singing in the African American Tradition: Choral and Congregational Vocal Music.* Woodstock, NY: Homespun Tapes, 1989.

Brennan, Elizabeth Villareal. *A Singing Wind: Five Melodies from Ecuador.* Danbury, CT: World Music Press, 1988.

Burton, Bryan. *Moving within the Circle: Contemporary Native American Music and Dance.* Danbury, CT: World Music Press, 1993.

Campbell, Patricia Shehan, and Ana Lucia Frega. *Canciones de America Latina: De Sus Origenes a la Escuela.* Miami, FL: Warner Bros., 2001.

Campbell, Patricia Shehan, Sue Williamson, and Pierre Perron. *Songs of Singing Cultures.* Miami, FL: Warner Bros., 1996.

Campbell, Patricia Shehan, Ellen McCullough-Brabson, and Judith Cook Tucker. *Roots and Branches: A Legacy of Multicultural Music for Children.* Danbury, CT: World Music Press, 1994.

Farrell, Gerry. Indian Music in Education. Cambridge, U.K.: Cambridge University Press, 1990.

Fukuda, Hanako. *Favorite Songs of Japanese Children.* Norwalk, CA: Highland Music Company, 1965.

Han Kuo-Huang, and Patricia Shehan Campbell. *The Lion's Roar: Chinese Luogu Percussion Ensembles.* Danbury, CT: World Music Press, 1992/1996.

Harpole, Patricia, and Mark Fogelquist. *Los Mariachis! An Introduction to Mexican Mariachi Music*. Danbury, CT: World Music Press, 1989.

Holmes, Ramona and Terese Volk. *The World on a String: World Music for String Ensembles*. New York, NY: Alfred Publishing Co., 2000.

Jones, Bessie, and Bess Lomax Hawes. *Step It Down: Games, Plays, Songs, and Stories from the Afro-American Heritage*. Athens, GA: University of Georgia Press, 1987.

Locke, David, Drum Gahu: *A Systematic Method for an African Percussion Piece*. Crown Point, IN: White Cliffs Media Company, 1987.

Nguyen, Phong Thuyet, and Patricia Shehan Campbell. *From Rice Paddies and Temple Yards: Traditional Music of Vietnam*. Danbury, CT: World Music Press, 1990.

Nyberg, Anders. *Freedom is Coming: Songs of Protest and Praise from South Africa for Mixed Choir*. Chapel Hill, NC: Walton Music Corporation, 1984.

Phaosavadi, Pornprapit, and Patricia Shehan Campbell. *From Bangkok and Beyond: Thai Songs, Games, and Customs*. Danbury, CT: World Music Press, 2003.

Sam, Sam-Ang, and Patricia Shehan Campbell. *Silent Temples, Songful Hearts: Traditional Music of Cambodia*. Danbury, CT: World Music Press, 1991.

Serwadda, W. Moses. Songs and Stories from Uganda. New York: Thomas Y. Crowell, 1974.

Shankar, Ravi. *Learning Indian Music: A Systematic Approach*. Elise B. Barnett, ed. Ft. Lauderdale, FL: Onomatopoeia, Inc., 1979.

Wilson, Chesley Goseyun, Ruth Longcor Harnisch Wilson, and Bryan Burton. *When the Earth was Like New: Western Apache Songs and Stories*. Danbury, CT: World Music Press, 1994.

Culture-Case Books/CDs in the Global Music Series
(Oxford University Press; each with individual lists of recommended books, recordings, films and videos)
Barz, Gregory, *Music in East Africa: Ngoma*.
Brinner, Benjamin, *Music in Central Java*.
Dudley, Shannon, *Carnival Music in Trinidad*.
Gold, Lisa, *Music in Bali*.
Hast, Dorothea E. and Stanley Scott, *Music in Ireland*.
Marcus, Scott, *Music in the Middle East*.
Murphy, John Patrick, *Music in Brazil*.
Reyes, Adelaide. *Music in America*.
Rice, Timothy, *Music in Bulgaria*.
Ruckert, George, *Music in North India*.
Sheehy, Dan, *Mariachi Music in Mexico*.
Stone, Ruth M., *Music in West Africa*.

Viswanathan, T. and Matthew Harp Allen, *Music in South India*.
Wade, Bonnie C., *Music in Japan*.
Wade, Bonnie C., *Thinking Musically*.
Witzleben, J. Lawrence, *Music in China*.

Viewing

Films, Videotapes, and DVDs

Amir: An Afghan Refugee Musician's Life in Peshawar, Pakistan. Royal Anthropological Institute, 56 Queene Anne Street, London W1M 9LA. Reunion of ethnomusicologist John Baily (film director) and Amir, who had known each other in Herat in the mid-1970s, prior to the Soviet invasion of Afghanistan; scenes of Amir's readjustment to life as a refugee, performing and learning music of his new surroundings.

Beats of the Heart. Dove Music, P.O. Box 08286, Milwaukee, WI 53208. Video series, including New York salsa, Indian cinema music, gypsies in Europe and Asia, religious music of the Appalachians, Tex-Mex music, Brazilian samba, Jamaican reggae, Nigerian konkombe, Thai tradition and popular music; each video is 60 minutes in length.

Black Orpheus. Sacha Gordine Production, Original screenplay by Jacques Vilot. Order from Home Vision. Story based on the legend of Orpheus and Eurydice set against the colorful background of the carnival in Rio de Janeiro.

Bomba: Dancing the Drum. Searchlight Films, 2600 Tenth Street, Suite 102, Berkeley, CA 94710. Centers on Rafael Cepeda, patriarch of African-descended bomba and plena rhythms and dance music and dance of Puerto Rico.

Carnival in Q'eros. University of California Extension Media Center, Berkeley, CA. A documentary of the carnival celebrations of a remote community of Quechua Indians in the Peruvian Andes, produced by John Cohen in 1990.

Chinese Opera. Audio-Forum, Suite M2, 96 Broad Street, Guilford, CT 06437. Part of the "Music in Society" series by Deben Bhattacharya, with samples of Beijing Opera, Cantonese Opera, and operas of Hangzhou, Suzhou, and Kunming; scenes of aria performances, makeup and costume preparation, martial and acrobatics rehearsals and performances.

Circles—Cycles Kathak Dance. University of California, Extension Media Center, 2176 Shattuck Avenue, Berkeley, CA. Introduction to the Kathak tradition of classical Indian dance, with total view of dancer and musicians; commentary by tablā playear Zakir Hussain.

Dancing with the Incas: Huayno Music of Peru. University of California Extension Center for Media and Independent Learning, 2176 Shattuck Ave.,

Berkeley, CA 94704. Highland musicians and musical genres in the cities of Lima and Cusco, including the continuity of "Inca" or pre-Columbian music among contemporary Peruvians, and music as a means of resistance to various threats posed by "the West" in Peru.

Discovery the Music of . . . Educational Video, 1401 Nineteenth St., Huntsville, TX 77340. Video series, including Music of Japan, Music of Latin American, Mexican American Musical Heritage, Sounds of Mexico, Music of India, Music of Africa, Russian Folk Music; each video is 20 minutes in length.

Djabote—Sengalese Drumming & Song from Master Drummer Doudou N'Diaye Rose. Multicultural Media, 31 Hebert Road, Montpelier, VT, 05602. Master drummer Doudou N'Diaye Rose on sabar drum, along with his Senegalese ensemble, are caught in characteristic movement and performance practice.

Exploring the World of Music. Narrated by Fritz Weaver. Annenberg/CPB Project, 1998. South Burlington, VT. In twelve parts, including "Sound, Music, and the Environment," "The Transformative Power of Music," and "Composers and Improvisors," featuring a wide variety of music and musicians.

Gagaku. Oklahoma University Foundation/Early Music Television, School of Music, Eugene Enrico, University of Oklahoma, Norman, OK 73019. Detailed explanations and demonstrations of instruments of the ancient Japanese court music ensemble, and dance.

Ghengis Blues. Wade Run Productions. New York, NY; distributed by New Video, 2000. Produced by Roko and Adrian Belic, this is the story of Paul Pena, a blind American blues musician, and his trek to Tuva to live among the inhabitants and compete in their triennial throat singing contest.

Haitian Song. Karen Kramer, Film Library, 22-D Hollywood Avenue, Ho-ho-kus, NJ 07423 (201) 652-1989. Portrait of the rituals of life in a Haitian village, with singing of local people, and processional ensemble of bamboo tubes, percussive iron hoe blades, and drums.

Hawaiian Rainbow. SVS, Inc., 1700 Broadway, New York, NY, 10019. Twelve performers or groups featured in the performance of music of ancient Hawaii. The focus is on contemporary songs of protest and alienation, including examples of ukelele, slack key guitar, yodeling, English-language songs accessible to tourists, steel guitar, and music of the Hawaiian Renaissance of the 1970s.

Hmong Music in America, Aspara Media, 13659 Victory Boulevard, Suite 577, Van Nuys, CA 91401, 1978–1996. Documentation of Hmong refugee families from Laos in their resettlement in the U.S., with songs and qeej music scenes from Providence, R.I., and California.

India's Master Musicians. Richard Bock, Los Angeles: Aura Productions, 1982. Performances by Imrat Khan, Lakshmi Shankar, Ashish Khan, Alla Rahkha, Lakshmi Viswanathan, Zakir Hussain, and Ramnad Raghavan.

The JVC Video Anthology of World Music and Dance. Smithsonian/Folkways Recordings, distributed by Rounder Records, 61 Prospect Ct., Montpelier, VT 05602. Series of thirty videotapes with accompanying nine books, including Introduction, East Asia, Southeast Asia, South Asia, The Middle East and Africa, Europe, Soviet Union, The Americas, and Oceania, with clips of instrumentalists, singers, and dancers in context.

Japanese Puppet Theatre. Oklahoma University Foundation/Early Music Television, School of Music, Eugene Enrico, University of Oklahoma, Norman, OK 73019. Behind the scenes and onstage with the musicians and puppeteers of the bunraku puppet theater of Japan.

Khyal: Classical Singing of North India. The Open University, Walton Hall, Milton Keynes MK7 6AA, U.K. Exploration of improvisation types in khyal performance, featuring Veena Sahasrabuddhe, recognized as the best of contemporary women singers, in diadactic segments as well.

Khmer Court Dance: Cambodian Royal Court Dances. Multicultural Media, 31 Hebert Road, Montpelier, VT 05602. Footage of Khmer dancers and musicians living in the United States in the performance of five of the most popular dances in the court repertoire; video is 74 minutes in length.

Kodo—Heartbeat Drummers of Japan. Jacques Holender, New York: Rhapsody Films, 1983. Kodo drumming techniques and performers' commitment to disciplined rehearsal and collective work.

The Language You Cry In: The Story of Mende Song. California Newsreel, 149 Ninth Street, No. 420, San Francisco, CA 94103. Joseph Opala, anthropologist, Cynthia Schmidt, ethnomusicologist, and Tazieff Koroma, linguist. A collaboration of the travels of a children's song from a Mende village in Sierra Leone to a Georgia Sea Island community of African Americans.

Latcho Drom. New Yorker Films, 16 West Sixty-First St., New York, NY 10023. Stage documentary of Romani (gypsy) music in the diaspora, from India to Egypt, Turkey, Romania, Hungary, Slovakia, France, and Spain.

Music of the Mande Parts I & II. Original Music Inc., 418 Lasher Road, Tivoli, NY 12583. Roderic Knight's 62-minute documentation of the West African harp, including construction of the kora and performance by the great kora player, Bai Konte, in The Gambia.

Powerhouse for God. Documentary Educational Resources, Watertown, MA. A documentary produced by Barry Dornfeld, Tom Rankin, and Jeff Titon about the Fellowship Independent Baptist Church in Stanley, VA, which focuses on the pastor, John Sherfey, his family, and his congregation and how they bring meaning to their lives through songs, prayers, sermons, and life sciences.

Rebetiko. Greek Video, Records & Tapes, Inc., 394 McGuinness Blvde., Brooklyn, NY, 11222. Features melodies of the bouzoukee and the baglama (long-necked lute) in a unique synthesis of Greek, Turkish, European, and Latin American musical elements.

Sworn to the Drum: A Tribute to Francisco Aguabella. Flower Films 10341 San Pablo Avenue, El Cerrito, CA 94530-3123, (510) 525-0942. Tribute to Afro-Cuban master drummer now based in Los Angeles, with excerpts of religious drumming traditions and Latin jazz style; 35-minute 16 mm film.

Those Who are in Love/Asiklar. Sinema Productions, 1740 Griffith Park Boulevard, Los Angeles, California, 90026, (213) 660-9622. Account of Turkish minstrels (asik) belonging to the Alevi sect of Islam, featuring the blind bard, Veysel, singing poems and playing the long-necked folk lute called saz (or baglama).

Too Close to Heaven: The History of Gospel Music, Volumes 1–3. Films for the Humanities and Sciences, Inc., Box 2053, Princeton, NJ 08543-2053, (800) 257-5126. History of important developments and artists in two hundred years of black religious music, with clips of Thomas Dorsey, Tramaine Hawkins, Andrae Crouch, and Kirk Jackson, with an extensive interview with musicologist and gospel singer Horace Clarence Boyer.

Wayang Golek: Performing Arts of Sunda (West Java). PA:L and NTSC, with booklet. Open University Worldwide, The Berrill Building, The Open Univeristy, Walton Hall, Milton Keynes, MK7 6AA, UK. Focus on the dalang (puppeteer) and musicians of a single family living in West Java, and the rod-puppet theatre form; also a section on topeng (masked dance).

Wisconsin Powwow. Smithsonian/Folkways Recordings, Washington, D.C. Produced by Thomas Vennum, Jr., a two-part film that depicts the recent powwow scene as it incorporates historical traditions and modern innovations.

Index

∞